Praise for

REBEL CINDERELLA

"Although the stuff of fairy tale—penniless immigrant factory worker marries old-money millionaire, then uses her fortune and influence to fight for the laboring classes—the story Hochschild tells in *Rebel Cinderella* is as taut and true as a well-tuned violin. Rose Pastor Stokes comes alive as a woman of passionate conviction and rare imaginative power, restored by Hochschild to her rightful place in the history of America's rise to world prominence in the first decades of the twentieth century."

— **Megan Marshall, author of *Elizabeth Bishop***

"Through the lens of a remarkable marriage, Adam Hochschild draws a vivid portrait of the Gilded Age—of immigrants, sweatshops, tenements, strikes, enclaves of patrician privilege, and a 'citadel of socialism' on a private island. At the center of it all is Rose, whose extraordinary story ends as anything but a fairy tale."

— **Jean Strouse, author of *Morgan: American Financier***

"Adam Hochschild recounts the incredible story of Rose Pastor Stokes, a Jewish immigrant from Eastern Europe who toiled in a cigar factory, met and married a rich socialite, and became an infamous socialist firebrand. The book is chock-full of fascinating characters and stories, with Stokes and her comrades often recounting their dramatic lives in their own words."

— **Tyler Anbinder, author of *City of Dreams***

"Lucidly written and painstakingly researched, this is a joy to read, cementing Pastor in her rightful place with other progressive figures of the time." — ***Library Journal*, starred review**

"Hochschild's captivating and fast-paced biography is a true delight and an excellent addition to women's history shelves." — *Booklist*

"Polished and accessible . . . few histories capture the era's combustible mix of idealism and inequality better." — *Publishers Weekly*

"Adam Hochschild writes movingly about an unlikely pair who also served as a potent symbol . . . Hochschild is a superb writer who makes light work of heavy subjects . . . Where information is scant or nonexistent, he deploys elegant workarounds that evoke a vivid sense of time and place . . . Hochschild's book shows us what a radical movement looked like from the inside, with all of its high-flown idealism and personal intrigues. Whatever protections we take for granted once seemed unfathomable before they became real."
— *New York Times*

"This vibrant biography portrays the riveting charisma of the socialist activist Rose Pastor Stokes . . . Hochschild captures the improbability and idealism of both Pastor Stokes and her era, a time when it seemed that stark divisions of class, race, and gender might be erased, in an instant, by love." — *The New Yorker*

"Adam Hochschild is among the most readable of historians . . . Hochschild has done a brilliant job of bringing [the Stokes's marriage] to life and in doing so, illuminating the complex social and economic history of a generation whose rabble-rousers and dreamers bequeathed us such reforms as Social Security, Medicare, child labor laws and the eight-hour day." — **Associated Press**

"A thrilling book. Adam Hochschild is a wonderful writer with a social conscience."
— **Bill Goldstein,** *Weekend Today in New York,* **WNBC-TV**

"Hochschild's historical account is both gripping and occasionally heartbreaking."
— *Shelf Awareness*

"A solidly researched and impressive biography."
— *Los Angeles Review of Books*

"A compelling read about a fascinating time in American history, one that bears some resemblance to today."
— *Minneapolis Star Tribune*

"[A] thoroughly engrossing, meticulously researched and well-illustrated biography . . . Despite the book's title, there are no fairy-tale heroes in it, which testifies to the subtlety of Mr. Hochschild's narrative imagination . . . Hochschild is as excellent at invoking such personal confrontations as he is at summarizing, with epigrammatic clarity, complex historical developments."
— *Wall Street Journal*

REBEL CINDERELLA

BOOKS BY ADAM HOCHSCHILD

Half the Way Home:
A Memoir of Father and Son

The Mirror at Midnight:
A South African Journey

The Unquiet Ghost:
Russians Remember Stalin

Finding the Trapdoor:
Essays, Portraits, Travels

King Leopold's Ghost:
A Story of Greed, Terror, and Heroism in Colonial Africa

Bury the Chains:
Prophets and Rebels in the Fight to Free an Empire's Slaves

To End All Wars:
A Story of Loyalty and Rebellion, 1914–1918

Spain in Our Hearts:
Americans in the Spanish Civil War, 1936–1939

Lessons from a Dark Time and Other Essays

Rebel Cinderella:
From Rags to Riches to Radical, the Epic Journey of Rose Pastor Stokes

REBEL CINDERELLA

From Rags to Riches to Radical,
the Epic Journey of
ROSE PASTOR STOKES

Adam Hochschild

Mariner Books
Houghton Mifflin Harcourt
BOSTON   NEW YORK

First Mariner Books edition 2021
hmhbooks.com

Library of Congress Cataloging-in-Publication Data
Names: Hochschild, Adam, author.
Title: Rebel Cinderella : from rags to riches to radical, the epic journey of
Rose Pastor Stokes / Adam Hochschild.
Description: Boston : Houghton Mifflin Harcourt, 2020. |
Includes bibliographical references and index.
Identifiers: LCCN 2019027932 (print) | LCCN 2019027933 (ebook) |
ISBN 9781328866745 (hardcover) | ISBN 9781328866769 (ebook) |
ISBN 9780358313168 | ISBN 9780358309536
ISBN 9780358522461 (pbk.)
Subjects: LCSH: Stokes, Rose Pastor, 1879–1933. | Feminists—United States—
Biography. | Women socialists—United States—Biography. |
Women political activists—United States—Biography. | Jewish refugees—
United States—Biography. | Women immigrants—United States—Biography.
Classification: LCC HQ1413.S69 A3 2020 (print) | LCC HQ1413.S69 (ebook) |
DDC 305.42092 [B]—dc23
LC record available at https://lccn.loc.gov/2019027932
LC ebook record available at https://lccn.loc.gov/2019027933

Book design by Margaret Rosewitz

Printed in the United States of America

DOC 10 9 8 7 6 5 4 3 2 1

For Georges and Anne Borchardt

Contents

VIII   *Contents*

REBEL CINDERELLA

Prologue:
Tumult at Carnegie Hall

MAY 5, 1916. Some three thousand people are packed into seats on both the sloping main floor and the four tiers of boxes and balconies sweeping in graceful arcs around the side and back walls. Men and women from an overflow crowd are standing at the rear of the hall. Another thousand people have been turned away at the door. But this is no ordinary evening in New York City's venerable temple of the arts. Policemen, uniformed and plainclothes, are stationed in Carnegie Hall's aisles, in the corridors, and on the pavement outside. They are here because they have anticipated just what is now happening: a young woman is publicly violating the law.

The crowd tonight has gathered to denounce the notorious Comstock Act, which makes it a crime to distribute material "of an immoral nature," including information about birth control. Onstage is Rose Pastor Stokes, a slender woman of 36, her reddish-brown hair pulled back in a chignon. Her voice carries a warmth and passion that has given her a rare ability to inspire almost any audience.

"We have met here," she says, "in protest against the law which operates to keep the knowledge of contraception from the mothers of the poor and blinks at the fact that the comfortable classes obtain that knowledge from their highly-paid physicians and from one another. We demand that the law which is a dead letter for the rich also become a dead letter for the poor." She mocks those who claim that birth control is "not only against the law of man but of the Almighty." Such "junior partners of the Lord seem to know it is God's will that children should come indiscriminately into the world; and that a large percentage of them should also be forced out of the world by humanly preventable conditions."

An immigrant, socialist, and union organizer, Rose Pastor Stokes spent 12 long years of her childhood and youth in sweatshops manufacturing cigars. Despite having less than two years of formal schooling, she has become one of the most renowned radical orators of her time. She has the crowd's rapt attention as she describes how she has received "letters from young mothers with two or three or four children who . . . desire to wait for a time when they can decently and safely take care of more children before bringing them into the world. Letters from mothers who have been warned by their physicians that another childbirth would mean the mother's death, but to whom those same doctors denied contraceptive information. . . . Such and many more have come to me day after day and are still coming. Some of them too tragic and too terrible to quote." She reminds the packed audience that she speaks with the authority of her own childhood, when she had "frequently the hard floor for a bed, and the weight of an unnamable nightmare as each succeeding year added another mouth to feed, then eliminated the father of those six little ones, in the unequal struggle for bread."

Although she is only one of several speakers at tonight's rally, she rivets the crowd and sets many newspaper reporters frantically scribbling in their notebooks when she declares that she will break this absurd law, now, on the spot. From the Carnegie Hall stage she begins handing out pieces of paper with the very details of birth control techniques that the authorities consider so dangerous. "Be the penalty what it may, I here frankly offer to give out these slips with the forbidden information to those needy wives and mothers who will frankly come and take them."

"Many young men and young girls rushed forward in a scramble for the slips," the *New York Times* would report the next morning. "Mrs. Stokes found herself in the midst of a pushing, unruly mass.

Chairs were overturned. . . . The cry went up from those who were in front of the stage that Mrs. Stokes was being arrested." In the commotion, "everybody shouted for the slips," another newspaper would say. "In its excitement the crowd overwhelmed Mrs. Stokes. Her hair was pulled from its fastenings and her shirt waist almost torn off."

Several scuffles broke out as impatient young men grabbed for the leaflets, which Stokes was trying to give only to women. As members of the audience eagerly dashed onto the stage, women's hats were crushed, people were knocked down, tables and the speaker's rostrum were smashed, and several women fainted. After 15 minutes of turmoil, a wedge of male supporters managed to rescue her from the surging crowd and take her backstage.

"I expect to be arrested," she assured reporters, sealing her fate still further, she thought, by telling them that she had also violated the law by sending birth control information through the mail. Several times, in the midst of the uproar, policemen were seen going to a telephone booth to call headquarters for instructions. But to her great disappointment, the police did not seize her. Even though at least 20 Americans had already served or would serve time behind bars for promoting birth control, Rose Pastor Stokes would not. She was not arrested the evening of her Carnegie Hall talk, nor in the days to come, nor on another occasion when she distributed similar leaflets on contraceptives in public.

And that was because of who her husband was.

Although all but forgotten today, no American marriage of its time won more public attention. It brought together a man and woman whose backgrounds differed so starkly that, if a novelist had invented them, we would find the tale wildly implausible. And it was not only because of the startlingly dissimilar families they came from. What other couple, for example, saw one partner received at the White House a few months after the other had been sentenced to ten years in a federal prison?

Rose Pastor Stokes first caught my attention some years ago, in a photograph from the 1920s. In the midst of writing a book about the Soviet Union, I noticed her among the American delegates to a meeting of the Communist International in Moscow. Even in that grainy black-and-white image she stood out: an intense-looking woman of medium height in a white blouse and long dark skirt. The juxtaposition of her name and the occasion startled me. Could she be connected, I wondered, to the immensely wealthy Phelps Stokes clan, several of whom were among the legendary 400 members—the number of people who could fit in Mrs. William Backhouse Astor Jr.'s ballroom—of New York's Gilded Age high society? That dynasty's name was tied to businesses that ranged from banking and real estate to mining and a railroad. And it was a Phelps Stokes who had built and owned the 100-room summer house that at one point was the largest private home in the United States. If this woman was part of that family, what was she doing in the Kremlin?

Later, when I began to explore her story, I found that she had indeed married into that very family—and that I was far from being the first person to notice this. For several years starting not long after that Carnegie Hall speech, according to a newspaper clipping service, her name was mentioned more often in the press than that of any other woman in the United States. (Only five Americans—all men—received more coverage.) Her marriage had been front-page news as well, and she and her husband would be the subject of thousands of later headlines. Their lives would inspire two novels and a movie.

Rose Pastor came from the kind of abject working-class poverty that was the lot of tens of millions of Americans of her time. No wonder the public's attention was caught by her 1905 wedding, at the age of 26, to the scion of one of the country's richest families. Leaping that chasm of class, people believed, surely would bring her great happiness. Millions of Americans living in crowded, grimy tenements without hot water imagined nothing but comfort in the splendid mansions that glimmered beyond their reach. Some were so fascinated by this rare couple that they compiled scrapbooks. A thick one full of brittle, yellowing newspaper clippings can be found at the New-York Historical Society today.

What made that marriage so intriguing? To begin with, it embodied an age-old fantasy in which an impoverished woman magically rises in status thanks to a fortunate connection with a rich and powerful man. A dream spanning the centuries, it can be found everywhere from the fairy tale of Cinderella to the musical *My Fair Lady,* from Samuel Richardson's *Pamela* (perhaps the first English novel) to our unceasing fascination with commoners who marry into the British royal family. It can be found in countless paperback romances in which a virtuous farm girl, chambermaid, or orphan overcomes malevolent rivals and other obstacles to win her prince or heir. In the United States of the early twentieth century such a fantasy had particular resonance, for the gap between rich and poor was the widest Americans had ever known.

Today, the appeal of making that magical leap from poverty to great affluence is once again resurgent. With stratospheric gains in income and wealth by the top 1 percent of Americans, we are on track to break all previous records of inequality. Some we may have already broken: by 2017, for instance, the country's three richest men—Jeff Bezos, Bill Gates, and Warren Buffett—owned more assets than the entire bottom half of the population, more than 160 million people. In our new Gilded Age, not only are neighborhoods more segregated than ever by wealth, but so is everything else, from aircraft cabins to places that never used to be segregated at all, like football stadiums now divided into ordinary seats and skyboxes.

So it is no wonder that it was a hugely popular TV show promising riches to the deserving, *The Apprentice,* that helped catapult a member of that top 1 percent (indeed, of the top .01 percent) into the White House. Donald J. Trump promptly added gold drapes to the Oval Office. He had already brought gold leaf to the ceilings, the moldings, and the marble pillars of his New York triplex and the coat of arms of his favorite Florida resort, not to speak of the gold seatbelt buckles and bathroom fixtures of his private aircraft. We are living in an age more gilded, almost literally, than the one before.

During the first Gilded Age, however, something beyond the perennial fantasy of sudden wealth also made people intensely interested in this couple. Rose Pastor Stokes was not only a charismatic orator, but someone completely at ease with people of any station in life. Her husband, Graham, was not the only member of his privileged circle who married outside his class in search of that very spark of life. Did he find it? Maybe, people wondered, *he* would be the one transformed. Who doesn't hope that a marriage will make both partners deeper, freer, happier?

One thing more drew me to their story. Although I've lived most of my life elsewhere, I was born in New York City, which still feels to me like the center of the world. Sometimes it seems to contain the entire globe. I remember walking across the top of Central Park on a warm summer evening a few years ago and feeling an unexpected delight at hearing four different languages in the space of ten minutes. Long ago Walt Whitman felt that same thrill: "City of the world!" he called it. ". . . All the lands of the earth make contributions here." I've long felt drawn to that city, which still feels like my city, during the first decade and a half of the twentieth century, a period of turbulence and hope before America entered the First World War. It was a remarkable moment that saw a flood tide of new immigrants, a flourishing of new forms of art, a zenith of crusading journalism, and dramatic strikes and demonstrations as working people and women demanded their rights. It was also a moment when many believed that on the horizon was a revolutionary upheaval that would wipe away forever the barriers of class, race, and inequality that so marred America's promise.

Rose Pastor Stokes was at the center of all of this, for she and her husband became part of the most spirited group of radicals, reformers, and dreamers this country has ever known. Their friends included the anarchist firebrand Emma Goldman, birth control pioneer Margaret Sanger, lawyer Clarence Darrow, "Wobbly" leader Big Bill Haywood, editor Max Eastman, labor crusader and socialist Eugene V. Debs, and writers Jack London, Upton Sinclair, W.E.B. Du Bois, Lincoln Steffens, and John Reed. Several of those men and women were in Carnegie Hall that evening in 1916, and others would be guests over the years at the couple's unusual island home. And all of this happened before a series of events would thrust Rose into the headlines in a way that no one, not even she, anticipated.

The couple's public lives crested, frustratingly, just before recordings and film might have captured them. Nonetheless, I found their voices in other forms, for they left behind not only their own pamphlets and articles but a revealing store of thousands of letters, a diary, and dueling memoirs, one never published, not to mention what others wrote about them: recollections from their extraordinary circle of friends and a cascade of newspaper stories beyond imagining. In addition, available today are documents Rose and Graham themselves were never able to read: dozens of surveillance reports by undercover operatives of the agency that was the predecessor of the FBI. All of this offers us a far more intimate window than we usually can have into a marriage in the past, from its Cinderella beginnings to an end that was anything but a fairy tale.

Rose's story begins on another continent.

1

Tsar and Queen

UNTIL THE FIRST WORLD WAR redrew national borders in Europe, Augustów, a trading center for cattle and the region's small, wiry horses, lay in imperial Russia. Today it is in the far northeast corner of Poland. Augustów was a garrison town when Rose — Raisel in Yiddish — Wieslander was born there in 1879. "I slipped into the world," she would later claim, "while my mother was on her knees, scrubbing the floor." One of her earliest memories was of the clatter of iron horseshoes on cobblestones as the tsar's cavalry swept across the town's wide market square. "One voice, ringing steel, commands. Men and horses swing and whisk and turn and gallop, stop suddenly, race, and disappear with a *cra-kerra! Kerreka-Kerreka!*"

Throughout the sprawling Russian Empire, there were often more troops in places with restive populations that were not ethnically Russian. In Augustów, that meant Poles and Jews. The latter had long been the officially sanctioned scapegoats for all the ills of the creaky realm of the Romanovs, with its corrupt and inefficient bureaucracy. Famine deaths? Jewish grain dealers hoarding all the wheat. Debt? Jewish moneylenders. Disease? Spread by the Jews, of course. Defeats on the battlefield? The Jews were spying for the enemy.

Though they often prospered in business, Russia's Jews faced almost insuperable barriers to obtaining a university education or a government job. Only one of the empire's five million Jewish citizens, for example, managed to become an army officer. With rare exceptions, Jews were restricted to the Pale of Settlement, a swath of territory spreading mostly across parts of what today is Lithuania, Poland, Belarus, and Ukraine. And even there, they were banned from certain districts and cities without special permission.

Augustów lay in a region of lakes, rivers, and a long canal. On these waters Rose's grandfather, known as Berl the Fisherman, plied his trade. She remembered his "thinly-bearded rugged face, with its high cheek-bones, generous mouth, and kindly grey eyes." He lived near a public well in a hut with a thatched roof, which held the traditional large Russian tiled oven used for both cooking and heating. "Some of my earliest recollections," Rose wrote, "are of a boat and oars and a wide expanse of shining water." She recalled her grandfather fishing from the boat with nets, women dressed in soft white muslin laughing as they bathed and washed their sheets in a river, and more women chatting as they rolled loaves of dough at a bakery. In the town's synagogue, there was "sunlight streaming in through a tall, high window, and a bird flying in the rafters." When her grandmother died in a typhus epidemic, her body was laid out on the dirt floor of Berl's hut, under a Persian shawl that had once been a wedding gift.

Despite those kindly grey eyes, Berl seems to have been a tyrant to his family of six children. He rudely broke up a romance between his daughter Hindl and a young Pole, forcing her instead to marry a Jewish bootmaker, a widower with a small child. The 17-year-old Hindl resisted—dirtying her face and dress when the bootmaker came courting, and fleeing to her father's hut when it was time to stand under the *huppah,* the wedding canopy, already surrounded by waiting guests. Berl slapped her face and dragged her to the ceremony—or so Rose heard. It was this loveless union that produced Rose. Before long, the bootmaker departed for America, leaving behind his resentful wife, their new daughter, and the small son from his previous marriage. From New York, he finally agreed to a divorce.

Above the bed where Rose's beloved grandmother died hung the only piece of artwork in the hut, a portrait of Tsar Alexander II. He was the reformer tsar, the emperor renowned for liberating Russia's serfs, millions of peasants who had been living in a state akin to slavery. Making a few cautious additional moves to modernize his country, he had shown considerably more tolerance for Jews than his predecessors had, ending some anti-Semitic measures including the harshest, a decree that sent tens of thousands of Jewish boys away for 25 years of military service. British Prime Minister Benjamin Disraeli called him "the kindliest prince who has ever ruled Russia." The Pale of Settlement and most other restrictions on Jews, however, remained in place.

In 1881, the year Rose turned two, on the very day he put his signature to a new set of reforms, Alexander was being driven along the embankment of a canal in St. Petersburg, the capital, when a revolutionary threw a bomb at him. The tsar was not harmed, but the bomb killed or wounded several Cossack guards and bystanders. As he then stepped out of his bulletproof carriage to see what was happening, another conspirator hurled a second bomb at close range. It exploded at Alexander's feet, injuring him fatally.

While the tsar's blood still stained the snow, the search for culprits began. There was but a single Jew among the small group of young assassins who were quickly captured, tried, and hanged, but that was excuse enough for what Russia's Jews had long feared would follow the enlightened Alexander's death. The cruel wave of repression that now erupted included the birth of a new league of anti-Semitic vigilantes and the worst pogroms in centuries. Several hundred Jews lost their lives to angry mobs that rampaged through towns, cities, and Jewish *shtetls,* or hamlets, raping women, looting shops and homes, and attacking Jews of all ages. Police or army troops would finally intervene to restore order, but only after waiting several days and sometimes joining the mayhem themselves. A flood of harsh new edicts followed: against Jews entering high schools, obtaining mortgages, holding political office, and more. The government imposed additional limits on where they could live. Thousands of Jews were forced to leave their homes.

Even before the assassination, Russian Jews had long been emigrating. Those who had already left included all five siblings of Rose's mother. Musical talent seemed to run in the family, and three of Hindl's brothers had become cantors in synagogues across the border in Germany. A fourth brother and a sister had gone farther, to London.

After the tsar's death, this exodus grew dramatically. In 1882, Hindl left her small stepson in the care of her ex-husband's mother, and she and Rose joined those who filled the railroad cars and dirt highways leading out of Russia, stopping first with the three cantors in Germany. For the three-year-old Rose, that country "was simply a sweet place where gardens and orchards bloomed, where children laughed, and men sang; where plenty graced the table." Then it was on to England. "Of our journey to London from whatever British port it was, I recall only a ride in the night, on a large, flat truck with iron-rimmed wheels that rattled over cobblestone roads. On the truck were huddled between twenty and thirty immigrants, hugging their large bundles."

In reconstructing her early life, the only information we have comes from the unfinished memoir she wrote much later, at a time when she wanted to stress the extreme poverty of her origins. So we hear, for example, about her grandfather's dirt-floored hut, but not about how he earned enough by fishing to get three of his sons some musical training, and apparently to supply all six of his children with enough cash to emigrate. Were his catches especially lucrative? Was there another source of income? Another house grander than the hut? Perhaps Rose herself did not know.

Whatever money her mother had ran out once they reached London. At first they lived with Hindl's brother, his wife, and their four small children in the slums of the East End, where the air was dense with coal smoke and everyone was crammed into two tiny rooms, which also served as the brother's work space. A shoemaker, he was earning an ever more precarious living as factories took over the trade. His wife's sister lived in the two rooms with them as well. Even when Hindl found work as a seamstress, the household still had trouble making ends meet. "I remember pangs of hunger—a gnawing that would make me restless when I tried to play," Rose recalled. She and other girls and boys "with pinched white faces and spindle legs, hushed and solemn," would stand outside the local baker's shop, noses pressed to the window. She shared a bed with several of her aunt and uncle's children, including an infant. One morning she woke up to find the baby dead.

Then they moved on to the home of Hindl's sister and her family, who were well-off enough to provide Rose and her mother a rare luxury: a room of their own. Although the two of them spoke Yiddish at home, Rose quickly picked up English. For the next year and a half she had her only experience of school. This brief stretch in the classroom gave her a lifelong love of English poetry, and she soon found a free source of it: the four lines of verse that appeared on the back of each ticket for the horse-drawn, double-decker omnibuses that crisscrossed London. Unable to afford books, she picked discarded tickets off the street and sidewalk and read them avidly.

Labor activism was stirring in London's Jewish community, especially among refugees from Russia's pogroms. One day, working in a tailor shop, her mother organized something Rose would later grow very familiar with: a strike. Angry that his women workers were looking out at the street and away from their stitching, the tailor whitewashed the shop windows. Hindl led her fellow workers in a week-long walkout—and they won. The whitewash came off. It set an example, Rose claimed, that she never forgot.

After a half-dozen years of the two of them living shoehorned into the households of their London relatives, Hindl married again, charmed by Israel Pastor, an upbeat, mustachioed young immigrant from Romania who liked to drink ale and sing. Rose took on her stepfather's last name. He had inherited some money from an uncle, and she was delighted when he bought her a tam-o'-shanter, silk stockings, and patent leather shoes. Gradually, though, the funds drained away into failed investments—first in a workshop making plate glass and then in one turning out caps. According to Rose, the first venture came to grief because of a conniving partner, and the second because a worker fell ill and the kindhearted Israel couldn't stop himself from paying for a doctor and medicine. He even supported the man's wife and child after he died. "My parents were unable to separate themselves from the workers." Can we believe this, or is this Rose the later labor organizer talking?

When Hindl became pregnant, Israel came up with a get-rich-quick scheme: he would go to South America, famous as a land of opportunity, and then send for his family. Back in London, Hindl and Rose, soon joined by a baby brother, had to take in an elderly woman boarder to get by. There was no time for school now. Rose and the two adults supported themselves by doing piecework at home, making black satin bows for women's slippers, while Rose rocked the baby's cradle with her foot. Only occasionally did she catch a glimpse of a different world, out of reach: the lush foliage of a park far from home or the "green leaves and gay flowers" surrounding the mansions of the rich, seen from the open top deck of an omnibus. Once she watched Queen Victoria, "a plain, heavy, beak-nosed old woman," ride by in her carriage in a parade celebrating her fiftieth anniversary on the throne.

Failing to make his fortune in Buenos Aires, Israel Pastor briefly returned to London, only to decide to try his luck overseas again, this time in the United States. There at last things seemed to go well, holding out the promise of a better life for all of them in the New World. From Cleveland, Ohio, he sent money for steamship tickets, and Rose, her mother, and the baby set off across the ocean to join him.

2

Magic Land

A SAFE HAVEN ACROSS THE ATLANTIC was the ultimate dream in the great Jewish exodus sparked by the assassination of Alexander II. "'America' was in everybody's mouth," wrote Mary Antin, also an immigrant from Russia. "Business men talked of it over their accounts; the market women made up their quarrels that they might discuss it from stall to stall; people who had relatives in the famous land went around reading their letters for the enlightenment of less fortunate folks; . . . children played at emigrating; old folks shook their sage heads over the evening fire, and prophesied no good for those who braved the terrors of the sea and the foreign goal beyond it; all talked of it, but scarcely anybody knew one true fact about this magic land."

We do not know the name of the ship Hindl, Rose, and the baby embarked on, but normally steerage passengers were separated by gender into two sections of a hold lined with stacked, narrow wooden bunks, each two feet or so up from the one below. If you wanted a mattress, sheets, or a pillow, you had to bring them. Several hundred passengers might share only one or two toilets and were allowed on deck, if at all, only at the whim of the captain. Steerage quarters shook with the churning of the ship's propellers just below, and smelled of engine oil, unwashed bodies, food scraps, tobacco, and vomit—for invariably many were seasick. The Pastors' ship had scarcely left the English coast, Rose recalled, "when a storm tore a great hole in the old vessel." The sea poured into their quarters below the waterline, and as "tables, benches, boxes and trunks began to swirl about, a great wailing went up." One woman dressed all in black held high a crucifix, shouting, "My God! My God! My God!" in Russian. After a two-day stop at Antwerp, Belgium, for emergency repairs, the ship set off again, for three weeks of pitching and rolling its way across the Atlantic. "Bodies were wrapped in canvas and buried at sea. Potatoes and herring, with bread and great chunks of salt butter (or what looked like butter) was the only food we were given."

The bedraggled trio first appear in US government records on the roster of those who came ashore on November 8, 1890, at Castle Garden, near the southern tip of Manhattan. This grim, circular, former fortress of red brick preceded Ellis Island as the main reception center for new immigrants. Its vast main hall reeked of those who had not been able to bathe for weeks on shipboard. Hundreds of bewildered men in fur hats and women in kerchiefs and shawls trooped in, carrying all their possessions in bundles or battered suitcases tied with rope. Con men bilked the gullible of their savings by collecting imaginary taxes or payment for telegrams to the old country that would never be sent. Rose, her mother, and the baby had little money to be cheated out of, however, for Israel Pastor had not sent them enough to cover their rail tickets to Cleveland. They got only as far as Philadelphia, where they had to wait a week before he could raise or borrow enough for the rest of the journey.

Finally united with her husband in Cleveland, Hindl, now 32, was amazed at the lavishness of their furnished three-room apartment. Rose remembered the scene:

> "Oh, Israel!" my mother turned her glowing face to him.
> "You bought all this!"
> "All this," he said, waving an arm at the new things.
> . . . Something in his tone brought another question.
> "Israel—is it all—paid for?"

It wasn't, of course, and he owed money to the grocer, the butcher, and the baker as well, who were already cutting off credit.

He had been trying to earn a living collecting secondhand goods and scrap metal with a one-horse cart, a common trade for new immigrants, just as driving a taxi would be for those arriving a century later. There was always the dream that the cart might someday be replaced by a small shop. For Israel Pastor, though, the cart yielded little. From her new bed that first night, Rose heard worried adult voices in the kitchen, making decisions that would change her life. Her mother would have to stay home to care for the baby while Rose went to work. Two days later, she and an older girl from the neighborhood went to apply for jobs at a nearby cigar factory. This was what she would do, with only a few short breaks, for the next dozen years. She was 11 years old.

The nation was not yet hooked on cigarettes, but American men loved cigars. In 1890, the year Rose started working, the country produced four billion of them. Wages were on a piecework basis, and fierce competition between manufacturers kept them low. Cutting and folding tobacco leaves and rolling them properly into cigars required dexterity, and employers increasingly hired women. They preferred immigrant women, who were eager for work, used to obedience, and had fewer troublesome ideas than men about trade unions. Those with little command of English were even less likely to complain about working conditions. As the tide of arrivals reached new heights that decade, owners often deliberately set up cigar factories in neighborhoods that were favored immigrant destinations.

Assembling the different grades of cigars, especially the higher-priced ones, took skill. You had to keep the large outer tobacco leaves, or "wrappers," under a damp cloth on your workbench, so that they remained pliable, but not soggy. You then spread a wrapper leaf flat on the bench surface with one hand while bunching up small "filler" leaves in the other, often blending two or three different types of tobacco for flavor. The tender tips of the filler leaves were thought to be sweeter, and had to be placed at the end of the cigar that would be lit, so their aroma would be in the smoker's first puff. If the cigar had a distinctive form, like a slight bulge in the middle, you had to shape the filler leaves accordingly. They could neither be placed crosswise where they might block the flow of smoke, nor be packed so loosely that hot air would be sucked through the cigar too fast and singe the smoker's tongue. Finally, you had to roll the filler in the wrapper leaf in a uniform spiral, covering the smoker's end of the cigar with an artful tuck of the wrapper, securing the seal with a drop of tasteless glue. Each cigar, of course, had to be the same length, weight, and shape. In most factories, you then placed the finished cigars in a U-shaped rack that held 50 of them. When it was full, you bound the bundle with string or a leather strap, adding a slip of paper with your name or seat number. A supervisor carefully inspected the cigars and docked your pay if they were not up to standard, or if you had used up too many of the more valuable wrapper leaves.

A coal stove heated the work space, but on a cold winter morning it could take several hours to warm up a whole floor of shivering workers. On sunny days in summer, the factories would turn into humid ovens—windows were often nailed shut, so that drafts of fresh air wouldn't dry out the wrapper leaves and make them brittle. The only relief from the heat was running cold water over your hands. Another discomfort of cigar work was the thick, penetrating smell—from the leaves themselves and from the oil in them that soaked into workbenches and storage bins and factory floors over the years. The odor found its way into your clothes and followed you home. Worst of all was the extremely fine tobacco dust. A brown coating of it lay everywhere: on floors and tables, on sills and panes of those nailed-shut windows—and in the air you breathed. As a result, cigar workers suffered the second-highest death rate from tuberculosis of any occupation in America; only stonecutters had it worse. As she arrived at the factory for the first time, Rose remembered, "the suffocating effluvium of tobacco dust strikes us in the face." All her adult life, she would be troubled by lung problems.

That first day, her employer told her, "Two weeks to learn. After that half-pay for six weeks, then full pay." In her first half-pay week, she earned 77 cents, equal to about $22 in purchasing power today. At one point she was surprised when the factory owner, out of apparent kindness, gave her a day off. Only later did she discover that he wanted Rose (three years under the legal minimum age for a worker) out of sight that day. He had learned, probably by paying someone off, that a government inspector was due to visit.

Rose would work in several cigar factories, large and small, over the following 12 years. At the next one she discovered her naïveté about something else. She was proud that the proprietor repeatedly praised her for being able to make twice as many cigars a day as the slowest workers. Too late, she realized that the owner was using her to set the pace for a speed-up. He soon announced that everyone's pay would drop from 14 to 13 cents per 100 cigars.

At home, the family lived among other Jewish immigrants who were similarly scraping by. "It was a hard winter. There was always someone losing a job, or hopelessly in search of one. Or the school-children were without shoes or decent clothing. Or there was nothing to pay the grocer who refused further credit. Or someone came to borrow an egg for a sick child. Or the eternal Installment Plan Agent had . . . threatened to take away everything. . . . Or a baby about to be born, and where will they get ten dollars for the midwife?"

The midwife came often to the Pastor household, for Hindl gave birth to five more children. This greatly increased the pressure on Rose to earn. After working a ten- or twelve-hour day, she sometimes went on to roll cigars until midnight in a smaller neighborhood workshop. Yet she seldom made more than eight dollars a week, equal to about $240 today. Her stepfather often made even less, and some of that had to be spent on fodder for his horse. Before long, horse and junk wagon were mortgaged, like the household furniture. During one blizzard, Rose quietly went without food for five days, so the others could have what little there was.

When her mother gave birth, it was Rose who had to carry water from the well and to clean the sheets and diapers in the washtub. The family's hardships were compounded by the Panic of 1893, when some 600 American banks and 15,000 businesses failed. Millions lost their savings and had to be fed by soup kitchens, and homeless families filled the streets, begging for food. More than four million people were thrown out of work, leaving nearly a quarter of all American workers unemployed. Indebted farmers plunged into bankruptcy. Angry groups of jobless workers tried to make their way to Washington, only to be stopped by federal troops. Those lucky enough to be still working often saw their wages and hours brutally slashed. The market for both Israel Pastor's scrap metal and Rose's cigars collapsed. The factory owner showed her a storeroom filled to the ceiling with unsold cigars and told her, "When I get rid of the stock on hand you may come back."

As the Pastor family ate still less, Israel took to drink and at times became violent with his wife and stepdaughter. "A blind brute force, raging and relentless, had entered our home to stay," Rose wrote. They took in a boarder to help with the rent, but he had his own problems and was soon gone. When the landlord evicted them during another blizzard, they moved to new quarters with money Rose borrowed from her boss. The saloon soaked up ever more of Israel's erratic earnings.

Somehow, in the midst of all her pregnancies and other travails, Hindl found time to read Yiddish poetry aloud to her children. Something else also nourished Rose's love of literature, the first book she possessed, and for months the only one: Charles and Mary Lamb's *Tales from Shakespeare.* "During my first year in America I read nothing but Lamb's 'Tales.' I had nothing else to read, looked for nothing else. It never occurred to me that there might be other books in the world. I had never heard of any." In this popular retelling of Shakespeare's plays for children, Rose was particularly drawn to Isabella, "the noble-minded heroine of *Measure for Measure,*" who "became my ideal of lofty womanhood. To be like her was the dream of my life." The chaste Isabella heroically resists the entreaties of the lustful, scheming Angelo to yield her virginity to him, does various good deeds, and as a result is rewarded with a marriage proposal from a duke. It would turn out to be an uncanny foreshadowing of Rose's own future.

Far from the realm of dukes and princes, Rose's employer for roughly half the years she worked in Cleveland cigar factories, Isaac Brudno, was a petty tyrant. "He would go from rack to rack; picking up handfuls of stogies. A mis-roll or two, a head or two badly sealed; a slight unevenness in length would call forth a violent fit of temper. He would hurl curses at the workers, break and twist the stogies out of shape, and throw them into the drawer of waste cuttings! A morning's work gone to the scrap-pile!

"'You call this stogie-rolling? Get out of my shop. Get out, this minute, or I'll pitch you through the window.'"

Rose later wrote a poem, "Song of the Cigar," that began:

> *Cut, cut, cut!*
> *The Sumatra as brown as a nut.*
> *Cut finely the selvage to-day,*
> *The foreman is looking my way;*
> *And I may be docked from my pay.*
> *Cut, cut, cut!*
>
> *Roll, roll, roll!*
> *Tho' dark as the shop is my soul,*
> *I may not look out at the blue,*
> *I'll make some mis-rolls if I do;*
> *And the foreman will break them in two.*
> *Roll, roll, roll!*

Rose was exaggerating little about the hardships of working for Brudno. Here is a factory inspector's description of this same workplace:

> The ventilation of the entire building very bad. . . . No means of collecting the scraps from the cigars; simply thrown on floor, walked over, swept up and sold to other firms to make the cheap scrap tobacco and clippings which are in very many cases used for chewing tobacco as well as smoking. While I was standing in the room an old man who was wrapping cigars took a violent fit of coughing and sat there spitting on the floor, right into the scraps of tobacco. Not one person in the place used a knife to trim the cigars. They all bit off the ends, and either swallowed

the saliva or spat it out on the floor. The mouths and faces of both men and women were stained with the juice. . . . One window in the rear of the second floor was open, but the air from the alley was so filled with the odor of decaying fruit and vegetables that it was impossible to leave it up for long.

Israel Pastor's drinking continued, and then Rose and her mother became desperate, for he disappeared. "No word, no clue. I worked impossible hours now at a frantic pace. . . .

"One evening I came from work to find him seated by the kitchen stove.

"'Hullo, Rosalie.'

"'Hullo, father.'

"Simply, quietly. As if he had not been gone for months without leaving any trace."

The same thing happened again and again. Finally, he left once more and did not return.

The last stanza of that poem of hers ran:

> *Count, count, count!*
> *To what does this day's work amount?*
> *One dollar and twenty-five cents*
> *And I must keep eight souls alive!*
> *Oh! how can man's faith in God thrive!*
> *Count, count, count!*

By the late 1890s, cigar rollers in Cleveland, like workers everywhere in the United States, were starting to hear about socialism. Rose lost one job when a manager found a book by the Belgian socialist leader Émile Vandervelde under her workbench. But she was disappointed by a few socialist meetings she attended, because "always I found a violent, wordy conflict in progress."

The other movement American workers were talking about was organized labor. Its great victories were yet to come, but one event not far from Cleveland had caught the nation's attention: a bloody

1892 strike at one of Andrew Carnegie's steel mills in Homestead, Pennsylvania. Workers had battled strikebreakers hired from the Pinkerton detective agency and landed on the factory grounds from barges on the Monongahela River, leaving at least seven steelworkers and three Pinkertons dead and many more injured. Some 8,500 National Guardsmen were called in to crush the strike.

For the moment, however, Rose found the union movement disappointing. Though Samuel Gompers, president of the American Federation of Labor, had begun his own working life in a cigar factory, the AFL saw itself as a guild of highly skilled craftsmen. When a group of Cleveland workers that included Rose tried to join its Cigar Makers' International Union, they were turned away. The union had no interest in those who made stogies, or cheap cigars, especially when so many were women and new immigrants willing to work for rock-bottom wages. The union movement was also not immune from America's ethnic tensions: AFL members at this time were overwhelmingly of German, British, or Irish ancestry, with no fondness for impoverished newcomers from Southern and Eastern Europe. Gompers backed tough restrictions on such immigrants.

In these long years in the factories, poetry became Rose's main solace. "Once your hand is trained," she wrote of cigar-making, "you can think the whole day." Or read. As she worked, a book was often propped up on her cigar bench. She published a few poems in a local newspaper and sometimes recited them at meetings of the Friendly Club, a group of Jewish single women. There, records show, she was elected to the odd-sounding post of "chairman of badges." At one performance evening she recited Edwin Markham's "The Man with the Hoe," widely popular as a protest against the exploitation of labor.

For this, she drew a sharp rebuke from the "women of leisure" of the city's wealthier German Jewish community who sponsored the club with the aim of educating and uplifting new immigrants. "Didn't I know that the poem is about a French peasant? . . . Didn't I realize that here in America we had no such peasantry? That here the farmers are free and rich?"

Rose shared the musical talent of her cantor uncles, and she was much in demand to sing at weddings and parties—and at work. "Someone would call out: 'Sing, Rose, sing!'" she recalled. "At the end of each verse, the whole shop would repeat the last line."

Although the poetry she wrote was in English, much of her singing was in Yiddish. A favorite song of hers was "Mayn Tsavoe," or "My Testament," by the anarchist poet David Edelstadt. She translated the first two verses as:

> *Ah, good friends, when I am gone,*
> *Bring our flag to my grave.*
> *The free flag, the red one,*
> *Dyed in the blood of workingmen.*
>
> *There in my grave will I hear*
> *My free song, my storm song*
> *And there I will shed tears*
> *For the enslaved Gentile and Jew.*

She sang hymns, ballads, folk songs, and German *lieder*—she was particularly fond of those by Franz Schubert. But "labor songs and songs of revolt had a special place in our hearts. They were the only expression of protest at hand. I sang as I came up the stairs in the morning, and sang as I left the loft at night. The boss would often hear me singing, but he never seemed to know what it was about."

A music teacher who visited the Friendly Club selected Rose "for solo work, and pronounced my voice a 'mezzo-soprano of rare range and quality,' and insisted that it be trained." But even at cut rates, the lessons were 50 cents each, and "after two lessons I am compelled to remember that fifty cents buys ten loaves of bread. I go to the studio no more."

Rose's long work hours left little time for romance. In her teen years and early twenties, her sole long-term infatuation was with a son of the owner of the Brudno cigar works, Ezra. He sometimes could be found in the family factory, but was clearly destined for higher things, for he attended college and then Yale Law School. Although she fantasized about him endlessly, imagining that he shared her love of literature (she wasn't wrong—he later would publish several novels), on only three occasions could she summon the courage to speak to him. The gap of class between them was too great.

One day a neighbor brought to the Pastor apartment some copies of a newspaper published in New York City. The *Yiddishes Tageblatt,* or *Jewish Daily News,* was the country's oldest and largest Yiddish daily. It featured a single page in English, Rose noticed, which invited readers throughout the country to send in letters. She did so, writing one from the factory during lunch hour, complaining jocularly that she made 200 fewer cigars that day thanks to the time it took to pen the letter. Not long afterward her words appeared in print, and she received a message "in the editor's own hand urging me to tell him more of myself, of the shop, of my life at home," and suggesting she try writing an advice column for young women. She was thrilled when she received a payment for the first one: a check for two dollars.

Under the pen name Zelda, Rose's "Heart to Heart Talk: Just Between Ourselves, Girls" was a chatty, cheerful mix of anecdotes, treacly poetry, and admonitions, such as "Don't let a day pass without its adding at least one stone to the building of your character." But she soon found that "the only hours in which I could earn the two extra dollars at writing were those torn from sleep." This left her exhausted and rolling cigars at a slower pace, a disaster for the family, since Rose was now the sole wage earner supporting her mother and her six younger sisters and brothers. She could not earn enough to feed them all, and so several were in orphanages or foster care. Her life was so little her own that she had no chance to see what the world outside the Cleveland slums even looked like. "I never saw a daisy," she would tell an audience years later, "until I was a grown woman."

Continuing the column was too much and she had to stop. But

when she did so, reported the editor, "hundreds of letters were being received from all parts of the country: What has become of Zelda?" Then came an extraordinary message from the newspaper's publisher—an offer of a job as a reporter in New York, at the princely salary of $15 a week, roughly double her cigar worker's earnings.

3

City of the World

IT WAS JANUARY 1903 WHEN the 23-year-old Rose stepped off a Pennsylvania Railroad train in Jersey City—there were as yet no tunnels under the Hudson River—and took a ferry to Manhattan. Someone who met her later that year described her as having "sparkling brown eyes and a pale, delicate face" beneath hair "like a bundle of red-brown combed wool." What a combination of awe, fear, and excitement she must have felt on seeing the great city's skyline spread out before her. As Emma Goldman would write of her own arrival in New York at about the same age, "All that had happened in my life until that time was now left behind me, cast off like a worn-out garment. A new world was before me, strange and terrifying."

Nearly ten times the size of Cleveland, the New York that loomed above the ferry dock was by far the nation's largest city; soon it would be the largest on the planet. It was already the world's biggest Jewish city. Truly Whitman's city of the world, in every sense it was a metropolis of superlatives: it had the country's greatest collection of millionaires; most illustrious array of libraries, theaters, and museums; biggest slums; tallest skyscraper; largest department store; and busiest port. It was on track to replace London as the world's financial capital, with the Bank of England already borrowing money on Wall Street. Separating Manhattan from Brooklyn and Queens, the

East River was claimed as the most heavily trafficked body of water anywhere. Spanning it was the Brooklyn Bridge, an engineering miracle held in place by feathery spiderwebs of cables made out of 14,000 miles of wire.

New York was the most polyglot city on earth, holding not just immigrants from places like Ireland, Sweden, or Portugal, but people who primarily identified themselves as Calabrians or Ruthenians or Dalmatians. Ethnic venues across the city ranged from the Czech National Hall to the Germania Assembly Rooms, as well as theaters in Italian, Spanish, Yiddish, and other languages. The *Yiddishes Tageblatt* where Rose had been promised a job was only one of several dozen foreign-language newspapers published in tongues from Greek to Arabic.

Some of what Rose saw in New York undoubtedly reminded her of Augustów: organ grinders and knife sharpeners on the sidewalks, or women at the Hester Street market wearing kerchiefs and aprons and hawking radishes, fish, chickens, pickles out of barrels, and challah for the Sabbath. "A great hubbub of human voices meets the ear as one nears the market" was how Rose described it. "Little boys, running with their baskets or bundles of wares, yelling at the tops of their voices; men using their lungs to the utmost capacity as they endeavor to call the attention of the women to the cheapness of the wares displayed on stalls, baskets or pushcarts. Teamsters whose lungs are wonderfully developed cry to the push-cart peddlers to get out of the way with their carts. Through all, the women's voices as they bargain loudly with the men or women at the little shops on wheels. And above the din the predominating cry, 'Women! women! women!' (the cry is in Yiddish: 'Veiber! veiber! veiber!')" The pushcarts sold everything from buttons and cloth scraps to garlic and freshly baked sweet potatoes from mobile wood-burning ovens. If you were too poor to invest in a cart, you could rent one for ten cents a day.

Other scenes—the palatial stone edifices of men's clubs, women in fur coats and hats with feathers or ruffles skating on the frozen ponds of Central Park—spoke of a different existence entirely. Far from the hardships of new immigrants, it was a world where fraternal societies in comfortable neighborhoods might raise funds for charity, or simply have a good time, by staging a "poverty ball." Guests came dressed in carpet scraps or worn-out clothing with rips and holes, and won prizes for the most ragged costumes.

The New York of 1903 was filled with things Rose had never seen: small steam locomotives puffing coal smoke while pulling elevated trains on tracks along frameworks of girders above the streets, thundering almost within reach of second-floor tenement windows, while teams of horses hauled trolleys along the streets below—both sources of power soon to be replaced by the magic of electricity. (The city's trolleys and elevated trains would provide more than a billion rides to passengers that year, more than all the railroads in the Western Hemisphere.) New York's 130,000 horses hauling freight wagons, fire engines, cabs, and fine carriages with top-hatted coachmen would take a little longer to give way to the internal combustion engine. By now, however, some of the new "horseless carriages," with spoked wheels and chauffeurs in open-air front seats, were already navigating among their four-legged competitors.

At night, the streets were bathed by the glow of nearly 60,000 lamps, most of them gas, lit at dusk by men carrying long poles with a flaming wick or cotton wad at the end. Policemen with high rounded helmets blew their whistles to try to clear traffic jams. A dense thicket of cranes, funnels, and masts lined the city's wharves; bowsprits overhung bustling dockworkers; steamboat whistles blew as the paddles of side-wheelers thrashed the water of the Hudson; and the giant Fulton Fish Market displayed a vast range of creatures from the sea. Underground, the earth pulsed with drills and jackhammers, as more than 7,000 laborers dug tunnels for a sprawling network of subway lines, the first of which would open the next year.

All this Rose would experience during her first weeks in New York. When she got off the ferry, however, the person she had expected to meet her, Abraham H. Fromenson, editor of the *Tageblatt*'s English page, was not there. In bringing her to New York, she ardently believed, he was doing more than simply recruiting a new reporter.

She had met him briefly a few months earlier when he made the long trip to Cleveland, supposedly "just to see me. After that meeting our friendship-by-correspondence took on a new color. There were declarations. . . . We shall be married and live happily ever afterward. . . . We shall be married and together work for the people." But after her arrival, she soon discovered that she was not the only woman to whom Fromenson had made such promises—and that he was already engaged. Years later, Miriam Zunser, a young journalist who befriended her in New York, recalled Rose's disappointment: "In our silent evenings together, in the Jackson Street park, or sometimes on the river bank, sitting between the posts of the Market Street pier, she would say enough for me to sense her suffering. Quietly we spoke, quietly we sang old English ballads, and quietly she wiped away her tears."

Fromenson did follow through on another promise, though: at the *Yiddishes Tageblatt*'s office, at 185 East Broadway, there was a job for her. The paper's English page had just gone from weekly to daily, and needed material for its columns. Anyone who has ever worked for a small, understaffed newspaper can easily imagine the editor's voice in the background, calling out, "Rose, we still have fifteen inches to fill!" The paper eagerly advertised her return: "Zelda Will Talk to Her Girls Tomorrow." In addition to resuming her advice column, Rose recalled, "I also became 'The Observer' and wrote sketches and impressions of the East Side; I made contributions in prose and verse under my own name. From time to time I published original aphorisms under the caption 'Ethics of the Dustpan.' . . . When the editor was absent, I wrote the English editorials."

She first lived in a flat packed with several generations of the family of Fromenson's secretary, sharing a bed with the secretary and her sister. This was not uncommon on Manhattan's Lower East Side, the city's most crowded quarter; one survey of the district in this decade showed 75 percent of families had three to five or more people sleeping in each bedroom. A 1906 study showed 51 blocks in New York with more than 3,000 residents each, 37 of the 51 on the Lower East Side. One block on Delancey Street, with 1,756 people per acre, may have been the most crowded in the world. The 1910 census would show 542,061 people packed into an area of slightly less than one and a half square miles. The more families that could be squeezed into each tenement, the more money its owner made. If they couldn't pay, they lost even those cramped quarters. Roughly 60,000 New York families were evicted from their homes each year.

Russian Jews dominated the Lower East Side, but Hungarian, Galician, and Romanian Jewish immigrants all had their own sub-neighborhoods. Butchers and restaurants were kosher. Although it had a bewildering variety of dialects, the common tongue was Yiddish, an offshoot of medieval German with added Slavic and Hebrew words. (The language reportedly once tripped up the powerful New York political boss Thomas Platt, who flew into a rage when 400 Lower East Side votes he had paid for didn't appear in his electoral tally. Platt's underlings had told voters to check off the "first column" on their ballots, but they had forgotten that Yiddish is written in Hebrew characters, from right to left. The surprised Prohibition Party found itself 400 votes richer.)

While Yiddish drama had been banned in Russia following the assassination of Alexander II, it flourished on the Lower East Side, which would soon be home to 20 Yiddish theaters hosting two million patron visits a year. Audiences munched on apples and peanuts, wept, laughed, jeered, hissed, and shouted advice to the actors. When the Russian-born Yiddish stage star Boris Thomashefsky died, 30,000 New Yorkers would march in his funeral procession.

The theater provided a respite from grim apartment life, in which hundreds of men, women, and children were squeezed into six-story walk-ups, seldom with any running hot water. In New York's dilapidated tenements, 350,000 rooms had no windows at all, or ones that opened only onto an air shaft. These shafts were normally so narrow you could reach across and shake a neighbor's hand. When windows onto the shaft were open in hot weather, any noise—a screaming argument, a baby crying, a couple making love, a woman giving birth, the pained coughing of one of the tens of thousands of New Yorkers with tuberculosis—carried through all the apartments in the building. Little light penetrated below the top floor or two of an air shaft, and in case of fire it acted like a chimney, quickly spreading flames upward. The bottom of the shaft was typically filled with stagnant water and rotting garbage, and in warm weather the stench, added to air already ripe with horse manure and coal smoke, could be overpowering.

Outside, laundry was strung across narrow alleys to dry, and, wrote one observer, a person on foot "had to pick and nudge his way through dense swarms of bedraggled half-washed humanity, past garbage barrels rearing their overflowing contents," and "underneath tiers and tiers of fire escapes barricaded and festooned with mattresses, pillows and feather beds not yet gathered in for the night." Sharp-eyed children roamed the streets scavenging coal and wood scraps for family stoves. To make ends meet, domestics and restaurant workers often stole food from their employers, and many a family whose utilities had been turned off for nonpayment found ways to tap a nearby water pipe or electric line. One new immigrant wondered, "Was this the America we sought? Or was it only, after all, a circle that we had traveled, with a Jewish ghetto at its beginning and its end."

The Lower East Side would be a fertile spawning ground for every variety of American socialism, anarchism, and communism, but none of this was reflected in the conservative *Yiddishes Tageblatt*. Writing for the paper gave Rose a quick education in how the world worked. "During an election period I observe strange comings and goings. Men closet themselves with the publishers in a small conference room. They come out flushed, glad, and excited. . . . Candidates for office come to the editorial rooms, rabbis, presidents of societies, every manner of East Side worthy. They all want something." And they got it. Money changed hands and favorable articles and editorials soon appeared.

From Rose, Fromenson wanted material for "the girls," as they were always called. She wrote about neighborhood shops, a trip to the country, women who were lucky or unlucky in love, a new Lower East Side park, a visit to a school, and her impressions as a "hayseed" in New York. Self-improvement and self-discipline were constant themes. She recommended novelists like Louisa May Alcott, George Eliot, Charles Dickens, and Charlotte Brontë. She told the "girls" that they should avoid "vulgar thoughts," revealing dresses, and kissing in public, and let themselves be courted only by good men. "A flirt is a creature all men despise, some men amuse themselves with, a few men fall in love with, and no man, worthy of the name, marries." So far as we can tell, Rose followed this advice herself. To one reader who wrote asking if she should yield to a man's urging, "Zelda" replied, "'Free love!' Do you doubt the terrible results of following this pernicious doctrine . . . Leave him!" Readers should help their mothers, she wrote, be content with their lot, scorn frippery like hats with stuffed birds, and not dream of great riches. "Those luxuries are beyond the station of the working girl."

Rose's $15 a week still could not support her entire family—two of her siblings remained in an orphan asylum in Cleveland—but it was enough, some six months after her arrival, to bring her mother and the other four children to New York. All of them moved into a small apartment near the *Tageblatt* office, which they shared with a boarder, a hunchbacked humor writer from the newspaper whom Rose was fond of.

Sometime during those early months in New York, a mysterious visitor—Rose seems not to have known his identity or motive—came to her desk at work and gave her the address of a nearby cobbler's shop, where, he told her, she could find her biological father. This shocked her; she had not seen him since he left Augustów when she was an infant. At a brief, awkward meeting, she did not tell him her name but he seems to have guessed who she was. To her dismay, she then heard that he quickly sold everything he owned and fled the city, apparently afraid that she and her mother might "make demands upon him." Efforts she made to find him again were in vain.

Although Rose failed to restore the relationship with her father, her columns often praised family ties. Closely connected to that was religion. She urged readers to pray daily, observe the high holy days and other Jewish traditions, and go "to the balcony" to worship—a traditional place for women in sex-segregated synagogues. All this was not a reflection of her own practice but of the fact that the *Yiddishes Tageblatt* was the country's main journalistic voice of Orthodox Judaism. Except for one childhood memory from Augustów, nowhere in her published or unpublished writing does she refer to setting foot in a synagogue unless invited to give a speech.

When it came to the question of whether Jews and Christians should mix, however, "Zelda" was so ardently uncompromising that she clearly was reflecting Rose's own feelings. Marriage was very much on the minds of her readers, and among the most numerous tradesmen on the Lower East Side were *shadkhanim,* or Jewish matchmakers. Rose repeatedly warned Jewish women against allowing themselves to be courted by Christian men. She also strongly opposed placing adopted Jewish children in Christian homes. "Our children MUST be kept away from all Christianizing influence."

It is hardly surprising that she thought Christians dangerous. Nothing she knew of the world suggested otherwise. For nearly a decade, France, for instance, had been convulsed by the Dreyfus case, where anti-Semites had trumped up charges of espionage against a Jewish army officer. The year Rose moved to New York saw the publication of the notorious anti-Semitic forgery *The Protocols of the Elders of Zion*. It would be widely reprinted in the United States and Europe in the coming decades. Moreover, every American Jew knew that Russia was now beginning a new cycle of pogroms, with the feckless, passive Tsar Nicholas II doing nothing to stop them. A vicious massacre in Kishinev in April 1903 spawned headlines and protests throughout the world. Russian mobs killed at least 49 Jews, raped or injured 600 more, and pillaged more than a thousand shops or homes. Some victims were beheaded or crucified or had nails driven into their skulls. As usual, the police did not interfere. Photographs showed rows of corpses and bandaged survivors. Rose responded in the *Yiddishes Tageblatt* by calling for an end to both "Jew-baiting and Negro-lynching" in the United States.

No pogroms ravaged America, but a wide range of college fraternities, men's and women's clubs, law firms, banks, and hotels explicitly or in practice barred Jews. Millions of Americans looked on them—especially the poorer ones now fleeing Russia in such large numbers—with fear or contempt. In a speech to his fellow senators, Henry Cabot Lodge of Massachusetts, a Boston Brahmin *par excellence,* warned against "undesirable immigrants" who were not from "kindred races," quoting a poem comparing them to the Goths and Vandals who pillaged Rome. His friend the historian Henry Adams declared that "the Jew makes me creep," and spoke in his autobiography of a "furtive Yacoob or Ysaac still reeking of the Ghetto, snarling a weird Yiddish." Adams also slipped a sinister Jew named Schneidekoupon (coupon clipper) into his novel *Democracy.* A third ill-spirited Henry, the novelist Henry James, deigned to visit the Lower East Side in 1904, but was disgusted by the Jews he saw "swarming" there, who reminded him of "small, strange animals . . . snakes or worms."

Earlier groups of Jewish immigrants had come mostly from Germany. They were far fewer in number, more educated and better off than the Russian Jews, and likely to practice the modernized Reform Judaism unknown in Russia. To both Reform Jews and Gentiles, the Orthodox Jews from Russia and eastern Europe, particularly those from the Hasidic sect, appeared drastically alien, the men with wide-brimmed black hats, long dark coats or caftans, beards, and curly sidelocks, the women with wigs or head scarves. While praying, particularly devout men wore *tefillin,* little square leather boxes containing pieces of parchment with verses from the Torah, attached to the arm and forehead.

American anti-Semitism was not without violence. One notorious episode had taken place less than a mile from the *Tageblatt* office, six months before Rose arrived in New York. Irish American workers at a plant that made printing presses began throwing garbage, nuts and bolts, and scrap metal onto the funeral procession of a prominent Lower East Side rabbi as it passed below their windows, and then turned fire hoses on the group as well. "Is this Russia?" shouted a man in the procession. More than 100 people were injured, some by falling metal and more when the police arrived and spent 30 minutes clubbing the mourners, while ignoring the factory workers. "You know what boys are," the factory owner said of his employees later. "Some of them have a dislike for the Jews." Neither the police nor the workers were ever punished.

Prejudice against Jews in America had grown markedly stronger during the last decades of the nineteenth century. The rapid industrialization following the Civil War concentrated great wealth in a new class of robber barons, leaving millions of workers and farmers behind. In economic crises like the Panic of 1893, which had so shaken the Pastor family, people looked for scapegoats. Many turned to a traditional one: the cabal of Jewish bankers like the Rothschilds who supposedly controlled the international gold supply. When William Jennings Bryan won the Democratic Party's 1896 nomination for president with a famous speech against the gold standard — "You shall not press down upon the brow of labor this crown of thorns! You shall not crucify mankind upon a cross of gold!" — it summoned up for many Americans the image of Jews as Christ-killers, Shylocks, and gold merchants. There was even a short-lived American Society for the Suppression of the Jews. "If this is a free country," asked one speaker at its first meeting, "why can't we be free of Jews?"

The enormous flood of immigrants would peak in 1907, when 1.3 million of them, Jewish and Gentile, arrived in a single year. They helped make the United States the world's economic powerhouse, but their coming deeply unsettled the Anglo-Saxon elite who had run the country since colonial days. Except for slaves, the Irish, and a small number of Asians, those who came to America in its first two and a half centuries had been primarily Protestants from Northern Europe. By 1890, however, the great bulk of arrivals were from Italy, Eastern Europe, or the Russian Empire, and were Catholic, Eastern Orthodox, or Jewish. Anglo-Saxon Protestants still controlled the heights of the economy but felt they had lost power over several major cities, like New York and Boston, now run by Irish Catholic political machines. By 1900, the majority of men over 21 in Manhattan were foreign-born. Furthermore, the immigrants spoke a Babel of languages, while the Yiddish-speaking Jews, Syrians, Greeks, Serbs, and Russians also used different alphabets. Someone whose forefathers came over on the *Mayflower* could no longer read the signs on hundreds of shops and businesses in New York.

Such people often felt, We *built* this country; who are all these newcomers? One disgruntled reaction of this sort appeared in a book published in 1902: "Throughout the [nineteenth] century men of the sturdy stocks of the north of Europe had made up the main stream of foreign blood which was every year added to the vital working force of the country . . . but now there came multitudes of men of the lowest class from the south of Italy and men of the meaner sort out of Hungary and Poland, men out of the ranks where there was neither skill nor energy nor any initiative of quick intelligence; and they came in numbers which increased from year to year, as if the countries of the south of Europe were disburdening themselves of the more sordid and hapless elements of their population." The author was a young Princeton professor named Woodrow Wilson.

Others had a different reaction. They felt that since these new immigrants were here to stay, they should be helped to become healthy, prosperous, proper citizens. Out of this feeling grew the settlement house movement, whose purpose, wrote one early activist, was to allow people "of education and culture . . . to help bring sunshine and refinement into the lives of the children of the neighborhood." The idea of settlement houses rapidly spread through the big cities of the American Northeast and Midwest. Idealistic upper-class volunteers established these outposts in slum neighborhoods to provide vocational and literacy classes, hot lunches for children, music lessons, medical help, and much more. Settlement house workers published voluminous reports documenting the problems new immigrants faced, like tuberculosis, child labor, and exploitation by landlords. They wrote earnest books with titles like *Our Slavic Fellow Citizens*. Research into industrial accidents by settlement workers played a role in the passage of early workers' compensation laws.

In New York, no neighborhood seemed to need more "sunshine and refinement" than where Rose was living and working, the Lower East Side. The first attempt to start a settlement house there, by seven Smith College graduates, occasioned a misunderstanding. The policeman who patrolled the block assumed that the seven young women he saw moving into a building were opening a brothel. He assured them that they would have no trouble with the law as long as he got his share of the take.

A book that helped stimulate the settlement house movement was the influential *How the Other Half Lives,* by the Danish-born journalist and photographer Jacob Riis. The world it portrayed was one Rose was intimately familiar with, but Riis shocked many middle- and upper-class readers with his gritty photographs of New York City's slums. Some in the upper reaches of the top half felt impelled to help those who lived in such surroundings. By 1905, American cities would be home to over 200 settlement houses, a number that would more than double within five years. The young workers who staffed them were overwhelmingly college-educated men and women of Anglo-Saxon background, often well enough off that they could afford to work without a salary. Most of them were devout Protestants: a survey of more than 300 volunteers found that 88 percent were active church members.

After Theodore Roosevelt became president in 1901, the spreading talk of reform further stimulated such idealism. One young woman who began teaching a dance and calisthenics class for girls at a Lower East Side settlement house two years later was his own niece, 19-year-old Eleanor Roosevelt. For her cousin Franklin, who was courting her, it was the first time he saw poverty and tenement life at close hand. "My God," he told her when he helped her take a sick child home to a crowded tenement one day, "I didn't know people lived like that!"

Many settlement house volunteers soon found themselves activists in a different and wider world. Staff members at Chicago's Hull House organized relief for railway workers caught up in a bitter strike, and, in an era when employers ruthlessly tried to smash labor unions, settlement houses often provided rooms where unions could meet. New York settlement volunteers were at the wharf to welcome a group of injured refugees from the 1903 Kishinev pogrom.

People began to talk of the importance of "vital contact"—a phrase soon much in the air—between those with higher education and those who lived in the teeming but vibrant city slums. Settlement house pioneer and social worker Jane Addams declared that "to shut one's self away from that half of the race is to shut one's self away from the most vital part of it." Princeton alumnus Ernest Poole, who went to work in the Lower East Side's University Settlement in 1902, was greeted by another college graduate already there with the admonition, "Make friends with these tenement people and listen, listen all the time. They've got a lot to teach us boys, so for the love of Jesus Christ don't let's be uplifters here!"

For volunteers like Poole, there was an exotic aura to the Lower East Side, whose narrow, cobblestone streets seemed so appealingly at odds with the restrained propriety of the social universe they had grown up in. Its allure was not unlike that which jazz and black culture would have for some well-off young whites of later generations. Whatever the mixture of altruism and imagined "vital contact" lay behind the creation of settlement houses, in an America where the gaps between classes and ethnic groups were so great, they were among the few places people from very different backgrounds could easily mix, talk, and learn about each other.

Anti-Semitism might be rampant in some quarters, but many of these young settlement house volunteers were philo-Semites. They found the Yiddish theater, with its passionate, kibitzing audiences, far livelier than Broadway. "We went to countless cafés," remembered Poole, "large and small, Russian, Polish and German cafés, Socialist, Anarchist, free love, freethinker and actor and poet cafés, where, coming from the oppression of Europe into the sudden freedom here to argue and shout and write as they pleased, young Jews were burning up their lives in this great furnace of ideas. Over black coffee and cigarettes they would talk fervently half the night and then, after three or four hours' sleep, go to the sweatshops where they worked from dawn till late evening." Poole soon learned Yiddish.

Many such volunteers worked at the University Settlement, one of New York's largest. It was quartered in an imposing, five-story, brick and limestone building ten blocks from the *Yiddishes Tage-blatt*. Rose did almost all her work for the paper either from her desk or by talking to the neighborhood's tradesmen, market women, and shop assistants, with whom she now felt at home. And so one Friday afternoon in the summer of 1903, the day before her 24th birthday, it made her highly uneasy when Fromenson, her boss, asked her to go to the University Settlement and interview one of its leaders, a man with an august, multibarreled Anglo name. She knew that the college graduates of that institution's staff came from a totally foreign universe. "I had visions of a stern old man with a long grey beard sitting on a throne, a sort of rich man's Jehova." At first she refused the assignment, but Fromenson insisted. "You get that interview this evening, young lady," he told her, "or don't come back on Monday morning."

4

Missionary to the Slums

JAMES GRAHAM PHELPS STOKES — Graham to his friends — had grown up in an entirely different New York from the one Rose now lived and worked in. In his childhood, his mother and father divided their time between a Madison Avenue mansion in the fashionable Murray Hill neighborhood; a Staten Island weekend estate with a dock, formal gardens, greenhouses, and a bowling alley; and a summer retreat in the Adirondack Mountains of upstate New York, a rustic complex of log and stone buildings on a wooded island staffed by ten servants. Each summer, Graham's parents chartered a specially equipped railway freight car to take three horses, a carriage, 25 trunks, and assorted other baggage from Grand Central Station to the Adirondacks. The family often traveled, and the return addresses on letters home spanned the world: Grand Hôtel Britannia, Venice; Élysée Palace Hôtel, Paris; SS *Rameses the Great,* Cook's Nile Steamer Services. On such trips, the nine Phelps Stokes children were encouraged to keep journals illustrated with picture postcards. As a young man, Graham was hosted by the banker J. P. Morgan on Morgan's oceangoing yacht, the *Corsair,* and by the railroad baron Cornelius Vanderbilt II during a two-week "housewarming" at the Breakers, his palatial estate in Newport, Rhode Island.

In 1894, a 500-man construction crew completed a new summer "cottage" in the Berkshires for the Phelps Stokes family. With 100 rooms and several castle-like turrets, it was at the time the largest private dwelling in the United States. Legend has it that one of Graham's brothers, in the class of 1896 at Yale, wired their mother that he planned to bring "some '96 fellows" home for the weekend. The apostrophe failed to appear in the telegram, and his mother replied, "Many guests already here. Have only room for 50." Another such tale claims that one of the younger children was bicycling outside one day when his mother called him in, saying that there was a storm coming and he'd have plenty of room to bicycle in the attic.

The fortune behind these various homes stretched back more than a century. It was rooted in a string of intermarriages over several generations among three families who all brought substantial assets to the table, named Phelps (shipping, banking, real estate), Stokes (marble quarries, wool importing), and Dodge (textiles, mining). One of the marriages between these clans was that of Graham's parents—his father was a Stokes and his mother a Phelps. On her father's death in 1888, she inherited a 45-room Madison Avenue mansion even grander than the one she and her husband lived in, as well as $2 million—roughly the equivalent of $50 million today. Still more money was left to a trust fund for her children.

The three families' names were yoked together not only in companies, like Phelps, Stokes & Co. (investment banking), Phelps Stokes Estates (New York apartment buildings), or the mining behemoth Phelps, Dodge & Co., but in the compound names of dozens of family members. Those of Graham and his eight brothers and sisters all ended in Phelps Stokes; there was a slew of Phelps Dodges; and an eccentric uncle of Graham's was William Earl Dodge Stokes. If these prized surnames disappeared when a woman married, they could be preserved in the names of children. So, for example, a son of Graham's sister Caroline and her husband, Robert Hunter, would be named Phelps Stokes Hunter.

First names also traveled down through the generations. An early Phelps patriarch had been christened Anson, in honor of a British admiral who circumnavigated the globe in the mid-1700s and captured a Spanish galleon full of gold. Three descendants would be named Anson Phelps Stokes and another three Anson Greene

Phelps Dodge. When one of the family businesses began manufacturing copper and brass goods, it would be in Ansonia, Connecticut, and another town named Ansonia appeared near a family-owned lumbering operation in Pennsylvania. Another family
enterprise, New York's Ansonia Hotel, would become one site of a
bitter conflict that figures in this story.

In the Phelps Stokes household, no extravagance was spared. At
one party, the crust of a large pie was broken open to release a flock
of doves, and Graham's mother once hired a private railroad car to
take a group of family and friends to the Grand Canyon and back.
But the family culture also included occasional acts of symbolic sacrifice. One Lent, Graham and his siblings went without ice cream so
that the money that would otherwise have been spent could provide
a scholarship for an Indian student at Hampton Institute, a black
college in Virginia. Every Christmas the family brought baskets of
food to the residents of a nearby slum or the children at the Colored
Orphan Asylum, on 143rd Street. And despite their multiple luxurious homes, the Stokes parents apparently encouraged their children
to acquire practical skills, for at some point—it is not clear when
—Graham learned bricklaying and carpentry.

For the most part, though, his childhood was one of sailing in
the Caribbean, first-class staterooms on ocean liners to Europe, in-
struction in horseback riding at Dickel's Riding Academy on Fifth
Avenue, and private schools. At one of these he was an enthusiastic member of the military cadet corps, becoming a company commander. When he went on to Yale, Graham again enrolled in a cadet program. At college he was one of two "class deacons"—friends
called him "Deac"—who led fellow students in prayer meetings.
He ran on the Yale track team and was voted the best dancer in his
class. Many a young debutante surely dreamed of whirling around
the ballroom in his arms at the great manor in the Berkshires, and
of someday making the house her own.

Graham, however, left no clue to any romances during his bach-
elor years. For unmarried men of his class and time, any sexual experience was likely to be furtive and paid for. Like many college
towns of that era, New Haven had a thriving red-light district, and

the city's police ledgers list hundreds of women arrested for "lascivious carriage," "nightwalking," or frequenting a "House of Ill Fame." But whether the class deacon ever set foot in such a house we do not know.

After graduating, Graham and one of his brothers took the sort of leisurely world tour that was a ritual for young men of their station in life. After that, he began training as a physician, planning to become a medical missionary—a surprising departure from what one might expect. It was hardly a rebellion, though, for his family were churchgoers and some ancestors had supported missionary work. One of his Dodge relatives was so devout that he had resigned from the boards of two railroads because they refused to stop running trains on Sundays.

It was as a Columbia University medical student that Graham first encountered New York's slums, and they shocked him. As part of his training, he was assigned to a horse-drawn ambulance from Roosevelt Hospital. One night, he remembered, "I had picked up an almost dead woman, long after midnight, at the bottom of a pitch-black airshaft into which she had jumped from a sixth floor window, far above, to escape her brutal husband." At the hospital, he saw many more women and children with ugly gashes and bruises from domestic violence. Poverty, he quickly realized, underlay everything. A mother whose small son had just drowned told him that she had no money, even for an undertaker. One agreed to handle the boy's body only if she signed over to him the benefits of her son's life insurance.

In a Lower East Side tenement, "a great barrack-like structure, six stories high" that housed some 600 people, Graham found "no toilet or bathroom facilities of any kind, except a single open sink on the landing of each floor, with a dim gas jet over it, and a row of shabby privy sheds in a small inner 'court.'" Some who did not want to descend six floors used the building's roof as their toilet. He found two married couples and a child sharing a bedroom nine feet square, with the child's bed suspended from the ceiling over one of the beds below. In another tenement, drinking water came from a well next to the privies.

Toward the end of his medical training, when he was still struggling to come to terms with what he was seeing, Graham took a summer vacation at his parents' island home on an Adirondack lake. He and his father were in the family sailboat when his father made a request that dismayed him. "My son," he said, "I think it is your duty to give up your proposed medical career and to help me in my business!" The elder Stokes's eyesight was beginning to fail, and none of his other children seemed suited to help. Graham had five sisters, but a woman as a business executive was unthinkable. Of his three brothers, one was studying for the ministry, one establishing himself as a successful architect, and the third still a schoolboy.

In the end, father and son reached a compromise: Graham would finish medical school but not open a practice as a physician. This would allow him time to help his father, but also to do some of the good works he dreamed of. Working from an office near Wall Street, in the same suite as his father, he became, among other things, president of two New York City real estate holding companies and a director of several more, vice president of the State Bank of Nevada, and president of two Nevada mining companies and of the Nevada Central Railroad. The latter was a 93-mile narrow-gauge line Graham's father had ordered built, to connect several lucrative family-owned mines in central Nevada with the transcontinental rail line across the northern part of the state. A local newspaper called one of the family mining companies "the wealthiest corporation in Nevada." Graham began traveling west once or twice a year, sending back reports to his father about shaft depths and the amount of silver and gold being recovered per ton of ore. Ironically, these visits became times when he could put his medical training to use. There were few doctors in the region, and miners and their families started calling on him for help.

But what might fulfill his wish to do good? One Sunday afternoon in the living room of his parents' home, his eye was caught by a newspaper article about settlement houses. Curious, he soon joined the board of the University Settlement Society, which was filled with reformers from New York's upper crust. Thwarted from becoming a medical missionary in foreign lands, observes one scholar of settlements, Graham "became instead a missionary to the Lower East Side."

Before long, he was deeply involved in planning a new building for the University Settlement. His architect brother's firm did the design, and his mother donated $5,000 toward its construction. Other members of the city's elite contributed as well. The building's five floors included a lecture hall, a kindergarten, and living quarters for volunteers on the top two floors. Since it was not proper to have unmarried men and women living in the same building, settlement house residents usually were either all one or all the other. Those at the University Settlement were men, some of them friends of Graham's.

With one foot in business and the other in social uplift, Graham dropped out of both these worlds in 1898 to rejoin another he was fond of, spending 13 months on active duty as a cavalryman during the Spanish-American War. He never made it overseas, but played on his squadron's polo team and took part—as troops often did in this era of stormy labor battles—in keeping order during a strike of Italian American workers building a dam for New York City's water system. In Graham's mind, these disparate worlds were not at all contradictory. Like charitable work, volunteer military service was common for young upper-class businessmen. In that same war Theodore Roosevelt recruited many Ivy Leaguers for his renowned Rough Riders cavalry regiment.

Still in his 20s, Graham thought of himself as a reformer, not a revolutionary. In his mind, eradicating poverty did not require the redistribution of riches belonging to families like his own. What the poor needed were basic skills. In one pamphlet—was it inspired by an inedible meal?—he urged settlement houses to provide cooking classes for women. "Thousands of laboring men returning to their homes tired and wearied from the labors of the day, find awaiting them, instead of a good and wholesome supper, food . . . abominally [*sic*] prepared. . . . When for instance a piece of steak has been broiled to the consistency of sole leather, or fried in grease until each particle of the meat is surrounded by an envelope of oil impenetrable to the gastric fluids, and when in addition its surface has been charred and thoroughly carbonized, it is no wonder that the workman of ordinary patience leaves his wife's table in despair to seek something palatable at the nearest saloon."

To his mind, the classes, like the sexes, were fixed in their proper places. "No work for social reform," he wrote, "can be lasting in its benefits unless it tends to spread and develop friendship and kindly feeling between the various social classes. So long as the rich as a class hold aloof from the poor . . . the gulfs that we hear so much of from our socialistic friends, as separating the social classes, will never be obliterated. If the classes could become the friends of each other, the 'gulfs' would not exist." Such kindliness, he believed, was to flow from the top down. "Intelligent and cheerful Christian people, by associating with children, and particularly the children of the poor, can help them to lead good and happy and useful lives."

Whatever the limitations of Graham's sense of *noblesse oblige,* he took his commitment to the University Settlement seriously. Several years out of medical school, in 1902 he moved into its building to live, which the *New York Times* noted with a front-page headline: "J. G. Phelps Stokes on Lower East Side."

On the evening in July 1903 when Rose walked from the *Yiddishes Tageblatt* office to the University Settlement, she felt so intimidated by the prospect of meeting someone from the unknown world of wealthy Protestants that she corralled a friend she ran into on the street, begged him to accompany her, and in the interview let him ask Graham most of the questions. But she was surprised, she would remember years later, to be "enchanted by the very tall slender young man who both in features and in general appearance was so like the young Abe Lincoln, and so full of sympathy for the poor." In her story for the newspaper, she wrote that there was "a look in his eyes as he concluded that suggested an unutterable longing to change the world . . . so that none might suffer." His face bore a "frank, earnest, and kind expression." He was, she declared, "a deep, strong thinker" and "a man of the common people."

At 31, seven years older than Rose and nearly a foot taller, Graham proved similarly smitten by his auburn-haired interviewer. As she was leaving, she recalled, "the tall young 'Lincoln' looked down upon me benignly from his height of six feet four inches (Lincoln's height, too!) to say good night, 'and I should like to read the interview before it is published.'" She mailed it to him the next morning. Two days later he came to the *Tageblatt* office and was disappointed to find Rose out to lunch. Too shy to immediately try to see her again, he made sure that several months later she was invited for tea with the University Settlement volunteers. There, he promptly asked her back for Thanksgiving dinner.

More such invitations followed, and she gradually learned about the settlement house, which served both Jewish and Italian residents of the Lower East Side. Its roof was a children's playground, and on the first three floors were classrooms for courses in English, history, economics, and other subjects, as well as space for art exhibits, concerts, and dances. There was a library of 6,500 books, a legal aid office, and something most tenements lacked: showers—no less than 41 of them, used by up to 800 people a day during the summer heat. The settlement sponsored a baseball team for neighborhood boys and ran two summer camps outside the city. Almost every volunteer managed a boys' or girls' sport or hobby club.

Although Graham had taken part in policing a strike while in uniform a few years earlier, his politics were changing, for he now found himself supporting organized labor. Like the other volunteers, he regularly attended the union meetings held at the settlement, going out to a nearby bar with the workers afterward. He not only lobbied and testified for a pioneering New York State law limiting child labor, but used his father's office to produce and distribute leaflets for the campaign.

On the settlement's top two floors, the aristocratic volunteers paid $45 a month for room and board and organized various activities just for themselves. Graham, for instance, led a group of men in a naked exercise class—something done at the time in imitation of the ancient Greeks. Yet the men also wanted to feel that they were sharing the life of the neighborhood. "Upon many stifling nights we dragged our mattresses up to the roof," remembered his colleague

Ernest Poole, "and we found a dim weird world up there, with the great hot glow of the city striking up into the sky but all around us dark shadowy roofs packed thick with acres of men and women and children, sleepers like ourselves."

Every night the volunteers ate dinner prepared by a staff cook at a long table where, Rose wrote, there "were always between thirty and forty residents and their guests. . . . Seated somewhere not far from Mr. Stokes at the head of the table, I would listen, but rarely speak. What was there that I could say to all those learned gentlemen and brilliant ladies — to professors, publicists, doctors, lawyers, scientists, educators, scholars!"

Over time, an astonishing array of people were guests at the University Settlement's table. They ranged from Jane Addams to the defense lawyer Clarence Darrow to the British novelist H. G. Wells to the muckraking journalist Lincoln Steffens. The Scottish labor leader Keir Hardie, a child of the Glasgow slums who had spent a decade working in coal mines, came for dinner, as did his colleague in Britain's House of Commons, Ramsay MacDonald, who would become his country's first Labour prime minister. For such visitors, an evening at the University Settlement offered the intellectual stimulation of talk with bright young Ivy Leaguers and the *frisson* of knowing you were visiting the city's most crowded slum.

There were relatively few women among these guests, but one of them was destined to become a friend (and, much later, a political enemy) of Rose. Ten years older than her, Emma Goldman was also a Russian Jew, born not far from Augustów. She had been inspired by Russian revolutionaries, particularly the women among them — and by the anarchists, male and female, she encountered after coming to the United States as a teenager. Goldman helped an early lover, Alexander Berkman, plan to assassinate an executive of the Carnegie steel mills at Homestead, Pennsylvania, who had ordered Pinkerton detectives to fire on striking workers. The attempt failed, and Berkman was sentenced to 14 years in prison. Goldman turned away from such tactics, but not from the anarchist movement and its vision of a decentralized, egalitarian society where both men and women could realize their full potential. Nor did she abandon Berkman, working (unsuccessfully) with several comrades on a scheme to free him by digging a tunnel. She herself spent a year behind bars for "inciting to riot" during a demonstration against hunger, finding prison "the crucible that tested my faith. It had helped me to discover strength in my own being, the strength to stand alone, the strength to live my life and fight for my ideals, against the whole world if need be."

Goldman shocked audiences by her fiery defense of free love and women's sexuality, as well as her claim that the only difference between marriage and prostitution was whether a woman sold herself to one man or many. In a straitlaced age, she believed that "sex expression is as vital a factor in human life as food and air," and would write of one lover, "In the arms of Ed I learned for the first time the meaning of the great life-giving force. I understood its full beauty, and I eagerly drank its intoxicating joy and bliss. It was an ecstatic song, profoundly soothing by its music and perfume. My little flat . . . became a temple of love." In photographs, however, the woman who wrote such lines does not quite look the part. She is a determined figure whose pince-nez gives her a no-nonsense, schoolteacherly air. One admirer describes her as having "a stocky figure like a peasant woman, a face of fierce strength like a female pugilist, a harsh voice, a dominating mind." A slightly outthrust chin telegraphs conviction—and defiance, as she faces a police photographer taking mug shots after one of her many arrests. A charismatic, mesmerizing speaker, she would become America's best-known anarchist.

In Goldman, Rose found a woman who lived, breathed, and defined her life by membership in a millenarian political movement —and who had spent time jailed for her commitment. She traveled under false names when the authorities were looking for her, and could always count on being sheltered by devoted comrades. In an era when women could not vote and faced other, huge barriers, Goldman offered a dramatic example of the power an outspoken woman could wield on the lecture platform. "I began to speak," Goldman wrote of her first public appearance. "Words I had never heard myself utter before came pouring forth, faster and faster. They came with passionate intensity; they painted images of the heroic men on the gallows, their glowing vision of an ideal life, rich with comfort and beauty: men and women radiant in freedom, children transformed by joy and affection. The audience had vanished, the hall itself had disappeared, I was conscious only of my own words."

Small wonder that Rose found Goldman an inspiration and the University Settlement "a seething center for the exchange of ideas," although initially she was too timid to discuss them with the volunteers or guests who seemed to know so much more than she. But her love of the printed word made her all the more eager to share their world, for almost all the volunteers were working on books or articles. She began teaching an occasional class at the settlement, and Graham invited her to join a group of volunteers who were studying the work of Lester F. Ward, a prominent sociologist.

This was the heyday of muckraking. A rising young author named Upton Sinclair was sending Graham, chapter by chapter, a draft of a novel he was writing based on seven weeks spent undercover in Chicago stockyards and meatpacking plants. Sinclair found, he wrote, "that by the simple device of carrying a dinner pail I could go anywhere." No one yet imagined the tremendous impact this book would have, but Rose was thrilled by the way Graham seemed in touch with the country's most exciting activists and writers.

Graham left no record of his own feelings, but he clearly saw in Rose some quality he had not found in the many eligible young women of his own background he had met over the years. And perhaps in some way he also found in her a connection to something he may have been seeking when he moved into the University Settlement: an America of immigrants, of factory labor, of grinding urban poverty, a nation that, whatever its simmering discontents, was somehow more "vital," in the word of the day, than the surroundings he had grown up in. After the dinners, he would see Rose home along gaslit streets, and soon he met her mother and the younger children in the small apartment in the Bronx, a step up from the Lower East Side, to which they had moved. A year after they first met, Rose invited him there for a modest meal celebrating her 25th birthday, and, as he told her later, "It moved me profoundly when you gave me a glass of milk, bread and butter, an egg, and a banana. . . . You were so simple and so solemn about it!"

Being with Graham made Rose acutely aware of her own lack of education. Among his friends who visited the settlement, for instance, was an older couple whose daughter acted in ancient Greek plays—in Greek. In 1904, the couple invited Graham and Rose to visit them at their summer home on a lake in Quebec. With difficulty, Rose saved and borrowed enough money for a train ticket, and was touched that Graham, who could have afforded a sleeping-car berth—indeed, his family could have bought the railroad—sat up with her in a coach seat all night.

Among the other houseguests in Quebec Rose found another woman who, like Emma Goldman, would become a role model. A decade older, Olive Tilford Dargan was born to parents who were both schoolteachers in Appalachia. She herself had started teaching as a teenager and, after spells in college and as a stenographer, began writing plays and poetry and married a fellow poet. For Rose, she was proof that a "working girl" of far from aristocratic background could find success as an author. She and Rose quickly became best friends, exchanging many visits and hundreds of letters over the years to come.

But most of her time on this vacation Rose spent talking with Graham. As was common for someone of his class, he had been baptized an Episcopalian, but he had long been intrigued by the idea that all religious traditions could be combined, and he had a particular interest in Hinduism and Buddhism. In Quebec, he and Rose took turns reading aloud to each other from Edwin Arnold's book-length poem, *The Light of Asia,* about the life of Buddha. Imagine who might have come to Rose's mind as she heard the story of the young Prince Siddhartha, born to a family of great privilege, who leaves home to seek cures for human suffering.

It was on this trip, a year after they first met, that Rose and Graham became engaged.

On their way home from Canada, in the village of Keene, New York, surrounded by forested Adirondack peaks, the couple spent a few days at the communal home of two more friends of Graham's, John and Prestonia Martin. Socialists and feminists, they were wealthy enough to employ a servant and to own a large house with outbuildings, perched on a hillside commanding spectacular views. In keeping with socialist idealism, however, the Martins expected their guests to take part in earnest discussions of philosophy and politics, and to contribute two hours of hands-on work each day. This could be chopping wood, clearing brush, gardening, fetching provisions by horseback, or washing dishes—men and women alike donned aprons. Once a week, everyone's clothes were placed in a large washing machine while, to the tune of "John Brown's Body," the guests sang, "The clothes go washing on." Fifteen to 25 guests drew chore assignments from a hat daily and proudly recorded them in a little notebook passed around at supper. Rose had never imagined anything like it: well-to-do professionals, artists, intellectuals, even a college president, all celebrating what she had worked so hard to escape—manual labor. But something else made a still bigger impression on her:

"I had never seen mountains before."

5

Cinderella of the Sweatshops

FROM THE MARTINS, GRAHAM WENT to visit his parents at their own Adirondack summer home 40 miles away. More timid than the youthful Buddha, however, he neither dared take Rose along nor reveal their plans to marry. However, the family did begin to hear, as she put it, "rumors of his interest in an 'Israelitish maiden.'" Soon after the couple were back in New York City, two unmarried aunts of Graham's, both active in Christian good works, were mobilized to take him on a trip, and, reliably considerate of his family's wishes, he agreed to go. "I am truly *delighted* to have you go off with the aunts to Mexico," his mother wrote him, "the longer rest and change is most essential for you." The visit "was designed," Rose said, "to provide him with a change of scene and—possibly of heart."

It is hardly surprising that his family was dismayed at the prospect of Graham marrying Rose. After all, one of his mother's ancestors had arrived in the Massachusetts Bay Colony in 1630 and subsequently became its governor, another had been the governor of colonial Connecticut, and a third the governor of both. His father's great-grandfather, an English cloth merchant, was already so wealthy when he moved to the United States in 1798 that he chartered an entire ship to bring along his wife, children, servants, and possessions. In several volumes about his forebears totaling more than 300 pages, Graham's father traced the family's bloodlines back to the Plantagenets, the dynasty that ruled Britain until the death of Richard III. "If my children fail of success in life," he wrote, "it will not be for want of distinguished ancestry." Such a clan had never imagined welcoming into its ranks an immigrant former cigar worker who had never finished elementary school.

The mission of the two aunts failed. News of the couple's engagement then came out sooner than planned, apparently because a telegraph operator—probably paid for the tip—leaked it to a reporter for the New York *Sun,* forcing Graham to make a public announcement. For the press, this marriage between rags and riches was irresistible. Many newspapers promptly filled a two-page spread with photographs of Graham and Rose, interviews with them and people who knew them, and excerpts from Rose's articles, advice columns, and poetry. Reporters rushed to her home and office, or waylaid her on the rattling elevated train in between. One journalist found her in the small living room of the Bronx apartment already talking with five reporters, two photographers, and a sketch artist.

Ever since the mythical Cinderella, covered with ashes from curling up next to her fireplace to stay warm, was rescued from penury by the attentions of a prince, the story of a downtrodden but virtuous young woman who marries into great wealth has had vast appeal. In reading such tales we are eager to know the ending. Will Cinderella be happily transformed once settled in the prince's castle? Or in some way corrupted? If things end badly, will she have to return to the ashes of her hearth?

In Gilded Age America, where the gulf between rich and poor was of unprecedented size, Cinderella fantasies had brought into being a whole genre of popular fiction. It flourished in the dime novels that were sold everywhere, including pushcarts on the Lower East Side. (If you didn't have ten cents, you could borrow the book for less from another pushcart that functioned as a lending library.) Between the 1880s and the 1920s, women consumed 15 million copies of the books of one such writer alone, Laura Jean Libbey. She wrote more than 80 novels, almost all based on the same theme: a pure and honest working girl in a drab, lowly job falls in love with a rich and good-hearted man. Events then separate them, but she success-fully overcomes obstacles such as kidnappings, storms at sea, jeal-ous rivals, spiteful relatives, and villains who try to steal her virtue, and in the end they are reunited and marry. Ironically, a week before she had met Graham, Rose had roundly condemned such stories in an advice column: "What excuse is there other than ignorance for any girl who reads the crazy phantasies from the imbecile brains of Laura Jean Libbey, The Duchess, and others of their ilk! . . . If you read those books—stop! stop!"

To the nation's press, the tale of Rose and Graham was a real-life romance novel for the age of tenements, sweatshops, and im-migrants. And if she was trying to escape upward, was he trying to escape downward? For their story spoke not just to the Roses of America, but to people who identified with Graham. In deciding to marry someone so different, so exotic, would he achieve that trea-sured "vital contact" with a layer of society more alive and less con-stricted than the world of wing collars and top hats in which he had grown up?

One more aspect of their match caught the public's attention. In the tens of thousands of words journalists lavished on the news, the gap between Gentile and Jew loomed at least as large as their differ-ence of class. When the *New York Times* put the story on its front page, it was headlined, "J. G. Phelps Stokes to Wed Young Jewess." Another New York paper reported that "no phase of the romance between Miss Pastor and Mr. Stokes has caused so much comment as their difference in religion." A few years later, when the first such statistics were tabulated, far less than 1 percent of Russian Jews in New York City married non-Jews. The few American Jews who did intermarry were generally more prosperous and educated men and women whose ancestors had come from Germany, Holland, or England a generation or more earlier. European newspapers were equally fascinated. The *Berliner Börsen-Zeitung,* typically, reported the remarkable news that the millionaire Stokes, whose ancestry it elaborated in detail, was marrying a "Russian Israelite."

In New York, the *Yiddishes Tageblatt*'s rival, the socialist *Forverts,* or *Jewish Daily Forward,* was quick to pounce on the articles Rose had written advising Jews not to intermarry. When a reporter asked her about one such column, she displayed a surefooted instinct for how to talk to the press, declaring that "it was obvious that the girl didn't love the man, whoever he was, and I was always opposed to loveless marriages." A Jewish writer named Jacob Lazarre denounced Rose as a "renegade." The question of intermarriage was placed on the agenda of a national conference of rabbis, who were already wary about the proselytizing of Protestant missionaries in Jewish neighborhoods. The editor of the *Hebrew Standard,* assuming that Rose would convert to the religion of her wealthy husband, denounced the "influence the young millionaire and his newly Christianized bride will exert over the children" of the Lower East Side. They should leave the area, he insisted, "and continue their 'uplifting' work among other sections of the population in greater need of it than the Jewish community."

Most New Yorkers, however, seemed fully enthusiastic about the unlikely match. An effusive editorial in the *Evening World* called it an "amazing marriage," quoted Shakespeare, and praised Graham's boldness: "All honor, in this generation of idle, rich and spendthrift young men, to one who has the courage of his convictions, the fervor of his faith and the daring of his devotion!" When Rose appeared with Graham in public for the first time, attending a speech he was to give to the Municipal Ownership League—not normally a venue for displays of great emotion—the crowd waved handkerchiefs and cheered for minutes before they would let him speak.

Graham's parents had been traveling in Europe when they received a letter from him telling them that "Miss Pastor and I want very much to be married. . . . I wish you knew Rose, that you might have the joy and the peace that she has brought to me." Although Graham had been the most obedient of sons when it came to following his father's wish to join the family business office instead of becoming a medical missionary, he alone, unlike any of his brothers and sisters, chose to marry someone from such a startlingly different background.

He had at first not dared tell his parents many details about Rose, and when they learned some from the Paris edition of the *New York Herald* and from a British newspaper, they were horrified. "You cannot realize what a very great disappointment it was to us," his mother wrote him from Italy, "to learn that with all the girls you have known," he had not chosen "one brought up in the same faith, same country and same surroundings as your own." She was sure Rose must be of good character, she said, and she wished the couple well, "but you won't mind my asking you to have the quietest kind of wedding." To the press, however, she diplomatically presented an upbeat face. "Stokes Family Approves His Choice of Wife," read one headline.

"Graham's engagement has quite put the Russian-Japanese war in the shade as an all-absorbing topic of conversation," his clergyman brother Anson wrote their mother. Despite her public statement, she was still fretting, replying to Anson, "Is it not astonishing that a *Phelps Stokes* should choose for his wife a poor girl of Russian Jewish parentage, ancestry unknown. . . . I really cannot understand how he could!" Anson, in turn, reassured her that Rose had "much simple, natural dignity" and that although she had "a Jewish look about [the] forehead and mouth," it was "not at all about the nose."

Mrs. Stokes had long shared the prejudices of the day. When honeymooning abroad 40 years earlier, she had written home that Kraków, "filled with Poles and Jews," was "one of the poorest and most squalid districts of Europe." From Vienna she reported that "the name 'Legion' might well be applied to the Jews." On all sides, "groups of this forsaken and outcast nation were seen engaged in conversation."

As reporters descended on the couple, Graham and Rose tried to minimize the contrast between them. He even vaguely implied that she was Christian, telling the *Times* that it was an "error" to think "that there is a difference in religious belief between Miss Pastor and myself. She is a Jewess, as the Apostles were Jews—a Christian by faith." Rose, talking to the *Sun*, insisted that she had long "been a Christian in spirit if there ever was one. Wasn't Jesus a Jew and weren't many of his apostles Jews?" The press dutifully lapped this up and quoted friends and fellow workers about how kind and charitable Rose was.

To another journalist, Graham described the couple's relationship in almost unearthly terms: "Miss Pastor and I have never considered ourselves as 'engaged,' in the ordinary acceptation of the term. There was no bond, no pledge given or required, for we are one person, not two. . . . Each of us recognized that in the other there was the same soul. . . . While I cannot prove that God brought Miss Pastor and myself together, I do believe we are under the direct influence of a supreme power."

For the next two decades, few months would pass when Rose and Graham did not appear in the newspapers. Searching for additional angles to the story, journalists talked with Rose's mother, who gave her blessing to the marriage. Not revealing that Israel Pastor had abandoned the family, she referred to herself as a widow. When Mrs. Pastor, with a parade of reporters coming to her door, complained to Rose that "millions of people who read the papers want to know what I am cooking in this little pot on my stove this morning," her media-savvy daughter told her, "Then it is important that you tell them exactly what you are cooking."

Although she had spent her life until now far out of the public eye, Rose adjusted to her new status with remarkable grace. More than one journalist who interviewed her commented on how at ease she seemed. Joseph Pulitzer's sensationalist *Evening World* immediately signed up this "genius of the ghetto" to write a series of six articles. With the paper selling more than 350,000 copies a day, for the first time she reached an audience vastly larger and more varied than that of the *Yiddishes Tageblatt*.

She was well aware that for most *Evening World* readers she was someone from another universe, and so she presented herself as a guide to it. She offered, for instance, a vivid description of the Lower East Side's Hester Street market, translating bits of Yiddish, capturing the flavor of its speech and insults: "You thief! You Siberian, you runaway horse thief!" Clearly she was aware of just how exotic a woman's extravagant bargaining with a fishmonger would sound to readers used to shopping at Lord & Taylor or Saks Fifth Avenue:

> A customer takes a flounder in her hands and attempts to get it two cents cheaper. She gets her arm wrenched off almost as he snatches the fish from her. . . .
> "Give me the money and take the fish — such a year should I have! What a flounder that is! I give it to you for eight cents; it cost me fifteen."
> "What? Seven pounds for eight cents? Pooh on you! What an idea! . . ."
> "A demon on your father! A dark fate on your head!"

The series offered glimpses of poverty: a weeping woman on a park bench who has been taken advantage of in a delicately unnamed way; sidewalk peddlers who can barely make enough to live on; a day laborer, desperate for work, who asks Rose in Yiddish if she needs a carpenter. She suggested no solution to such suffering other than simple human kindness.

In one of the articles, about her childhood in London, she described how her mother gave her a penny so she could buy a few of her favorite chocolate candies. Then into the candy shop came a beggar, who said he had had nothing to eat. His feet were bare, and the street was thick with snow. When the shop owner turned him away, Rose ran after him through the streets, found him under a lamppost, and gave him her penny. He said, "God bless you, my child." The tone is redolent of Dickens, but the Dickens of *A Christmas Carol* rather than of *Oliver Twist*. Rose was trying to persuade her readers — surely imagining Graham's family among them — that although she came from another world, she was noble, goodhearted, and unthreatening. In the six long articles she never mentioned her years working in cigar factories.

The press coverage continued, unrelenting, and rare was the description that did not manage to find a way of saying that Rose looked Jewish. "She is rather short in stature, with a slender, pretty figure and a wealth of golden-brown hair, which she wears hung loosely in the back," said the *Evening World*. "Her eyes are dark brown and full of light. She has the forehead of her race." The *Sun* noted that "Miss Pastor is a blonde of the Jewish type, with a ripple of gold in her hair." The personal appearance of Graham—thin, somber, and nearly a head taller—was seldom mentioned.

The wedding was set for July 18, 1905, Rose's 26th birthday. But first she took Graham on a trip—properly chaperoned by a friend from the *Tageblatt*—to Cleveland, to see where she had grown up, attend a Passover Seder, and meet some of her friends. At a cigar factory, he reported to his family, they were "delightfully received by her old employers and associates. . . . Dear Mother, Rose has developed a wonderful soul in the midst of her hardships, and it is a deep deep blessing to know her."

As the date for the marriage approached, people wondered what kind of ceremony was in store. Would Rose promise to "love, honor, and obey" her husband? This was certainly a match far different from those of Graham's siblings: one sister had married a viscount, and a brother an heiress. The Stokes parents, already facing an avalanche of press coverage, now feared a corps of reporters descending on the wedding itself.

This was not, however, the family's first experience with unwanted publicity. William Earl Dodge Stokes, a volatile, litigious New York real estate mogul with a handlebar mustache, was the brother of Graham's father. In a way the rest of the family dreaded, he regularly made the news. He sued relatives who were fellow trustees of a charity, was himself sued for usury, battled with a contractor in court, sued a cousin over a disputed loan (who, in turn, sued him for libel), was taken to court by his lawyers for nonpayment, and got into a drunken brawl in his own house. When it came to women, W.E.D. Stokes preferred them young. At 42, he married a 19-year-old and later produced many more headlines with a stormy divorce and child custody battle. A playboy in an extravagant era, he gave one notorious dinner where all the guests received small covered baskets which, when they were commanded to open them, revealed bullfrogs that hopped out and wreaked havoc among soup bowls and wine glasses. Stokes also was well known for carrying a pistol or two, laying them on the table beside his plate when he ate. With strong ideas about superior and inferior races, he was not likely to be happy about his nephew marrying a Jew. But Stokes family loyalty ran deep, he was Graham's Uncle Will, and he had to be asked to the wedding. Would he behave?

Although Graham had described himself and Rose as being a single soul, he clearly thought of her as marrying into his world. When he wrote her, he addressed her as "Girlie," and nothing about Rose led him to assume that she would be other than a traditional wife. She herself seemed to expect the same, and to feel that he and the glamorous social circles he was a part of would be the glowing center of their marriage. "I soon grew to worship him," Rose told a reporter this year, talking of how she had met Graham. When she wrote to him while he was in Nevada on a brief business trip, she called him "dear darling Saint!"

However, in the weeks before the news of their engagement became public, Rose had done something surprising. Knowing that her life would never again be the same, she quit her *Tageblatt* job and, using another name, went back to work making cigars. It was as if Cinderella, glass slippers in hand, had temporarily returned to the ashes of her fireplace. Graham later claimed that this was his idea, but that seems highly unlikely. Instead, Rose's description of her feelings rings truer: "I wanted to sit at the bench again, to renew the old labor, the old relationships. Perhaps I felt that never hereafter would my own regard me as one of them. . . . I could not bear the thought that my marriage might prove a barrier between my class and me." She had not rolled cigars since coming to New York, but now she took a job in a factory on Third Avenue. "It is good to be again among my own. We talk, we sing, we race—I am one of them. But I was a bit of a mystery to them. They cannot understand why I am there. They tell me so. 'You ought to get a better kind of job. . . . The way you talk and all—Why, you, you could even get work in a department store.'"

She had been away from manual labor more than two years, however, and her body was not up to the task. Her hands and fingers swelled painfully, and Graham insisted that she stop. When she went to the factory to collect her final pay and say goodbye, she was greeted with an uproar. "Cutters rattle, knives beat on rolling-boards, shouts, calls, feet stamp, hands clap! I am bewildered." The news of her engagement had just hit the headlines, and despite her assumed name, the other cigar workers had figured out who she was. "'A millionaire! Don't forget us, Rose! Come to see us, some-times.' My face is burning. I feel a bit ashamed."

There was a final, ironic footnote to this chapter of her life. "And now that I am to 'marry a millionaire,' and am no longer a strug-gling unskilled worker in a stogie factory," she wrote, "I am invited to join the American Federation of Labor!!!" She and Graham both spoke at a meeting of the local she was admitted to, accompanied, as always now, by the press. Her voice "trembled with emotion," a journalist reported, as she recalled the hardships of her dozen years in the trade, and the low wages that often forced three generations of a family to all be at work rolling cigars in order to survive.

Graham's speech took a different tone. "I believe that trade union-ism is a good thing," he told an audience that surely needed no con-vincing. ". . . I believe in a spirit of charity being exercised by the union men not only toward one another, but toward their employ-ers." He also sounded as if he did not see his forthcoming marriage as being one between equals. "The work in the interest of human-ity that I have been carrying on," he declared, "I hope to carry on in a more extended way with the assistance of Miss Pastor when she is my wife."

The wedding took place in Noroton, on the stretch of Connecti-cut shoreline known as the Gold Coast for its array of luxury homes. The main building on Graham's parents' property there was called the Brick House, a recent replacement for the 100-room "cottage" in the Berkshires. Although somewhat smaller, it still had 13 bedrooms for servants alone, a columned entrance hall, a billiard room, two el-evators, and three guest cottages. On the estate's ten and a half acres were a sunken rose garden, shade trees, walking paths, greenhouses, a squash court, and a terrace overlooking Long Island Sound. A flock of gardeners took care of the grounds, and the staff included a butler named Barton. Several of Graham's brothers and sisters had homes nearby. His architect brother, Isaac Newton Phelps Stokes, would have a three-story half-timbered English Tudor manor house from 1597 disassembled, packed in 688 crates, shipped to Connecticut, and put back together again so he could declare that he was living in the oldest home in the United States.

In her memoir, Rose describes herself as being in a daze during the weeks of wedding preparations, but claims that she demanded, "'I want the word "obey" eliminated from the service.' The request has upset plans somewhat. The local minister has refused to conduct the service. He cannot leave out 'obey.' Such a thing has never been done before! He will not take responsibility. There are family councils." The written record, however, tells a somewhat different story. Graham did indeed write to his mother and brother Anson explaining that both he and Rose felt strongly about leaving out "obey." Anson's initial doubts were quickly overcome, and there is no record of the local Episcopal minister complaining. According to the *New York Times,* "The rector, the Rev. Dr. French, performed the marriage ceremony. He was assisted by the bridegroom's brother, the Rev. Anson Phelps Stokes, Jr."

Most of the 200 guests arrived in two special coaches attached to a morning train from New York. On a day of record-breaking summer heat they were transported from the station to the small, ivy-covered church in carriages and omnibuses. Among them were many members of the Stokes, Phelps, and Dodge families, including Graham's cantankerous Uncle Will, who, to everyone's relief, did not mar the occasion. He would later claim, however, that he stopped several of Rose's younger siblings—"two or three little Jakys and Ikes"—from pocketing silverware. Rose's mother and her children were dressed in white, and the guests also included friends of the couple from the University Settlement staff, the *Tageblatt,* and the Lower East Side. In a concession to her in-laws, Rose wore a small cross around her neck. When Graham's mother arrived at the church in her carriage, she was outraged that a cluster of newspaper photographers were waiting, and, according to one reporter, "Mrs. Stokes objected very strongly, so strongly that she got up out of her seat and cried out loudly, 'Don't! Don't!' Before the camera men got a good chance, Mrs. Stokes had alighted and charged them. . . . The cameras fled."

Rose was nervous. "I literally ran up the aisle and down again, I was told. Perhaps I did. It was something disagreeable to be gone through quickly." Yet witnesses say that she walked up the aisle arm-in-arm with Graham. Afterward, they received their guests on the Brick House terrace. At the lunch that followed, according to the *Times,* "the only difference between the men from the east side and their fashionable brothers was that those from the tenements had braved the weather in frock coats and high hats, while their wealthy brethren had, as a rule, thought Summer clothing appropriate." Even the Stokeses' staff slyly made fun of the Lower East Siders. An immigrant friend whom Rose had invited recalled:

"One of the butlers filled our crystal goblets with effervescent liquor.

"'What is this?' I asked jestingly.

"'Beer,' he answered disdainfully, as he covered the champagne label with his hand."

After Rose had pieces of wedding cake boxed and mailed to some of her fellow cigar workers in Cleveland, the newlyweds changed their clothes. Rose donned a black straw hat and Graham a cap. The guests showered them with rice as they climbed into Uncle Will's large open car, and America's most improbable couple left for a honeymoon in Europe.

6

Distant Thunder

THANKS IN PART TO THE unceasing flow of immigrants, the America from which the newlyweds sailed the day after their wedding had become the world's largest economy. Theodore Roosevelt was beginning his second term in the White House. Known to all as TR, he was certain he was the man for this promising moment in his country's life. His brisk, outdoorsman's exuberance conveyed a can-do optimism that any problem could be solved, any dream realized. "He wore a tall black hat," wrote one journalist, "and he strode along the platform with the physical power of a landslide." If there was a question to be faced, he had a law to propose, an executive order to issue, or a blue-ribbon presidential commission to appoint.

It was high time, TR felt, to flex his country's muscles on the world stage. He had become president only a few years after leading the famous Rough Riders cavalry in the Spanish-American War of 1898, in which the United States trounced a decrepit European empire and acquired its first colonies. On his watch, construction started on the American-controlled Panama Canal, and he toughened the Monroe Doctrine, warning European countries against any intervention in Latin America. In 1907, he would send his Great White Fleet of modern steel battleships, 348,000 tons of naval firepower, steaming around the globe, with enough deafening gunnery displays to make it clear that his nation was now a major power.

A seventh-generation New Yorker, TR was the ultimate patrician reformer, moving in the same circles as the Phelps Stokes family. Before reaching the White House, in fact, he had spoken at the ribbon-cutting ceremony inaugurating the new University Settlement building that Graham had helped plan. As a state legislator, president of the New York City Board of Police Commissioners, and governor, Roosevelt had battled corrupt politicians. As president, he pushed for the regulation of railroads and insurance, public health measures, civil service reforms, national parks, and more. But to Americans like Rose and Graham who were increasingly concerned about poverty, achievements like the Pure Food and Drug Act and the birth of the US Forest Service did not address the country's deepest problems.

Known as "the man on horseback" from his cavalry days, Roosevelt thundered against the trusts that dominated the economy, and he broke up a few of them. Despite defiant rhetoric against "the malefactors of great wealth," however, he proved to have little interest in taking any of that wealth away from them. In the war between capital and labor, TR was, in the end, what critics called "the man on two horsebacks." His Republican Party, after all, was the chief beneficiary of the flood of corporate contributions now shaping American politics. Roosevelt's 1904 presidential campaign reaped hundreds of thousands of dollars from executives of companies ranging from New York Life Insurance and General Electric to Standard Oil and the New York Central Railroad. And a new class of skilled lobbyists had gained influence in Washington and in state capitals, making sure that business got the favors it had paid for.

To workers, the government offered little. Workplace safety laws were few and industrial accidents plentiful. Everything from collapsing mine tunnels to exposed gears and moving belts that snagged the limbs of exhausted factory laborers claimed the lives of roughly 35,000 Americans every year. Far more lost hands or fingers, were burned by toxic chemicals, or were maimed in other ways. Legal protection for labor organizing was almost nonexistent: 200 workers were killed and nearly 2,000 injured in workplace disputes every year.

Trusts, monopolies, and powerful corporations continued to thrive. A single railroad, the Philadelphia & Reading, for example, owned or controlled 63 percent of the country's anthracite coal. When some of the men who mined that coal went on strike in 1902, demanding higher wages, shorter workdays, and recognition of their union, the railroad's president declared that such matters should be decided "not by the labor agitators, but by the Christian men to whom God in His infinite wisdom has given the control of the property interests of the country."

Tycoons like Andrew Carnegie and John D. Rockefeller controlled vast industrial empires. A severe gap between rich and poor has long dogged American life, but in the early 1900s inequality soared to previously unknown heights, with real wages in decline for most people. By 1915, the richest 1 percent of the population would own 35.6 percent of the nation's wealth. Many workers felt, in the words of a popular union song,

> *They have taken untold millions that they never toiled to earn,*
> *But without our brain and muscle not a single wheel could turn.*

Some who turned those wheels were restive. A few weeks before Rose and Graham married, a new organization came into being that would later play a part in Rose's life. On June 27, 1905, 200 activists met in Chicago to form the Industrial Workers of the World, or IWW, which soon became known as the Wobblies. In a smoke-filled meeting hall, western miners in cowboy boots, East Coast immigrant factory hands speaking half a dozen languages, and a small sprinkling of radical intellectuals celebrated the birth of "one big union" that would unite all labor, wage war on capital, and speed toward a new and fairer society. "The working class and the employing class have nothing in common," said the IWW's constitution.

Instead of celebrating Labor Day in September, the IWW celebrated May 1, long the traditional holiday of revolutionaries. The

Wobblies turned no worker away, male or female, black or white, Gentile or Jew. Any immigrant who had belonged to a union in the old country was instantly given membership. The appalled Samuel Gompers of the more conservative American Federation of Labor labeled the IWW a "fungus" on the union movement. The Wobblies not only drew in the unskilled, but also recruited among the unemployed. Wobbly organizers worked street corners where day laborers gathered and the freight trains that migrants and hobos rode in search of work. On western cattle ranges there was even a Cowboys' and Bronco Busters' local. The IWW had more flash than breadth, for the number of people who actually held a red membership card would never be large. (At its peak the group claimed over 100,000 followers, but most of the time paid membership was probably less than a quarter of that.) Nevertheless, the Wobblies would help workers achieve gains everywhere from sawmills and gold mines to steel plants and clothing factories. Unusually for the day, Wobbly organizers included women, who targeted occupations where women predominated, such as telephone operators and textile workers.

A Wobbly speaker on the street might attract an audience by repeatedly shouting, "Help! I've been robbed!" Only when a crowd had gathered would he or she add, ". . . by the capitalist system!" and launch into a recruiting pitch. The union was unmatched for its boldness, the snappy graphics of its posters, and the fearlessness of its organizers, who never hesitated to battle corporate detectives on the picket line or in railway yards. Sometimes, in order to cross police lines, they even posed as strikebreakers. When an Iowa judge demanded that a Wobbly before him prove that he was a real worker —and not an outside agitator—by displaying the calluses on his hands, the man replied, "Take down your pants, judge, and let me see where your calluses are!"

IWW offices often had a piano. Many of the songs in the union's famous *Little Red Songbook* were written by Joe Hill, an organizer who would later be convicted of murder on much-disputed evidence and killed by a Utah firing squad in 1915. Joe Hill's songs often scorned religion, as a poor substitute for justice here on earth.

Would you have mansions of gold in the sky,
  And live in a shack, way in the back?
Would you have wings up in heaven to fly?
  And starve here with rags on your back?

Although Rose would sing many of these songs in years to come, she and Graham were anything but starving in rags as they crossed the Atlantic on the fast and elegant new White Star liner *Cedric*. Their promenade deck stateroom was a far cry from the cramped steerage bunk of her voyage west 15 years earlier—although on this eastbound trip Rose made a point of visiting the steerage quarters daily, to play with the children there. In Europe, Graham's mother had arranged for a Packard limousine to ferry them around the continent. Rose introduced her new husband to her London relatives (he later paid for the passage of some of them to New York). She even found the lamppost under which she had given her penny to that barefoot beggar in the snow. She wanted to show Graham where she had lived, but "as we approached the court, I become aware of a group of women near the very door to the old house. Prepared by the London press that heralded our coming apparently, they are organized to receive us! I am too conscious of the automobile, of Henri the chauffeur, of my custom-tailored costume and my fine black straw hat with its ostrich plume. . . . We get back into the car and drive away."

Their honeymoon included several months of museums, castles, ancient ruins, "the Bay of Naples, Rome, and again galleries; a bewildering wealth of art." At one point a "strange, feathery, rose-tipped cloud at sunset . . . proves to be Mont Blanc, and brings me in the moving car to my feet with a great shout." Graham was active in a prison reform group, and they took time out from touring for him to attend an international conference on prisons in Budapest.

They returned to New York in the autumn of 1905. Rose had insisted they live on the Lower East Side, but the apartment Graham leased there was of luxurious size for a mere two people: six rooms and a bath, on the seventh floor of a building that had a great rarity

in this part of town, an elevator. Newspapers and magazines continued to examine their lives in minute but admiring detail, publishing photos of the apartment's rooms, the view from its windows, the
curtains Rose hemmed, the pots and pans she cooked with. "She is
a tall, slender young woman," reported a correspondent for *Woman*
magazine, who found Rose's face "framed with a glory of rippling
brown hair, and lighted by leaf-brown eyes in which is the most
spiritual expression I have ever seen in a living face; it is like that in
the pictures of Joan of Arc and St. Cecelia."

Harper's Bazar revealed that she used paper napkins instead of
table linen in her new home in "the Russian quarter," and had no
servants except a cleaning woman who came on certain days. Like
almost every journalist who interviewed her—Rose seems never to
have turned one away—this reporter was eager to say that Cinderella's glass slipper fit perfectly: "Her eye was gentle, her movement
graceful, her manner restful; she had poise, that inevitable accom-
paniment of character."

Rose carefully curated her public image, and she and Graham
subscribed to a clipping service for stories that mentioned them. He
claimed never to read these articles, but she saved them all. Many
times in the years ahead she would write to a newspaper—or several
of them, if a wire service story was involved—when she felt she had
been misquoted, and she filed away those corrected stories as well.
Invisible to the press now, however, was the immense relief that financial security brought her. "I learned," she would later write, "that
three adequate meals a day made an astounding difference; that a
few pounds added to my weight added incredibly to my sustaining
powers, to my ability to work and play in joy."

The new apartment was piled high with books, the press reported, and Graham had a massive mahogany roll-top desk. At her
more modest one, Rose, with the help of a friend she had hired as a
secretary, answered an unceasing flood of letters from people wanting money, advice, or her autograph. After the enormous publicity
their marriage had shone on Graham's wealth and on their shared
concern for the poor, hundreds wrote to one or both of them asking for help: a loan, aid in promoting a new cure for tuberculosis,

backing for a copper mine in Washington State, a hand with mortgage payments on an Illinois farm, an investment in a cheap new whole-grain food, or assistance in patenting a new type of turbine (diagram enclosed), for "the road to the Patent Office is beset with thieves, and I have a wife and baby and an unsteady job." A letter from Grangeville, Idaho, offered for sale a portrait of George Washington and a violin guaranteed to be a Stradivarius, the writer promised, while another asked for two years of support "to instruct a staff of men and women in the science of Unopathy." Such pleas would pour in for years to come.

With Rose's new celebrity status came a national audience. Major newspapers and magazines asked her for articles or book reviews. At first she wrote under the name Rose H. Phelps Stokes. Soon, as if perhaps deciding that was assimilating to Graham's family by one name too many, she reverted for the rest of her life to Rose Pastor Stokes.

Petitioners continued to besiege them, sometimes lining up outside the apartment door. Overwhelmed, Rose initially seemed uncertain what to focus on. She still did some work at the University Settlement, but found it jarring to then attend luncheons and dinners at the Stokes mansion on Madison Avenue with people like the Episcopal bishop of New York, newspaper baron William Randolph Hearst, and other business moguls. Even so, many such people seemed captivated by her, one of them Andrew Carnegie, whose sale of his industrial empire had made him, by some measures, the richest man on earth. He "put a hand on my arm and inclined my ear," Rose recalled. "'Shsh!' he whispered. 'Don't tell anyone! But I don't believe in God!'"

A great pressure had been lifted from her shoulders, for Graham's money was now there to support her mother and the six younger children. She stayed in close touch with them, and indeed, in the couple's next home, mother and children would be there too. In marrying Rose, Graham knew, he was in some ways marrying her whole family.

With his relatives, however, Rose found things more awkward.

His mother, rumor had it, had heaved a regretful sigh at the wedding when her son said "I do," and not a single family member had come to see them off from dockside on their honeymoon. Rose would soon form a close, lifelong friendship with Graham's sister Helen, a painter with a deep concern for social justice, but the rest of the clan clearly had no idea what to make of her, nor Rose, at times, of them. She was amused, for instance, by the "dainty bits of cardboard"—the calling cards that were *de rigueur* for visitors of their class to present or leave at one another's houses. There were many such callers at the couple's new apartment, from the president of Yale and his wife on down, curious to have a look at the former cigar worker who was now part of the Phelps Stokes dynasty. Graham's sister Ethel, whose husband was a well-to-do businessman and the great-nephew of a former secretary of state, invited Rose to several meetings of the National Flower Guild. This consisted, as Rose later put it, of wealthy women who "were supplying the poor in the tenements with window-boxes 'at a very low price,' and sending their no-longer-fresh boudoir bouquets to the sick in the hospital wards. The spectacle filled me with a fierce impatience."

Settlement house work left her increasingly frustrated. In a 1906 article, she complained of "wealthy women very expensively dressed attempting to encourage the so-called unfortunates by visiting them and telling them what they should do. Not long ago, in one of the principal settlement houses of New York, a very fashionably dressed woman, a lorgnette dangling from her finger tips, opened the door of a working girls' club, uninvited, and, raising her lorgnette to her eyes . . . remarked in the hearing of all, 'What a very attractive-looking lot of working girls these are!'"

Graham, too, became increasingly frustrated by the limits of traditional charity, as if marrying Rose had opened him up to a wider view of the world. Both of them came to feel that the work of places like settlement houses was no better than putting superficial bandages on deep social wounds. Such organizations, wrote Graham in a letter to the *Times,* could risk being means "through which men who are unjust in business and private life seek to mitigate some of the evils which their extortions have caused." (Indeed, one of the largest donations for the University Settlement's new building had come from John D. Rockefeller.)

Rose, as would always be the case, was more blunt. "Sometimes I wish I could wipe all philanthropy off the face of the earth," she said as a guest speaker at a Syracuse University alumni banquet, where the audience included many executives and philanthropists as well as the university's chancellor, a vocal defender of trusts and corporations. "If it didn't exist people would see conditions as they are, for these charities act only as a blind." In another talk, she likened traditional charity to a small boy with a tin pan trying fruitlessly to empty a pool of water fed by an unseen fountain. Could more militant labor unions, she and Graham started to wonder, be the key to attacking systemic poverty? They began going to meetings of the Women's Trade Union League.

One experience exposed Rose to a face of American injustice that was new to her. Graham was a trustee of Booker T. Washington's Tuskegee Institute, one of the first higher educational institutions for black Americans, and for its 25th anniversary celebration the couple traveled to Alabama in a chartered train with the other trustees. "Through the trip south," Rose wrote, "I kept Graham in distress because I insisted that I would go and sit in the 'Colored' instead of the 'white' waiting-room, whenever the train stopped." Her husband was always more cautious. "'Don't, please don't,' Graham pleaded. 'It will do no good in the world, and you'll only succeed in getting yourself arrested.'" In Atlanta, where the party stopped to attend a lunch marking the opening of a new library, Rose was told that black people were not allowed in the building. She walked out, this time persuading Graham to join her.

Whatever their uncertainties about how best to eradicate poverty in the United States, there was one country where Graham and Rose and their friends were completely sure about what needed to be done. The country was Russia; it was a tyranny, and that tyranny had to be overthrown.

Periodically, injustices in some distant part of the world capture the American imagination—witness, for example, the attention lavished on apartheid in South Africa in the 1970s and '80s. Russia had that role at the turn of the twentieth century. Americans were fascinated by this vast empire with its peerless writers like Leo Tolstoy and Anton Chekhov, but outraged by the way rampaging Cossacks slaughtered Jews, by the chain of prisons and villages of exiles stretching across Siberia, and by the haughty and remote tsar and tsarina, living in grand palaces and on yachts, apparently heedless of the suffering around them.

The empire's notorious penal network had been the subject of a widely read 1891 exposé, *Siberia and the Exile System,* by explorer-journalist George Kennan (a cousin of the future diplomat and historian). His publisher promoted the book as the "*Uncle Tom's Cabin* of Siberian exile." In hundreds of lectures throughout the United States, Kennan told audiences about the horrors he had witnessed, often appearing in convict's clothing: a Russian peasant blouse and cap, an overcoat against the icy Siberian winters, and shackles on his ankles. Listeners and readers were moved by his tales of courageous freedom fighters locked up for years or executed, and many were inspired to join an organization he helped found, the Society of Friends of Russian Freedom. After one Kennan lecture in Boston, a man in the audience with a thick thatch of white hair and a white suit was so outraged that he rose from his seat in tears and said, "If such a government cannot be overthrown otherwise than by the use of dynamite, then thank God for dynamite!" It was Mark Twain.

Rose and Graham heard much about Russia from two close friends who had been there and whose differing backgrounds were strikingly parallel to their own. Leroy Scott was a shy, soft-spoken graduate of Indiana University with a slight stutter. His family was wealthy enough that when young Leroy wanted to get a start in journalism, he could do so at a newspaper owned by his brother. Later, for a time he worked as acting director of the University Settlement, where he also coached the boys' basketball team. His wife, Miriam, was a Jewish Lower East Sider who ran the children's playground on the settlement's roof. Like Rose, she was an immigrant from Russia who had gone to work young to help support her fam-

ily. She was fluent in Russian as well as Yiddish, which proved a
boon to her writer husband when the two of them went to Russia
to gather material for Leroy's magazine articles. Miriam sometimes
dressed as a peasant woman with a shawl over her head, to avoid at-
tracting undue attention. In homes and cafés, while her husband
scribbled notes she translated conversations with workers, former
political prisoners, idealistic students who had "gone to the people"
in the countryside, villagers suffering from hunger, and revolutionaries living underground. Miriam soon began publishing her own
articles and short stories about Russia as well.

Like the Scotts, millions of people across the United States felt it
was high time for Russia to rid itself of the tsar and become a democracy. A National Committee for the Relief of Sufferers by Russian
Massacres raised over a million dollars for the victims of pogroms,
while Leroy Scott worked with another committee of notables gathering funds for Russian famine relief. Others collected signatures on
petitions demanding freedom for Russian political prisoners.

Through something of an underground railroad, Russian revolutionaries on the run from the tsar's secret police made their way to
America. One had even escaped from a Siberian prison hidden below the false bottom of a sauerkraut barrel. These refugees brought
new tales of suffering and raised more funds, while telling their stories to audiences everywhere from tenement basements to Carnegie
Hall. Surprisingly, a few of those the Scotts interviewed on their
travels came from the nobility, heartwarming proof, it seemed, that
in a society even more stratified than the United States, the battle
for justice could be waged by people of all classes.

Rose found it intoxicating, for example, to meet Catherine Breshkovsky, a dissident who had spent 22 years in prison or Siberian exile before escaping the country, and whose visit to America Emma
Goldman helped arrange. Breshkovsky stayed with Goldman in
New York while raising $10,000 ($50 of it from Graham), to be sent
to Russia to buy arms for revolutionaries. She captivated Americans by her upper-class background and the fact that she had begun
teaching herself English in a tsarist prison. Opening a school for the
laborers on her family's estate, she later watched in horror as troops

brutally suppressed a revolt by them. When her husband said he was not willing to suffer death or exile in the cause of revolution, she left him; she had also, regretfully, given up her baby to a sister-in-law, so as to be free to agitate. While traveling with forged papers, she was arrested and thrown into solitary confinement. There, she learned to tap in code on pipes, to communicate with other prisoners. "She was going back to Russia to help the Revolution," wrote Rose. "Perhaps she would be captured, perhaps die in prison. It did not matter to her. . . . So Russia's revolution had one of its leaders in this gentle white-haired woman, member of the Russian aristocracy. How impressed was I."

Such meetings, incidentally, were something the couple almost certainly did not discuss with Graham's Uncle Will, for W.E.D. Stokes had a very different Russian connection. Among his avocations was breeding racehorses at a stud farm in Kentucky, a hobby he had long shared with the man who took the Russian throne in 1894 as Tsar Nicholas II. Stokes attended his coronation, and the tsar appointed him a special adviser on equine matters, which entitled him to wear a plum-colored uniform with green trim on official occasions. Nicholas also bestowed several medals on Stokes, and the two men sent each other prize mares to improve the breeding stock of their respective stables. Stokes named one of his fastest horses after Nicholas II's ancestor, Peter the Great.

With their passion about the country, Americans enthusiastically devoured the work of Russian novelists. Among them, perhaps even surpassing the elderly Tolstoy in popularity, was his friend the young Maxim Gorky. With only a few months of formal schooling, Gorky had worked at jobs ranging from shoemaker's helper and dockworker to dishwasher on a Volga River steamboat. This life among the down-and-out led him to his pen name, for *gorky* means "bitter." His stories, plays, and novels, which dramatized the stark divide between Russia's elite and its underclass, won him fame at home and abroad. While Americans and Western Europeans had plenty of abject poverty in their own countries, there was something reassuring about being able to lionize a writer from an empire where the suffering was so much worse. Although little read today, "for much of the early twentieth century," the Harvard literary historian Donald Fanger wrote recently, "Maxim Gorky was probably the world's most famous writer." His short stories were published in many American magazines and newspapers. Two of his novels and the text of his widely performed play, *The Lower Depths,* were on American bestseller lists, and one novel had appeared in daily installments in the *New York Herald,* with the paper proudly advertising that the book had been suppressed in Russia.

In 1905, the year Rose and Graham married, interest in Russia rose yet more when that country was shaken by revolution. A Russian Orthodox priest—who also seems to have been a police informer—led a huge march of workers on the Winter Palace, the imperial residence in St. Petersburg, carrying religious icons, portraits of the tsar, and petitions asking him for reforms. Although the demonstration was peaceful, the chief of the security police, the tsar's uncle, was alarmed by the sight of some 200,000 marchers converging on the palace from different directions and ordered his men to open fire. There was blood on the snow as horse-drawn sledges piled with corpses hurried through the city. No one knows the full toll of "Bloody Sunday," but one estimate puts it at 500 killed and 3,000 wounded.

In the United States, the tsar who had allowed this to happen was denounced from hundreds of pulpits and in impassioned articles and poems that flooded the newspapers. Buffalo Bill Cody, the cowboy showman, announced that he was dropping the Cossack act from his Wild West show. In New York, a large march protesting the massacre wound its way up the East Side, cheered on by tenement dwellers from windows and fire escapes, to end with a rally in Union Square. And under the headline "The Massacre As I Saw It," Hearst's *New York American* printed a front-page account by Gorky. "The bloody dawn of the day of freedom will be followed by more slaughter," he wrote, "but in the end the people will triumph."

Further uprisings broke out around the tottering empire, among them a dramatic naval mutiny where rebel sailors took over the battleship *Potemkin* in the Black Sea and ran up the red flag of revolution. More red flags fluttered over makeshift barricades of boards, shop signs, carts, and barrels on the streets of Moscow. Revolutionaries assassinated a grand duke. In many cities general strikes were directed by *soviets,* or workers' councils, a phenomenon that spurred excitement around the world. In October the tsar reluctantly granted some reforms. "The news of the Russian Revolution of October 1905 was electrifying and carried us to ecstatic heights," wrote Emma Goldman. ". . . The radical East Side lived in a delirium, spending almost all of its time at monster meetings and discussing these matters in cafés, forgetting political differences and brought into close comradeship by the glorious events happening in the fatherland." Would this repressive regime at last be replaced by a genuine democracy?

Gorky had been thrown into the notorious prison inside St. Petersburg's Fortress of St. Peter and St. Paul, but managed to smuggle out a letter that was published in the popular *Collier's Weekly.* A storm of international protest led to his release. Soon after, Rose, Graham, and their friends were filled with anticipation when they learned that the newly freed novelist was about to make a trip to America.

7

Island Paradise

THE YEAR AFTER THEY MARRIED, the lives of Rose and Graham took a surprising turn: from their Lower East Side apartment, they moved to an island.

Three acres in size, it was a wedding present from Graham's mother. It lay in Long Island Sound, just off Stamford, Connecticut, connected to the shore by a 400-foot causeway. Then, as now, a private island within easy commuting distance of New York City did not come cheaply. It was originally called Waite's Island; Rose renamed it Caritas Island, after the Latin word variously translated as "charity" or "care" or — her preference — "brotherly love." Over the coming years an extraordinary parade of artists, writers, labor leaders, and revolutionaries would sign their names in the Caritas Island guestbook.

Graham's architect brother Newton designed the shingled 14-room home to which those visitors trooped, and where the couple was soon joined by a stray dog they adopted and named Peter Pan. Their house had a pillared front porch, interior walls of unfinished wood, rag rugs, and earthenware dishes. In the spacious living room was a large fireplace with a sunken hearth. Outside were purple asters, goldenrod, wild roses, daisies, and a grove of trees. Adding a salt tang to the air, surf beat against a small beach where Rose learned to swim. With Graham's approval, she moved her mother and four of the younger children into the house, as well as a friend from the *Tageblatt* to provide Mrs. Pastor, who was not completely at home in English, with some Yiddish-speaking company whenever Rose was away. A dock provided moorings for five sailboats. Photographs show guests fishing, picnicking on the grass, playing croquet, flying kites, shooting with bows and arrows, and dressing up for amateur theatricals.

The couple intended the island to become a center for a community "of congenial people engaged in the same work," as Graham put it to a curious reporter. He proposed the idea to several University Settlement friends, offering them housing, apparently rent-free. The first to accept were Leroy and Miriam Scott, who planned to move to the island once a separate, smaller home could be built for them. For Rose, living on Caritas Island, with close friends soon to move in next door, meant a way of life a universe away from the Cleveland cigar factory she had left less than four years earlier. At last, she wrote joyfully to a friend this year, she had "come out of the abyss for the first time in my whole life! . . . God is surely good! and my Beloved and I are so grateful."

Unlike the couple's first apartment, their new home with its parade of overnight guests had live-in servants, one of whom a visitor described as "a young Bulgarian peasant woman who plodded, barefooted, about her daily chores." As they embraced this comfortable life, Rose became, by virtue of her marriage, the first known woman of Jewish descent to be listed in the *Social Register,* the definitive almanac of America's upper class.

Paradoxically, the same year Rose and Graham began living on Caritas Island, they also made a move in a dramatically different direction: they joined the Socialist Party. Both had felt drawn to the movement for some time. Her husband, Rose wrote years later, "read much Socialist theory," while she, by contrast, "being a worker with no schooling, looked up to Graham in all matters theoretical: He '*knew*'; I was learning." On May Day, 1906, both were stirred by a speech they heard given by one of the most noted radical orators of the day, J. Stitt Wilson, a Methodist minister who would later become mayor of Berkeley, California. For Rose, who had little appetite for Marx or other theorists, the conversion to socialism was more emotional than intellectual. For Graham, however, socialism was a superior idea, whose truth should be self-evident to those sufficiently educated and intelligent. "Socialism has hitherto appealed altogether too much to relatively inefficient and unpractical people," he wrote to one friend from an old New England family who was now a Columbia professor, "and altogether too little to men and women of initiative, efficiency and power." There is no doubt in which group he placed himself.

What *was* socialism, anyway? Over the previous century the word had been claimed by as many disparate sects as had "Christianity." As with the kingdom of heaven, in 1906 no one had yet seen a society that called itself socialist, so believers could imagine whatever they wished. The word suggested a blueprint, often of the vaguest sort, of a yearned-for future. People differed on the best pathway to that future. Would it require violent revolution or merely the increasing public ownership of industry? Either way, everyone agreed in describing the end result in the most glowing terms. Because the people would own and control the economy, there would be no more of the boom-and-bust cycles that regularly threw millions of Americans out of work. There would be no more concentration of wealth at the top while the bottom half of the population remained miserably poor. There would be full equality for women and people of all races (although for many socialists, that was, at best, an afterthought). Small farmers would thrive (although socialists differed over whether they would own their own land), and labor unions would set safe and fair working conditions. Intractable problems of all kinds would be solved: "Socialism Would Cure Tuberculosis" read a headline in a socialist newspaper Rose would soon be writing for. As for a police force, Graham would declare, under socialism "it would hardly be necessary." There would be generous pensions, care for the elderly, free kindergartens, and certainly no more strikebreakers. And of course there would be no more war, for the solidarity among workers throughout the world would transcend petty national rivalries.

Above all, socialism would mean a society shaped not by the

ruthlessness of Gilded Age robber barons, but by human brother-hood. No wonder socialists found many supporters among evangelical Christians, and that it was a minister who inspired Graham and Rose. So splendid was the socialist dream that Mark Twain, the great skeptic, once said, "I can't even hope for it — I know too much about human nature."

Not only were there many different visions of socialism, but there was a bewildering variety of socialist groups, for countless new immigrants preferred to go to meetings in German or Italian or Slovak or Finnish. The largest socialist organization in the United States was the Socialist Party,* founded in 1901. By four years later it was expanding so fast that a worried President Roosevelt, writing to a journalist friend, called it "far more ominous than any populist or similar movement in times past." In 1912 the party's candidate would win 6 percent of the popular vote for president. Before long the Socialists would have one member of Congress, 79 mayors, thousands of city council members and other municipal officials, and 33 state legislators in 14 states, including six in Oklahoma, a party stronghold. Socialists would control cities as varied as Minneapolis, Milwaukee, Schenectady, and Butte, Montana. The pro-Socialist *Appeal to Reason* — known to its enemies as "the Squeal of Treason" — would have a peak circulation of 750,000 and for a time be the nation's most widely read political weekly. At the party's peak, it had the support of 13 American daily newspapers, eight of them in languages other than English. The several hundred socialist weeklies and monthlies around the country ranged from the *People's Friend* of Rogers, Arkansas, and the *Western Comrade* in Los Angeles to the *Górnik Polski* in Pittsburgh and Chicago's *Parola Proletaria.*

The conversion of Rose and Graham to socialism only enhanced their status as celebrities. The country's leading lecture agency, the James B. Pond Lyceum Bureau, whose clients had included everyone from the young Winston Churchill to P. T. Barnum, offered them a contract, although the couple declined. After being wel-

---

* Except in a few direct quotations, when capitalized in this book, Socialist refers to the American party or one of its members.

comed into the Socialist Party, they were quickly conscripted to campaign for its candidate for governor of New York, John Chase, a former shoe factory worker. The three of them traveled across the state together, calling each other "comrade" on the platform. Rose spoke as a worker who had experienced injustice firsthand; Graham as someone who was shocked by the poverty he had seen in New York City, had studied different visions of society and had found socialism the best; and Chase, a skillful raconteur with a wide, elegantly trimmed mustache, kept audiences laughing with funny stories. His only campaign expense, he joked, was two cents for a stamp on his letter accepting the Socialist nomination, so he was sure to gain more votes per dollar than the Democratic candidate, newspaper king William Randolph Hearst.

"It was a great night for the workingman," reported the New York *Sun* of one campaign rally, "and the capitalists got many a hard wallop." In the end, Chase won only a small percentage of the vote, but the campaign proved a major turning point for Rose. For the first time, she fully discovered her talent as a public speaker. She realized something else as well: she could connect with audiences in a way that Graham, despite his many years of formal education that still awed her, could not. On the platform, one witness remembered, "he hemmed and stammered and made grotesque gestures."

Rose, on the other hand, had an instinctive sense of how to hold a crowd's attention. "I made no notes and had no set speech," she later wrote. "I coined my words as I stood and faced the audience. Speeches differed in approach as my audiences differed. . . . I [was] determined to learn to think on my feet." She was always nervous beforehand, but found it "a profound joy to me to be able to reach so many." In a way she had never imagined, she was fulfilling old fantasies, of singing for an audience of thousands. Indeed, she possessed a singer's control over her voice. One listener described it as "now calm and low, now impassioned and full of fire."

Whatever Graham's immediate family felt about the couple's conversion to socialism, they largely kept their emotions in check, except for the irascible Uncle Will. Graham's new beliefs, his uncle wrote him, were like those of converts who "leave Methodism for

Presbyterianism, then Episcopalianism, then take up Catholicism and become the most extreme Catholics." He assumed Graham would run through a cycle of extremes and then return to the fold. "You are yet young, and the sooner you become a Nihilist and a Terrorist the better for you. . . . The quicker you go through these changes and these 'isms' the better."

Increasingly, Rose and Graham were swept up in their work for the party. They helped found a group that would become the vehicle for much of their speaking, the Intercollegiate Socialist Society, designed to spread the gospel to colleges and universities. Before long, it grew to have chapters on 60 campuses. Ironically, Rose, who had never even gone to high school, was the speaker most in demand. She also became a delegate to the Socialist Party's national convention, and Graham won a place on its seven-member national executive committee, writing letters on party business that began "Dear Comrade" and ended "Fraternally Yours." (The Stokeses were unaware of just how many of their fellow activists were in fact private detectives, reporting to worried employers. For example, recently discovered papers indicate that two of the three men in a Socialist delegation sent on a mission to a Denver labor union office in 1907 were undercover detectives.)

Even though Graham's new socialist convictions led him to resign from numerous traditional charitable and reform boards, he was still a dutiful son, spending time each week at his desk in the office that oversaw the family-owned New York apartment buildings, Nevada mines, and more. It was as if this was a normal household chore that had to be done even though there was a world to be remade. Nonetheless, he and Rose had firmly come to believe that the capitalist system itself was the main source of human misery. In December 1906, he wrote his "darling Mother" that he doubted whether "you recognized the injustice of the system which provides you with your great income at the expense of others; and whether you recognized the relation between this system and the terribly widespread suffering which you endeavor so earnestly to relieve."

Rose, typically, was more joyful when she wrote a friend that same month, speaking of her island paradise as a place where "one can rest and gather strength and inspiration for the work that lies before." This battle for a socialist future would be, she declared, "a great, glorious fight. The only thing worth living for in these inspiring days."

The year that Rose and Graham joined the movement also saw Maxim Gorky's long-anticipated trip to the United States. To all who hoped for change in his benighted homeland, it seemed a crucial moment. Although the Russian Revolution of 1905 had in the end been brutally suppressed, Tsar Nicholas II had given in to one of its demands by allowing the election of a legislature. But the new body was largely toothless, for it could be dismissed by the tsar. Much more needed to be done, American radicals felt, and now at last the most famous literary voice of Russia's revolutionaries, under surveillance by the empire's secret police for nearly two decades, was on his way to an America where he had so many admirers. More than a thousand people met his steamer when it docked in New Jersey, and a phalanx of police, ship's officers, and longshoremen was needed to get Gorky through the cheering crowd to a waiting carriage. Banquets, speeches, and receptions were on the agenda. The Russian novelist was hoping to raise a million dollars to support revolutionaries in his native land, and the committee that formed to help him do so included some of the best-known Americans of the day. A cartoon in one newspaper showed a friendly Statue of Liberty bending down her torch to light one carried by Gorky labeled "For My People."

Although capable of mesmerizing American listeners by reciting Edgar Allan Poe's "The Raven" in Russian, Gorky did not speak English. The Russian-born Miriam Scott, however, was on hand to act as his interpreter. While the writer's New York hosts were delighted to have him in their city, several were nervous. Russian diplomats in Washington had attempted to have the novelist barred from the country. They were unsuccessful, but from a secret sympathizer inside the embassy Gorky's American friends learned some alarming information that could turn the writer's visit into a public relations catastrophe. The only question was when the news would break.

From the moment he arrived, Gorky was treated like royalty.

"The American nation seemed concentrated upon one great and ennobling idea," wrote H. G. Wells, visiting at the time, "the freedom of Russia, and upon Gorky as the embodiment of that idea." The novelist dressed the part of a proletarian, wearing black trousers tucked into high boots and a peasant's long, belted shirt. He saw the sights of New York, declaring that the Hudson River reminded him of the Volga flowing past his native town of Nizhny Novgorod. He was awed by the skyscrapers, which "seem to kiss the clouds." Leroy Scott took him to the Barnum & Bailey Circus at Madison Square Garden. At a welcoming dinner the day after his arrival, he sat next to Mark Twain. The toastmaster was former University Settlement executive director Robert Hunter, now married to Graham's sister Caroline. A party later that evening went on into the early hours of the morning and featured, in Gorky's honor, Russian cigarettes and tea poured from a samovar. As he explained to the gathering, he was doing nothing more than Benjamin Franklin had once done in Europe: asking for help in a struggle for liberty on another continent. He then amused his listeners by picking up his host's hunting rifle and miming the shooting down of foes of the revolution. Among the guests at the party were Graham and Rose.

Four days after his arrival, what Gorky's American friends had been fearing finally happened. On its front page, complete with photographs supplied by the Russian embassy, the *New York World* headlined the fact that the attractive young woman traveling with Gorky was not his wife but Maria Andreyeva, an actress from the Moscow Art Theater who had appeared in the writer's plays. The two had been living together for several years. Leroy Scott had briefed newspaper reporters about this as they waited for Gorky to disembark from his ship, and the journalists had informally agreed not to embarrass the author by mentioning it. The tsar's government, however, was bent on wrecking his mission. After all, not only did he want to overthrow the regime, but his trip had come at a particularly awkward moment: having just lost a war to Japan, Russia was in deep financial difficulty and was desperately trying to raise loans in the West.

Another war lay behind the embassy's success in persuading the

World to publish its exposé, a ferocious rivalry between two newspaper titans. Joseph Pulitzer's *World* and *Evening World* were locked in a fierce battle for readers with Hearst's *New York American* and *Evening Journal.* In Russia, Gorky had signed a contract with the Hearst chain, which meant he could neither write for other American publications nor grant them exclusive interviews. The editors of the *World* were eager for revenge. Once their story was out, it was repeated and embellished in other newspapers, as columnists and editorial writers rushed to denounce Gorky for this shocking breach of propriety. A few defended him, one noting that Queen Victoria had received the shah of Persia, who had a whole harem of wives. But another newspaper promptly pointed out that when meeting the queen, the shah had at least had the courtesy to leave his harem behind.

The startled novelist explained to anyone who would listen that he had long been amicably separated from his wife. Since the Russian Orthodox Church made divorce extremely difficult, and in particular did no favors for revolutionaries, neither of them had been able to formally marry their new partners. Gorky's wife sent telegrams to the press supporting his story, all in vain. The unfortunate Gorky and Andreyeva were immediately evicted from their New York hotel, whose proprietor declared, "I am running a family hotel, and I can't have these people in my house any longer." As soon as the manager of the next hotel they went to discovered who his guests were, the same thing happened. The couple then moved to a third hotel, but returned around midnight from a socialist meeting to find all their baggage piled on the sidewalk in the rain. As Andreyeva held a dripping bouquet of flowers given to them at the meeting, Gorky told a reporter that, if need be, he would sleep on the street, as he had often done in Russia.

The first people to offer the thrice-evicted couple a place to stay were Leroy and Miriam Scott, who, while their Caritas Island home was being built, shared a building near Washington Square with some other writers. Soon afterward, John and Prestonia Martin hosted the novelist for several months of writing at their Adirondack summer home, the place where Rose had seen mountains for the first time.

Gorky's fund-raising mission was stymied, and banquets, rallies, speeches, and a reception that Theodore Roosevelt had planned to host at the White House were all canceled. Even Mark Twain, no apostle of bourgeois piety, regretfully withdrew from the writer's support committee. One widely reprinted newspaper attack specifically condemned Graham as one of several "rose water and angel-cake Socialists" who had endorsed a "polygamous humanity" by backing Gorky. In the world of American radicals, however, esteem for Rose and Graham grew because they remained among his supporters. The *Worker,* a New York socialist newspaper previously suspicious of Graham's class origins, praised him for "standing by the Gorkys when so many others were scared away by the outcry of the capitalist press." For her part, Rose told the *Evening World,* "We must accept him as the great man he is. Will the disclosure that the woman who accompanied him to this country is not his wife change my attitude toward him? Certainly not!" If the punctilious Phelps Stokes clan was upset by such comments, their distress was surely eclipsed by the fact that Uncle Will just at this moment made the headlines yet again, as the object of a paternity suit.

On July 3 and 4, 1906, with Miriam Scott doing the translating, Maxim Gorky was one of the first visitors to the new Stokes home on Caritas Island.

8

A Tall, Shamblefooted Man

THE SAME YEAR GORKY CAME to America, 1906, a horrifying scene took place in a restaurant in St. Petersburg, the Russian capital. A holiday celebration was under way, with champagne flowing, women wearing their most elegant dresses, and men their military decorations. As a band started playing, the crowd of diners rose to sing the national anthem, "God Save the Tsar." However, a young man in a student's uniform, sitting with his mother and fiancée, did not stand. An officer at the next table walked over and ordered him to rise. He refused. There was a shouting match, a scuffle, and then two shots rang out. As terrified, ashen-faced restaurant patrons fled into the snowy street, they could see the officer standing over the student's dead body. Four days later, he was released from police custody, unpunished.

Among the diners were two young Americans, Anna Strunsky and William English Walling. Having first met in the United States, they had crossed paths again in Russia, where they were each gathering material for magazine articles. The shock of seeing the student killed brought them closer. As the melodramatic Anna wrote to her brother, "Our love which had been filling our hearts from the hour of our first meeting suddenly burst into speech. It was baptised in blood." They were married on their way home—in Paris, with a grandson of Karl Marx as a witness. On the marriage certificate, both listed their profession as *écrivain,* writer.

Walling, known as English to his friends, had been a housemate of Graham's on the upper floors of the University Settlement, and the two were close. In a striking parallel to Graham and Rose, he was a wealthy Protestant and Anna a Russian Jewish immigrant. She had come to the United States when she was nine.

Like Graham, English Walling stood to gain a large inheritance. His was a prominent midwestern family with interests in banking, streetcar lines, and real estate. In 1880, when he was three, his maternal grandfather, William Hayden English, one of the richest men in Indiana, was the Democratic candidate for vice president. He and his running mate, Winfield Hancock, narrowly lost the election to the Republican ticket headed by James Garfield, but his speech accepting the nomination would be required reading for his grandchildren years later. After studying at the University of Chicago and Harvard Law School, English Walling used family ties to the governor of Illinois to gain a job as a state factory inspector, which allowed him to see the sanitary and working conditions of the day from the inside. After visiting one cookie factory, he declared he would never eat Fig Newtons again. The work led him to a lifelong belief in strong trade unions.

Anna had spent her teenage years in San Francisco, where she had started a California chapter of the Society of Friends of Russian Freedom. The desire to report firsthand on the country of her birth then led her to St. Petersburg. "I cry, Long live the Revolution," she wrote to a friend, "and would gladly shed my blood in the field." In photographs the Wallings make a handsome couple, but there is no mistaking English's class background, given his dark suit, double-breasted white vest, and watch chain. The dark-haired, stunningly beautiful Anna has a round-eyed, slightly sad, and vulnerable face. A contemporary described her "intense seriousness, unrelieved by any sense of humor. . . . Nobody in the world ever said 'socialism' with so much intensity, overflowing like a huge wave the infinite beach of life."

Once in Russia, she began taking notes on the rebels she and English were meeting, for a book to be called *Revolutionary Lives,* which she hoped to write together with him. "We are equals," she told her mother-in law proudly. English, however, seemed to expect her to be little more than his assistant. Anna was "not exactly masterly in keeping address-books," he complained to his father, adding, confidently, that he would in any case "always have a stenographer or secretary of my own." From St. Petersburg, Anna journeyed alone to the city of Gomel, to gather interviews about a bloody three-day pogrom that had just taken place there, leaving more than 100 Jewish shops and businesses burned, hundreds of Jews homeless, and an unknown number dead. She told friends and family to watch for her article on the subject, but a writer's block that would dog her for the rest of her life intervened, and it took years before she could finish the piece, by which point magazine editors were no longer interested. By contrast, her husband poured out a stream of articles, read eagerly by Rose, Graham, and their friends, including one containing what may be the first published American reference to Lenin. English then wrote a widely reviewed book about Russia.

In several trips there, the couple raced around St. Petersburg by sleigh to mass meetings, interviewed Leo Tolstoy (who predicted a revolution, but not a good one), and sheltered in their hotel room a man on the run from the police. ("He arrived shortly after midnight," Anna wrote, in an account that remained unpublished, "a tall, gaunt man, with his head bandaged; his face paralyzed; his large, dark eyes burning with fever and his hands trembling so that he could hardly drink the tea which we set before him.") At another point, the pair were jailed for a night. English had no shortage of self-regard, and believed he had penetrated to the country's soul. "The Revolutionaries tell me what they will tell no one else," he wrote to his parents, claiming that there was "no single man to whom Russia is so open."

Meanwhile, from a continent away, Graham invited them, as he had Leroy and Miriam Scott, to live on Caritas Island. From Russia, Anna replied, telling him how delighted they were to be asked "to share permanently in your island," where they could throw themselves "heart and soul into the glorious hopeful American movement alongside you." Soon a house for the Wallings began going up next to the one for the Scotts. Graham, surprisingly handy for someone who had grown up surrounded by butlers, maids, and chauffeurs, did some of the masonry and woodwork for the Wallings' house himself, with help from two immigrant workmen.

And so three couples, each consisting of a wealthy Anglo-Saxon Protestant man married to a Russian Jewish woman of much more humble background, were soon living on the island together. The three women, in fact, had been born within a few hundred miles of each other in the Pale of Settlement. All six were now passionately involved in the socialist movement, and Rose liked to refer to their mates not as husbands but as "comrade-lovers." They all believed, or at least liked to think they believed, in a day when gender stereotypes would be transformed. Then, as English Walling put it, "sports, heavy drinking, cynical talking and vile stories will no longer appeal to men, just as sentimental romance, mere prettiness, timidity and softness will no longer appeal to women." When Anna became pregnant, she spoke of the unborn baby as "my little International." In a United States that has seen many intentional communities, Caritas Island was one of the more unusual.

The Russian Revolution of 1905, with its heroic images of workers wielding power through *soviets* before being crushed by the tsar's armed might, was one stimulant to the growth of American socialism; another was a severe recession and financial panic in 1907. Throughout the United States there were runs on banks and trust companies, many of which failed. Police pushed back crowds of desperate men and women trying to withdraw their life savings before these vanished. Unemployment soared, while families doubled up and tripled up, sometimes squeezing close to 20 people into a three-room tenement apartment. The safety net was almost nonexistent, with the country spending less than half a percent of its gross domestic product on social welfare measures of any kind.

The economy improved only when J. P. Morgan, the world's most powerful banker, then visiting Virginia, ordered his private railway car hitched to a steam locomotive and rushed back to New York City so he could strong-arm fellow bankers and friends like John D. Rockefeller into infusing money into the banking system. The crucial meeting took place amid the Gutenberg Bibles, Renaissance bronzes, and smoke from Morgan's cigar in the library of his grand home on Madison Avenue and 36th Street. It was, incidentally, next door to the house of a friend with whom he shared a love of yachting: Anson Phelps Stokes Sr., Graham's father. A greater disaster was averted, but public confidence had been shattered. That it required a small group of plutocrats, in no way responsible to voters, to prevent the economy from crashing to further depths left millions of Americans open to the idea that there was something fundamentally wrong with the capitalist system.

Although the great majority of socialists were working class, when it came to talking about these beliefs, Graham was only truly comfortable with aristocrats like himself. In 1906, for example, he had used the guest rooms of his parents' lavish Noroton, Connecticut, estate, the site of his wedding reception, to host a startlingly elite conference on socialism. This was not just a matter of the surroundings or the elegant carriages that met the train bringing people out from New York City, but of the pedigrees of the 20 or so participants. Among them were Graham's brother-in-law Robert Hunter, the son of a wealthy midwestern wagon manufacturer; Joseph Medill Patterson, whose grandfather had owned the *Chicago Tribune* and been mayor of the city; Gaylord Wilshire, publisher of *Wilshire's* magazine and the man after whom Wilshire Boulevard in Los Angeles is named; and several other upper-class reformers. Graham's socialist-minded sister Helen and Rose were the only women present, and Rose was almost alone in the group in having a working-class background. When she addressed the gathering, the New York labor lawyer Morris Hillquit was struck by how at home she appeared, calling her "a Jewish factory worker of rare charm, who in the aristocratic surroundings of the Noroton 'Brick House' looked and acted more to the manner [*sic*] born than almost any other member of the assembly."

Journalists, invited to one day of the conference, were intrigued by the spectacle of these "millionaire socialists" gathering in such a luxurious setting. Graham's parents were vacationing in Europe, where his mother was dismayed to read in the press about the goings-on in her own house. She wryly suggested that her clergyman son Anson might want to hold a gathering of bishops at the Brick House to "take the taste away."

Others suspected that the group's radicalism might not run that deep. The humorist Finley Peter Dunne used his famous character, the Irish bartender Mr. Dooley, to mock the millionaires, who included "th' well-known Socialist leader, J. Clarence Lumley, heir to the Lumley millyons. This well-known prolytariat said he had become a Socialist through studyin' his father." Mr. Dooley sized up the situation: "I'm sthrong f'r anny rivilution that ain't goin' to happen in my day."

Increasingly, however, Rose and Graham did seem ever more determined to make a revolution happen in their own lifetimes. They not only quietly helped finance socialist organizations and publications, but Rose contributed articles to some of them. When the Socialist Party established a daily newspaper in New York in 1908, the *New York Call,* for several months she edited a weekly half-page for women, writing some of the pieces. She also resumed doing an advice column for women in the Yiddish press, but this time in the *Yiddishes Tageblatt*'s rival, the socialist *Forverts,* now surging ahead of the *Tageblatt* in circulation. Taking advantage of her new fame, the *Forverts* editors syndicated her column in English to several Hearst papers.

One of Rose's newspaper pieces went far beyond advice. She entered a prison to interview—and befriend—a murderer.

Sarah Koten, a 22-year-old Russian Jewish immigrant, had gone into training as a nurse for a Manhattan doctor who ran a small, private maternity hospital on East 93rd Street. He lived upstairs in the same building and offered her a bedroom there as well. One night, she said, he had slipped into her room when she was sleeping, given her chloroform, and raped her. Weeks later she realized she was pregnant. She brought a charge of criminal assault against him—a rare and brave act for a working-class woman of her time. But the case was dismissed after less than ten minutes when the doctor produced two witnesses who testified "that her character was not good."

The district attorney refused to pursue the matter further. "All right, judge," Koten said she declared in court. "You won't give me justice—I'll be my own judge." Shortly afterward, she left a telephone message that the doctor was needed by a patient at a certain address. Across the street, Koten waited until he arrived, then approached, pulled a revolver out of a black handbag, and shot him in the heart. For good measure, she fired a second bullet that severed his jugular vein, then sat down on the curb to await arrest. At a nearby police station, the coroner pointed at the doctor's body and asked her, "Are you the murderer of that man?" She replied, "He is my murderer, coroner."

The case of a pregnant woman who could face the electric chair seized New York's attention. Some newspapers described Koten with denigrating stereotypes. The *Sun,* for example, declared that "there is little that is attractive about Sarah Koten. She is squatly formed, square shouldered, thick waisted and dumpy. She looks like any one of a hundred peasant girls from the north of Europe you might see any day shuffling from the gates of Castle Garden laboring under a bundle of clothing. Her eyes are black and dull, her lips are thick and her nose is wide." A later story described her as "a dull, plodding peasant type."

But public opinion would change when a second woman came forward with a similar story about the dead doctor. A former patient, she said that while under his care, he had drugged and assaulted her. She, too, had then tried to kill him, but he had seized her revolver before she could pull the trigger. The case quickly took on feminist overtones.

Like Rose, Koten came from Russia and had once been a factory worker. Rose became involved immediately. She went to the Tombs, as the main New York City prison was known, and spoke with Koten. "In less than five minutes she was talking freely (Yiddish makes such a difference)," Rose wrote in a *New York Call* article that was reprinted in other newspapers, "and her story welled up from within her between breaks of sobbing and blinding tears."

Koten laid out her whole saga for Rose, including the fact that the doctor had wanted to perform an abortion when she told him she was pregnant. She said she felt no choice but to kill him: "He will never, never ruin other women's lives as he ruined mine!" Rose not only published the fullest account of Koten's experience, but remained active in her support for months. The trial was postponed until after Koten gave birth in prison. "I will pay all of the expenses of Miss Koten's defense," Rose told a reporter, "and as soon as she is acquitted will take her to my home at Paradise Island, near Stamford, and will let her remain there as long as she sees fit." The journalist had garbled the name of Caritas Island in his story, but after Sarah Koten was at last released with a suspended sentence—an almost tearful judge declared her "more sinned against than sinning"—the prospect of time on the island must have seemed to her indeed like paradise.

In this era before television and radio, with movies still in their infancy, the best way to take advantage of one's celebrity to reach an audience was public speaking. Rose and Graham were now giving speeches sometimes three or four nights a week. They spoke to men's clubs, women's clubs, church suppers, a meeting in Boston of 60 clergymen, a demonstration of the unemployed, the Odd Fellows, the Woman's Christian Temperance Union, as well as to distinctly unsocialist groups like the Daughters of the American Revolution. All were curious about this remarkable marriage. Typically, Rose would describe her time as a cigar worker, while Graham would explain how his medical experience with some of New York's poorest had led him first to settlement house work and then, convinced that "something at the bottom was wrong," to socialism.

The range of their audiences was a challenge that thrilled Rose. "I felt I could remove mountains," she later wrote. "Nothing was too difficult, no campaign so hard and trying, but that I could come through it stronger and more buoyant." When she talked to middle-class suburban groups, she evoked a vivid picture of life in inner-city tenements and sweatshops. When she spoke to workers, she included the tale of how happy she had been to hear a factory owner flatter her for rolling cigars so fast, only to realize that she had provided him the excuse to drop the piece rate. When she spoke at the Chautauqua Institution summer colony in upstate New York, whose residents were heavily religious, she adjusted her message accordingly: "We call to mind the story of the man who fell among thieves on his way to Jericho. Suppose that after robbing and injuring him as they did, the thieves had returned and given him back a small portion of what they had taken, to help him recover his health. Would that be justice? . . . The wolves of Wall Street become the very meekest lambs of charity after they have taken the greater part of the spoil for their own enrichment."

As a speaker, Rose continued to outshine Graham. Their message "was attractively presented. This was especially true of Mrs. Stokes," noted a Brooklyn newspaper. "Mrs. Phelps Stokes made quite a hit at Barnard last night," a worried Republican wrote the president of Columbia University, suggesting that the college invite someone to speak against socialism. "She is immensely effective as a speaker," reported the *New York Times.* "Her voice is vibrating and high. It is not strong, but by very distinct enunciation she makes herself heard perfectly." (Like so many journalists, this one made sure to remind his readers of her ethnicity. She had, he wrote, "the melancholy associated with her race.") A student who heard her at Colgate University found that "Mrs. Stokes is a wonderful lecturer—there is charm in the manner of her speaking that makes a potent appeal to the hearer's heart. Her clear, tense, lucid style and the ring of fervent sincerity in her voice, produce a profound impression upon an audience." Her childhood years in London had left behind an appealing trace of a British accent.

Rose spoke from the heart, and sometimes, such as when addressing an audience in Milwaukee during the winter of the harsh 1907 recession, she broke down sobbing. As Graham's sister Mildred recalled, "She was very emotional and I have known her to burst into tears at the table and have to leave because seeing such good and plentiful food made her so sorry for those who didn't have it." She greatly widened her own sense of America on these speaking tours, seeing new parts of the country, learning from those she spoke to, entering a coal mine in Pennsylvania, for instance, to see the dark, low-ceilinged, tunnels, knee-deep in water, where the miners worked.

In the fall of 1908, the couple's speaking took on new purpose when Graham ran as a Socialist candidate for the New York State Assembly from the Lower East Side. Despite his militant denunciations of the "able-bodied men who live idly upon the product of the toil of others," his lanky, awkward figure did not set alight the audiences of "comrades" he spoke to. These weeks, however, broadened Rose's sense of what she could do as a speaker. Campaigning for Graham at dozens of rallies gained her experience before crowds that ranged from a meeting of 3,000 women cigar workers to impromptu gatherings she addressed from a fire escape or the back of a horse-drawn wagon. She spoke in English or Yiddish as the occasion required. "She is as much at home on the stump," observed one newspaper, "as she is in her study or on the lecture platform."

To the mainstream press, which eagerly covered their joint speaking appearances, the pair remained Cinderella and Prince Charming. The radicals who flocked to hear them may not have been completely immune from the Cinderella myth, but for socialists this couple who so obviously loved each other symbolized something else as well: that, in the dreamed-of future, all barriers of class and ethnicity would be dissolved.

Graham may have been a distinctly uncharismatic campaigner, but Rose's eloquence more than made up for that, and when the two of them appeared together, audiences often went wild. After they both spoke to an election rally at Rutgers Square on the Lower East Side, an enthusiastic, shouting crowd unhitched the horses from the couple's open carriage and pulled it several times around the square themselves. What could better symbolize the hope of human brotherhood than such a marriage of rich and poor, native-born and immigrant, Gentile and Jew?

Earlier that year, Graham and Rose had taken part in the convention that nominated the Socialist Party's candidate for president, the charismatic railway union leader Eugene V. Debs of Terre Haute,

Indiana. Rose would become particularly close to Debs; ten years later she would be, literally, at his side during one of the most difficult moments of his life.

Like her, Debs had little formal education. One of ten children, he had left school at 14 to go to work cleaning grease from the wheel assemblies of freight engines, then became a fireman, shoveling coal into the hot mouth of the furnace that burned beneath a locomotive's boiler. Railway labor was ill regulated and dangerous. Everything from derailments to exploding boilers killed more than 2,000 and injured more than 20,000 railwaymen each year. One friend of Debs's died when he fell under a locomotive. Workers were frequently maimed or crushed between freight cars that had to be coupled and uncoupled by hand. In 1894, Debs had helped lead a strike against the Pullman sleeping car company. Some 14,000 army troops, National Guardsmen, and police suppressed it, killing as many as 30 people and seriously wounding hundreds more. His belief in socialism was born of the books he read and the discussions he carried on during the six months he spent in jail for his role in the strike. But despite his reading of Marx, his creed always reflected more of the New Testament than of *Das Kapital*. During a longer stay in prison years later, he would hang a picture of Jesus, with a crown of thorns, on his cell wall.

Six and a half feet tall, almost always in a bow tie and a three-piece suit that left his shirt drenched with sweat in warm weather, Debs would pace back and forth across a stage, his piercing eyes fixing one person after another in the crowd. He would lean far forward as he spoke and throw his arms wide as if to embrace them all, while his long face seemed to carry all the cares of the world. The socialist writer and editor Oscar Ameringer described how "children used to flock to him as they must have flocked to the Carpenter. I remember gray-bearded farmers, who as American Railway Union strikers had followed him to defeat, rushing up to their Gene, crying 'Gene, Gene, don't you remember me anymore?' And Gene remembered them always, threw his long arms around them, pressed them to his heart until their eyes moistened in love and gratitude to the leader who had lost them their strike, their jobs and their home.

"Gene Debs was the dreamer, poet, and prophet of the weary and heavy-laden. He was the stuff of which the prophets of Israel, the fathers of the Christian Church, the Ethan Allens, Nathan Hales, Abe Lincolns, and John Browns were made."

Debs gave generously to those in need: money, when he had any, even clothes from the suitcase he carried on his endless travels. "It was like a sacrament to meet him," wrote one friend, "to have that warm, rapierlike attention concentrated on you for a moment." He spoke not just of health care and decent pensions, but of the way socialism would transform all human relations. "That old man with the burning eyes actually believes that there can be such a thing as the brotherhood of man," another socialist once said. "And that's not the funniest part of it. As long as he's around I believe it myself."

A generation later, in his panoramic *U.S.A.* trilogy, the novelist John Dos Passos would write of Debs:

> He was a tall shamblefooted man, had a sort of gusty rhetoric that set on fire the railroad workers in their pine-boarded halls
>> made them want the world he wanted,
>> a world brothers might own
>> where everybody would split even:
> *. . . I don't want you to follow me or anyone else. If you are looking for a Moses to lead you out of the capitalist wilderness you will stay right where you are. I would not lead you into this promised land if I could, because if I could lead you in, someone else would lead you out.*
> That was how he talked to freighthandlers and gandy-walkers, to firemen and switchmen and engineers, telling them it wasn't enough to organize the railroadmen, that all workers must be organized. . . .
> those were the men that chalked up nine hundred thousand votes for him in nineteen twelve and scared the frock-coats and the tophats and diamonded hostesses at Saratoga Springs, Bar Harbor, Lake Geneva with the bogy of a socialist president.

In 1908, Debs barnstormed the country, covering more than ten thousand miles in his Red Special train. It carried a brass band and a baggage car full of socialist literature, with more boxes of pamphlets and bright red Socialist Party lapel buttons stacked in the coaches. Railway switchmen gave the train the fast track, and locomotive engineers blew jubilant blasts on their whistles when they recognized the Red Special barreling past, red pennants and bunting streaming from the roof, wheels, and rear platform. Supporters in buggies and farm wagons lined up to cheer from the trackside. In San Diego, 15,000 people paid to hear Debs speak. Though it was 4 a.m. when he arrived in Santa Barbara, a large crowd of socialists was waiting for him in the railway yards. He talked to miners, sharecroppers, students, factory workers, often by the thousands, with no loudspeakers. In Woodstock, Illinois, he stopped to have a chat with the sheriff, who had become something of a friend while Debs's jailer during his six months behind bars years earlier. Once he gave 17 speeches in a single day. In October, when the Red Special arrived in New York, police reserves had to be called in to deal with the 4,000 enthusiastic men and women who crowded to greet him under the vaulting glass-and-wrought-iron roof—then one of the largest in the world—of the old Grand Central Station.

Socialists of every sort turned out to welcome Debs to the nation's largest city, including the members of the 250-voice United Workmen's Singing Society. Women wore red sashes and caps, and members of both sexes waved red handkerchiefs. One supporter remembered how he stood next to the socialist leader "on a truck that slowly plowed its way through a roaring ocean of people as far as the eye could see, all up and down dark tenement streets." As a candidate for the state legislature, Graham was on the platform when Debs addressed a throng of 7,000, who cheered and waved red flags for 15 minutes before letting him speak.

Debs was also scheduled to be guest of honor at a banquet arranged by New York Socialist Party leaders, but was too exhausted to appear. Still, the faithful gathered, others spoke, and, as always at such events, an appeal for funds was made, this time by a socialist clergyman who mounted a table to better address the 500 diners. Rose seized the headlines when she, too, climbed onto the table.

She had no money with her, she told the crowd, "but I and many women here are wearing jewels which we really do not need." She placed a large pearl stickpin on the table and then added, "I have a brooch at home and I never wear it. That, too, I'll give." This unleashed "great applause," the *Times* reported, "and then from several parts of the room women cried out their gifts. A gold purse, a ring, a gold watch, a chain. . . . Mrs. Stokes was so overcome that she burst into tears."

Both Debs and Graham lost their races on election day, but socialists remained confident that their movement had a luminous future. Rose was certain that Graham would always be with her as they moved toward it. "Oh, what a wonderful cause we are working for, my Precious!" she wrote him this year from Caritas Island when they were apart. "What a lifting of loads there will be when our cause triumphs. That is the joyous thought! That someday, all our striving, all our straining will gain for the world that peace that passeth understanding. And I know it shall come."

9

By Ballot or Bullet

Rose, graham, and other socialists might imagine a more glorious future, but what battles could bring it closer? On the evening of November 22, 1909, a dramatic conflict broke out in the very heart of American capitalism, New York City. And most of the combatants were women.

The opening scene took place in the Great Hall of Cooper Union, the pillared auditorium of a private college that is more famous than the college itself. Abraham Lincoln had given an important speech there against the expansion of slavery, and later presidents had also chosen it as a forum. This evening it was packed to overflowing with young women angry over abysmal working conditions in the city's garment industry. Most were Jewish immigrants. Older labor leaders, almost all men counseling moderation, including Samuel Gompers of the American Federation of Labor, monopolized the stage for two hours. Then 23-year-old Clara Lemlich rose, interrupted a male speaker, and demanded to be heard. A Socialist Party member who had fled to the United States as a teenager after a Russian pogrom, she had been arrested many times for labor activism. Lemlich was small, but her black eyes flashed as hands from the audience lifted her onto the platform. "I am a working girl," she cried out in Yiddish. ". . . I am tired of listening to speakers who talk in general terms. What we are here for is to decide whether we shall or

shall not strike. I offer a resolution that a general strike* be declared
—now."

An uproar swept the hall. Hats and handkerchiefs shot into the
air. After five minutes the tumult died away, and up went a thousand
hands and the repetition in unison of a traditional Jewish oath: "If
I turn traitor to the cause I now pledge, may this hand wither from
the arm I now raise." The room exploded with cheers and shouts of
"Strike! Strike!" More than 20,000 clothing workers walked off the
job the next day, and in the following weeks that number kept rising. It was the largest work stoppage New York had ever seen and
the first major American strike consisting primarily of women.

It is no surprise that it was among garment workers—in particular the women who made shirtwaists, or blouses—that a strike began. The New York City garment makers, who produced well over
half the country's clothing, normally worked 56- to 59-hour weeks
—stretching to 70 hours in busy seasons, or unpredictably shrink-
ing to nothing if demand fell. Clothing factories, almost entirely
unregulated, were cramped places where lint filled the air and wages
were low. Fire hazards were everywhere and fire escapes flimsy—
something that would soon have tragic consequences.

The majority of New Yorkers in the needle trades were Russian
Jews. Managers did their best, however, to sow ethnic discord, foil-
ing one strike by telling Italian workers that the Jews were walking out because they didn't like working with them. In 1909, only a
small minority of clothing workers had the protection of a union.

Rose swiftly made the cause her own. "She was on the platform,"
wrote a *Collier's* magazine reporter, "a score of girls surrounding her,
listening rapt. 'Nothing can be gained unless you hold together,' she
told them—just what any number of other people had told them,
but somehow it hadn't made the same impression. A few minutes
more and the signing [up to join the union] began." From her own
years of rolling cigars, Rose also understood that for young women
working for male supervisors, wages and hours were not the only is-

---

* Meaning a strike against all factories in a branch of the clothing industry,
rather than just against one employer.

sues. She told the same journalist, "There are foremen in certain factories who insult and abuse girls beyond endurance." Similar veiled
comments from other organizers of this strike make clear that this
was a matter of what today we would call sexual harassment. Foremen and employers had particular leverage to demand sexual favors,
the historian Nan Enstad explains, "in piecework, where the kind of
piece one was assigned to do could make a difference in pay of up
to 50 percent."

In visits to meeting halls around the city, Rose tried to keep up
the spirits of the "girl strikers," as newspapers called them. After the
police beat up one group of picketers, she was the main speaker at a
Lower East Side protest rally. She addressed as many as ten gatherings a day, at one point bringing her mother—her own experience
of a strike in London not forgotten—to talk as well. She sounded
ever more apocalyptic. As Rose put it in a newspaper article, one day
at a "supreme, despairing moment," the employers' ownership of industry would be "wrenched from their grasp, forever."

This strike proved a harbinger of a long wave of American labor strife. Over the next turbulent decade, few months would pass
without tens of thousands of workers walking out, often destroying
machinery in the factories they were striking. Police and National
Guardsmen regularly wielded guns, batons, and fire hoses to battle them, while parades of supporters included hundreds of women
wearing sashes emblazoned with slogans across their right shoulders.
In New York City alone, from 95,000 to 300,000 workers would go
on strike annually. In Los Angeles the following year, a labor militant would plant a suitcase full of dynamite in the building of the
harshly anti-union *Los Angeles Times,* killing 21 people and injuring
more than 100.

The origins of the turmoil were clear enough. Groups like the
Industrial Workers of the World and the Socialist Party had placed
the dream of more equality on the table. Yet the ways the nation fell
painfully short of this were daily laid bare, for investigative reporters
like Lincoln Steffens and Ray Stannard Baker—both of whom Rose
and Graham would soon know—were energetically documenting
the underside of American life. These muckrakers wrote about child

labor and the millions of dollars in kickbacks and bribes that flowed into the pockets of city officials; about the harsh discrimination against black Americans that made a mockery of the promise of full citizenship; and about the powerful railroads and oil companies that seemed to be vacuuming up all the country's wealth for themselves. Their exposés were published in nonfiction books, novels, and, over the course of a decade, in nearly 2,000 articles in popular magazines. Despite these revelations, however, working people at the bottom of the ladder were finding few changes for the better and some for the worse, for many had lost jobs and savings in the recession of 1907. "My people do not live in America," declared one immigrant, "they live underneath America."

Reformers and social workers estimated that the average annual income needed to adequately support a family of four in New York was, at the bare minimum, $800 a year, equal to roughly $25,000 today. Yet half of all male clothing workers earned less than $400, and average wages for women or immigrants were still lower. Furthermore, much of New York's clothing was manufactured in small workshops crammed into tenement rooms, workers overflowing into hallways in winter and onto fire escapes in warm weather. "Morning, noon, or night it makes no difference," wrote the crusading journalist Jacob Riis about the Lower East Side, "the scene is always the same. . . . Men stagger along the sidewalk groaning under heavy burdens of unsewn garments. . . . Up two flights of dark stairs, three, four, with new smells of cabbage, of onions, of frying fish, on every landing, whirring sewing machines behind closed doors betraying what goes on within, to the door that opens to admit the bundle and the man."

As the New York garment strike flamed into being after the Cooper Union meeting, dozens of clashes erupted between picketing strikers and police or strikebreakers—some of them off-duty prostitutes and pimps hired by factory owners. Striking workers sometimes hurled rotten eggs at strikebreakers, and two bold activists reportedly cleared strikebreakers out of one factory by slipping into the building, taking the freight elevator up, running onto the shop floor, and yelling, "Fire!" More than 700 strikers were arrested and hauled away in horse-drawn paddy wagons. Rose went to court repeatedly to help organize bail, once staying until 3 a.m.

The strikers were heartened by some unexpected help from a sprinkling of wealthy women. "The police became afraid to arrest anyone," recalled one reporter, "for they never knew what rich man's daughter they might be taking into custody." In their elegant hats, pearl necklaces, and fur coats against the snowy winter weather, these supporters joined union members on the picket lines and in marches. The press nicknamed them the "mink brigade," and the strike was a landmark in making Americans outside the working class aware of what factory life was like. Even J. P. Morgan's 36-year-old daughter, Anne, took part, donating money to the cause, although she quarreled with the socialists among the strikers, whom she considered fanatics. Helen Taft, the college-student daughter of President William Howard Taft, now in his first year in office, visited a picket line and was shocked by what she learned about the workers' lives. "Really, I'll never put on a shirtwaist again without a shudder," she declared. ". . . I shall certainly speak to papa about the terrible conditions."

This unusual solidarity owed something to the campaign for women's suffrage, a cause that both Helen Taft and Anne Morgan backed enthusiastically. Although largely a middle- and upper-class movement, its activists knew what it was like to organize against stubborn resistance and felt something in common with the strikers, despite the chasm of class differences. In addition, the companies being struck were not owned by the likes of Anne Morgan's father, but by smaller entrepreneurs, the great majority of them Jewish. At the Colony Club (which, incidentally, barred Jews from membership), an elegant women's gathering place on Madison Avenue only a few blocks from the Stokes and Morgan mansions, striking women were invited in to talk to society matrons and raised $1,300 for their cause.

Rose did not attend, telling the press she preferred to be on the picket line. "Altogether too much is made of the fact that a few prominent women are interested in the fight," she wrote to a friend. "The working girls must not be made to feel that they must depend upon outsiders for their victory. They must learn the extent of their own strength." At one point strike organizers dispatched her to two clothing factories on Broadway between 12th and 13th Streets. A reporter was on hand to record her attempt to persuade a strikebreaker not to cross the picket line. It was a rare occasion when someone got the better of her in an argument.

"What is there in the future for you without the union?" Rose asked.

"I'm in hopes that some rich man will come along and marry me," the strikebreaker answered. "Things like that occasionally happen."

Word of Rose's activism spread, and 100 women cigar workers on strike in Cincinnati sent her a telegram asking for help. Strike duties in New York kept her from traveling that far, but she did go to Philadelphia to speak to a meeting of clothing workers there. "Mrs. Stokes told of the situation in New York," said a newspaper, "and asserted that the strikers there were winning."

This would prove too optimistic. There were indeed some victories, among them an agreement covering 1,200 workers in four factories, which union leaders credited Rose with helping bring about. Many other small factories settled with the union as well, but the largest manufacturers held out. Frigid cold, bail expenses, police harassment, and beatings by hired thugs took their toll, and the strike was called off in February 1910, two and a half months after it began. Still, the outpouring of support had strengthened both the fledgling International Ladies' Garment Workers' Union and the Socialist Party, whose members won many union posts. And the strike had firmly placed Rose on the national stage. Now 30 years old, she was no longer seen primarily as the wife of James Graham Phelps Stokes.

In the wake of the strike, Rose invited a union delegation to stay at Caritas Island while they tried to organize clothing workers in nearby Stamford, Connecticut. Unfortunately none of these guests left a record of how they felt—after days spent dodging harassment from hostile employers who didn't want their workers unionized— about returning to an island home to be served dinner by a maid.

Others, however, have written about life on Caritas. All were charmed by Rose. Horace Traubel, an older radical poet and Walt Whitman's literary executor, who spent a summer on the island, wrote her besotted notes that read almost like love letters. ("Rose, any time I see your handwriting it makes me feel homesick. Why should I feel homesick? . . . A man's home is where his love is.") The Scott and Walling families now occupied their own houses on the island, but the Stokeses' larger home was always filled with visitors, some of them long term.

While on one of their lecture tours, for example, Graham and Rose met an ardent young socialist named Rockwell Kent, then supporting himself as an architect, not yet the well-known painter he would later become. Hitting it off with him and his wife, they stayed up almost the entire night talking. Soon after, they invited the Kents to live with them on the island, and the couple remained there for nearly a year. "We were received with open arms," wrote Kent. He described Rose as "imbued with passion." Graham he found "a tall, spare man with a countenance memorable, by its sunken cheeks and dark-rimmed, deep-set, burning eyes, as that of one who had made all mankind's sufferings his own."

Kent converted a small brick-and-stone garage into a stall for his horse. Each morning he galloped several miles to a railway station, left the horse in a nearby livery stable, and took the commuter train into New York. After a day of architectural drafting, he would be back on Caritas for dinner. During the year the couple lived on the island, Kathleen Kent gave birth to a baby boy. "The baby was a source of great delight to Rose," wrote the artist, grateful that she and Graham "made that child and its mother their responsibility as long as they might be in need."

There is no sign that Rose and Graham ever considered having children themselves—something that would have been expected of a scion of a family so proud of its ancestry. Unlike their friend Emma Goldman, whose lusty missives to her lover Ben Reitman abound in invitations to put his "Willy" in her "t-b" (treasure box), letters between Rose and Graham in this period are loving but not physically passionate. We have only a few clues to their sex life together, and these would not emerge for many years. Although Kent believed that they ardently wanted a child, there is no other evidence of this. Indeed, later in her life, when campaigning to decriminalize birth control, Rose declared that she herself had broken the law by using contraception. Most likely, with a world to save and Rose's young brothers and sisters installed on the island, she and Graham felt they already had enough children in their lives.

Moreover, when growing up Rose had seen the hardships that a seemingly endless succession of births brought to her mother. And by now she had also seen firsthand the difficulties children could pose to a woman intent on a career as a writer and public figure. Her close friend Anna Walling was conspicuously set back in her literary ambitions by two miscarriages, a baby who died, four surviving children, and an irritable, self-centered husband who was little help with them. A cook and nanny eased some, but not all, of the problem. "Only the prisoner who walks to execution can feel such inevitableness of misery," Anna once said of childbirth. Overwhelmed and pregnant again, Anna wrote to a friend, "Someday I shall emerge from the nursery." Emma Goldman jokingly reproved her: "Forget your babies! What a strange girl you are to have so many kiddies." By contrast, Goldman, whom Rose greatly admired, had remained childless.

The life of another island guest also clearly showed something about the tensions between motherhood and revolution. Elizabeth Gurley Flynn was an IWW organizer, and in the spring of 1910 she was 19 years old and pregnant by a fellow Wobbly in whom she had lost interest. She was agitating in Spokane, Washington, where she was thrown in jail. There was a furor over the authorities imprisoning a pregnant woman, and to Flynn's disappointment, a jury acquitted her of conspiracy charges. When Graham and Rose brought her to live on Caritas a few months later, she was a single mother with a ten-week-old infant. She reveled in the unfamiliar luxury of having her own room and bathroom, and the leisure to read in the sun while her baby boy slept in a basket. After he was weaned, however, she was able to go back on the road for the IWW only because her mother and sister took over raising him. (When a strike Flynn was organizing kept her in one place long enough, her mother and child would sometimes move there too.)

Flynn had spent part of her childhood in a kerosene-lit South Bronx tenement with no central heating or hot water. Her family's flat overlooked a railyard, and she got an early lesson in class solidarity when, in tough times, locomotive crews tossed down chunks of coal to neighborhood children. Her family was Irish, and as a child she heard tales of that island's anti-British rebels, including a few of her ancestors. ("Until my father died, at over eighty," she wrote, "he never said 'England' without adding, 'God damn her!'") For Rose, she was probably the first close friend who had grown up in extreme poverty but was not Jewish. Flynn joined the IWW before she turned 16. With a bright red scarf contrasting with her blue eyes and dark hair, she could attract a crowd anywhere, and when she spoke, wrote the journalist Mary Heaton Vorse, "it was as though a spurt of flame had gone through the audience."

Flynn and Rose would remain friends for the rest of their lives, and would work together in several campaigns. Although younger, Flynn represented a way of being that would have ever-greater allure for Rose: a life constantly on the move, and one defined by membership in a cause. As Flynn once wrote, "In those days no traveling Socialist or IWW speaker went to a hotel. It was customary to stay at a local comrade's house. This was partly a matter of economy. . . . But, more than all else, it was a comradeship, even if you slept with one of the children or on a couch in the dining room. It would have been considered cold and unfriendly to allow a speaker to go off alone to a hotel. It was a great event when a speaker came to town. They wanted to see you as much as possible."

An extraordinary array of other visitors came to Caritas, sometimes for a weekend, sometimes for months. They included the black intellectual W.E.B. Du Bois, whom English Walling took swimming in Long Island Sound; Rose's closest friend, poet and playwright Olive Dargan; the pioneering feminist author Charlotte Perkins Gilman; Irish-born labor orator Mary Harris "Mother" Jones; and the immensely popular novelist Jack London.

Another writer who spent time on the island was Upton Sinclair, whose best-selling novel *The Jungle,* an exposé of Chicago meat-packing plants, Graham had read in manuscript as Sinclair was writing it. Although Sinclair had hoped that his portraits of such shocking events as an exhausted worker falling into a giant rendering vat would rouse a horrified public to socialism, instead most readers were dismayed at the thought of what they might be eating. *The Jungle* helped push Congress to pass the Meat Inspection Act and the Pure Food and Drug Act. "I aimed at the public's heart," Sinclair said, "and by accident I hit it in the stomach." (Even ardent socialists, however, proved to have stomachs. "After reading it I forthwith became a vegetarian!" wrote Flynn.) Sinclair also worked closely with Graham and Rose in the Intercollegiate Socialist Society. The diminutive author would turn out some 90 books over the course of his life; one photograph shows him with a stack of them taller than he is.

More island guests provided a link to Russia, which Graham and Rose, like others on the American left, continued to see as ripe for upheaval. The young journalist Arthur Bullard, for instance, had joined rebels at the barricades in Moscow during the Revolution of 1905. His worried father, a minister, wrote to him, "Take care, my son. It is always the innocent bystander who is hurt." Bullard replied, "Don't worry, father, I am no innocent bystander." Rockwell Kent also reported encountering on the island a mysterious stranger said to be in hiding from the police; more details we do not know.

Another Caritas visitor was the distinguished photographer Clarence Hudson White, who captured many of the others with his camera. His pictures show a striking contrast between Graham — usually solemn in a coat and tie — and Rose, who in one shot is dancing exuberantly on the lawn, a knee high in the air and her raised hands whirling a long scarf. Kent called Caritas "the very citadel of the Socialist movement."

Could a movement of the dispossessed really have a citadel on a privately owned island? And, moreover, on one in a particularly elegant corner of the country? After all, only eight miles away, on the opposite shore of Long Island Sound, was Sagamore Hill, the grand, sprawling home of Theodore Roosevelt. (At one point, a three-mile-long convoy of Navy ships appeared in the intervening waters to salute him with cannonades.) Graham was often asked why, given his beliefs, he hadn't shared all his money with the poor, a question that clearly made him uncomfortable. To one reporter, he claimed that his income was "probably not exceeding $2,500 a year," apparently his salary from the family-owned complex of real estate companies. To another journalist he acknowledged receiving an additional $2,000 annually in investment income, all of which, he said, he donated to socialist causes. He wrestled with such questions as a matter of conscience. When, for instance, his father offered him a position as a trustee of his maternal grandfather's estate — something for which Graham would have been paid a $20,000 fee, plus $2,000 a year — he turned it down. When not on Caritas, he and Rose got around not in a chauffeured car like his parents, but by motorcycle, Graham driving and Rose in the sidecar.

Graham's parents were anything but poor, of course, but they kept close control of their fortune as long as they were alive, loaning or doling out money as needed to their children. In 1908, for example, Graham asked his mother if she could provide "a gift or loan of a few hundred dollars? We are desperately in need of funds." This was for unpaid bills from his New York State Assembly campaign that year. Many other letters of his ask her for money for improvements to the Caritas house or other expenses. This she gave him in small installments, in a way that can only have felt infantilizing. Graham apparently never objected.

While not owning much more than the island themselves, he and Rose could still enjoy the fruits of the family's wealth by staying with his parents on Madison Avenue when in New York and vacationing with them in Europe and Florida. Graham seemed quite able to compartmentalize the strangeness of it all, appearing on a speaker's platform with Eugene Debs before wildly cheering workers one day and heading for his downtown business office the next, to deal with meetings and paperwork about leases, dividends, mortgages, audits, and insurance. His father was now in ill health, with ever-worsening eyesight, so more of this work landed on Graham's desk. Even in the midst of that 1908 election season, in fact, the family sold a large mine in Nevada, where a newspaper identified Graham as "the moving spirit" behind the deal.

Although always the warm and well-mannered daughter-in-law, Rose could never completely forget one world while in the other. "I have already trod on idle toes," she wrote to a friend from a Palm Beach vacation with Graham's parents in 1909. "[I] confronted one of these idle women with the facts of exploitation — and saw the light in her eyes grow as hard as the precious stones she wore. I cannot hope to win them, but when the chance offers I can't help telling them the blood and lives they cost." On another Florida holiday, she recorded, "Left pamphlets in room, for maid." And after one European trip with the elder Stokeses, on the ship home she and Graham gave lectures on socialism to the passengers and crew.

Whatever their struggles to harmonize their lives with their politics, as the first decade of the twentieth century came to a close, the couple sounded ever more radical. Those who heard them wondered where this militancy would lead. On one ocean voyage, they outraged fellow travelers and made it into the press once again by refusing to stand for "The Star-Spangled Banner." Talking to the *New York Times* in 1910, Graham condemned the interest and dividends that went to "non-producers." This "ruling class" wealth, he insisted, should be "distributed among the workers who created it" rather than to "an idle class of absentees." How, the reporter asked him, should this be brought about? Graham replied that he hoped socialism could come without bloodshed, but "if revolt, if armed and bloody revolt, was justified in 1776, it is infinitely more justified today, in view of the infinitely greater wrong that is today done to the people."

Rose, for her part, gave a long interview to a *New York World* reporter who came to the island and described her as "more slender, more tense, more mistress of herself than she was at the time of her marriage." Speaking of the oppression of workers as "white slavery," she predicted that before long the slaves would rebel. Even the Socialist Party was moving with "extreme caution." The working class will take power, she declared, "with the ballot if possible," but "with the bullet if necessary."

Rose and Graham on their wedding day, July 18, 1905.

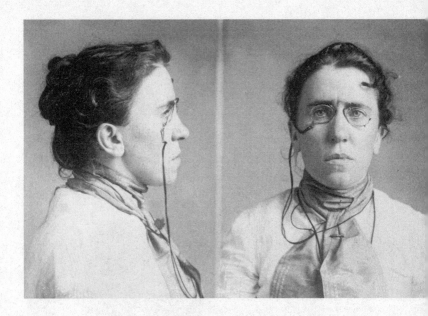

Firebrand orators Emma Goldman (*above*), during one of her many arrests, and Elizabeth Gurley Flynn. Maxim Gorky, the Russian novelist whose visit to America stirred great controversy.

Above: Sixteen-year-old Rose, third from left in back row, with fellow Cleveland cigar workers. *Below:* Graham's parents with their children, children-in-law, and grandchildren at their Adirondack estate in 1907. Graham is standing, hands crossed on counter; Rose is second from right among those seated on floor.

Above: A shipload of immigrants approaching New York. *Below:* Children's nursery at the University Settlement.

Rose, c. 1906. Her engagement the previous year spawned headlines at home and abroad, and press coverage of her would be lavish for nearly two decades to come.

Whether in a West Virginia coal mine (*above*) or a Lower East Side garment work-shop (*below*), tens of millions of Americans labored long hours for low pay.

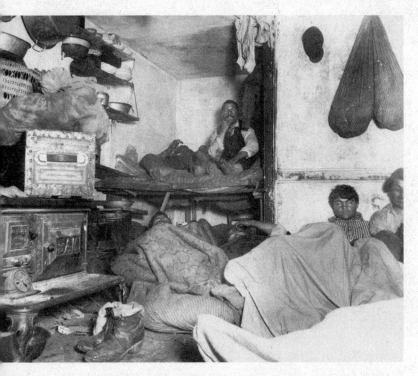

Above: Immigrants in a New York tenement. *Below:* The Phelps Stokes 100-room summer "cottage" in Stockbridge, Massachusetts, at its completion the largest private home in the United States.

Rose was deeply involved in two major strikes of New York garment workers, in 1909–10 and again in 1913.

Rose and Graham in their home on Caritas Island, c. 1909. Others soon began noticing signs of strain between them.

Above: Eugene V. Debs, socialist visionary. *Below:* Journalist John Reed; Rose's closest friend, writer Olive Tilford Dargan.

Labor uprisings were often met with force. *Above:* Troops deployed in Lawrence, Massachusetts, in 1913. *Below:* Chicago police arrest a striking garment worker in 1910.

The deadly Triangle Shirtwaist fire of 1911; legendary troublemaker Big Bill Haywood of the Industrial Workers of the World; children of striking Lawrence clothing workers welcomed by sympathizers in New York.

In 1913, more than a thousand striking silk workers from Paterson, New Jersey, marched (*above*) to Madison Square Garden, where they put on a pageant (*below*) about their strike, written by John Reed.

Above: The arrival of American troops in Europe in 1917 was a severe setback for pacifists. *Below:* Peace parade on Fifth Avenue, August 1914.

The vast Ansonia Hotel on Broadway was owned by Graham's playboy uncle, William Earl Dodge Stokes. Furious that Rose had urged his waiters and maids to strike, he eagerly informed on her to the Justice Department's Bureau of Investigation.

H. J. JENTZER   NEW YORK CITY   APRIL 2 1918   March 24th

IN RE: ROSE PASTOR STOKES
Violation of Espionage Act

SUNDAY

Agent received word from W. E. D. Stokes that Rose Pastor Stokes at various times at her residence at 88 Grove St., New York City, held meetings with socialists and I. W. W., and if a search was made of the premises some valuable information could be secured.

Above: Armed Bolsheviks in Petrograd, 1917. The Russian Revolution produced a massive crackdown on American labor unionists and progressives. *Below:* The office of a left-wing group in Cambridge, Massachusetts, after a raid by government agents, 1919.

10

A Key to the Gates of Heaven

THE BLAZE BEGAN AS SWIFTLY as a summer storm. Within minutes it engulfed the building's top three floors while horrified spectators on the sidewalk below could see tongues of flame billowing out of the windows. Screams pierced the air. Fire engines raced to the scene, but their ladders could not reach the upper floors. Then came something still more terrifying: one after another, figures began tumbling out of the ninth-floor windows, to land on the sidewalk with sickening thuds. Almost all were women, most of them young, leaping to their deaths to escape the roaring fire. From the street, people caught sight of one couple at a window, silhouetted against the flames. They embraced, kissed, and leapt, the woman first, the man after her. The water from fire hoses that gushed into the gutters turned red with blood.

It was late on the afternoon of March 25, 1911, when the inferno erupted high up in a crowded clothing factory a block from New York's Washington Square, apparently ignited by a discarded match or cigarette. It fed quickly on wooden beams and work tables, on flammable machine oil in barrels and spilled on the floor, and on overflowing wicker baskets of "cutaways"—leftover scraps of cloth. From the tenth floor, the top one, which housed the company's executive offices, the owners and other officials scrambled to safety on the roof of an adjoining building. On the doomed ninth floor, women in white blouses and dark, ankle-length skirts had been lined up elbow to elbow, finishing the day's work stitching sleeves, collars, and buttonholes at long tables packed with humming electric sewing machines. There was no sprinkler system, only scattered pails of water. Some workers managed to escape into, or on top of, an elevator before smoke and flames shot up its shaft, but others who desperately rushed for a rusted fire escape were less lucky. It collapsed under their weight and crashed nearly 100 feet to the ground. At least 20 were hurtled to their deaths, some impaled on the spikes of an iron fence. Worst of all, the door from the crowded ninth floor to a stairwell was illegally locked — supposedly to keep workers from stealing cloth or leaving early, but perhaps also to keep out union organizers. The foreman who had the key was not on the floor.

It was a Saturday, and the cutters, trimmers, and seamstresses, working amid a hubbub of Yiddish, Italian, and English, were employees of the Triangle Shirtwaist Company. They were looking forward to Sunday, their only day off. In the strike of clothing workers that had ended the previous year, Triangle had been one of the largest companies targeted. In response, the firm had fired workers who were union activists and organized its own company union. Its owners had shifted work to factories outside the city and paid thugs to beat up women on the picket line. Eventually, they granted slightly improved wages and hours, but refused to recognize the union — or agree to install sprinklers or better fire escapes. The factory had already experienced at least three small fires.

Now, on the sidewalk, shocked policemen in their tall helmets — the same ones who had roughed up many of these women when they were on strike months earlier — wept as bodies, long hair on fire, continued to crash at their feet. Nineteen more victims, hidden from sight, leapt to their deaths down the elevator shaft. Still others were trapped on the ninth floor, their charred skeletons later found amid the sewing machines. As smoke wafted over the city, patrol wagons and ambulances could not handle all the corpses; peddlers volunteered their pushcarts. Some victims were mothers and daughters, some were sisters. Two thirds were Eastern European or Russian Jews, almost all the rest Italian Americans. The dead were taken to a makeshift morgue at a pier and laid out with their heads propped on pillows and their mangled bodies hidden under white sheets. Their names and ages told the story of hopeful journeys across the ocean: Essie Bernstein, 19; Vincenza Billota, 16; Abraham Binowitz, 30; Albina Caruso, 20; Tillie Kupferschmidt, 16; Maria Giuseppa Lauletti, 33; Rose Mankofsky, 22; Bertha Wendroff, 18; Sonia Wisotsky, 17; Rosaria Maltese, 14. Of the 146 dead, all but 15 were women and almost half were teenagers. Seven bodies were burned too badly to be identified.

The Stokeses and their friends were riveted by the tragedy. Anna Walling reached the scene while the fire was still blazing and for once managed to get a magazine article written and published. So did Miriam Scott, who tracked down the stories of some of the victims. One 18-year-old woman, who earned $6 a week, had bought a steamship ticket on the installment plan to bring her sister from Russia; she died on the collapsed fire escape. Another was sending money to her elderly parents in Romania. At home was a letter written and addressed to accompany the next payment, but her wages —the day of the fire was payday—went up in flames with her.

Eleven days later, on a cold and rainy morning, more than 120,000 men, women, and children marched in the funeral procession, starting near the scene of the fire and proceeding up Fifth Avenue. An estimated 300,000 people lined the streets as it passed. The public was further outraged when the Triangle owners were found not guilty of manslaughter—and even collected a fire insurance payment. In the years ahead, New York State would pass more than three dozen new laws about fire safety and working conditions. The Triangle fire proved a landmark, for it made dramatically clear to millions that the crusade for workers' rights in which Graham and Rose were engaged was not just a question of sharing society's wealth more fairly, but a matter of life and death.

Two miles uptown from the burned-out Triangle factory and across the street from Grand Central Station, the Hotel Belmont was one of New York's most elegant. Its public rooms were adorned with frescoes, crystal chandeliers, and marble pillars. Financier August

Belmont Jr., builder of both the hotel and the early New York subway system, kept a private subway car with luxury fittings on a siding below his hotel. On May 7, 1912, at 7:15 p.m. in the Belmont's bar, where some customers stood with one foot on a brass rail while others sat at small tables laden with olives and drinks, a waiter brought a black whistle to his lips and blew a loud blast. It was immediately answered by similar whistles from the hotel's several dining rooms. Patrons were startled, but the waiters, in white shirts and black coats, napkins over their arms, knew what to do. Organized by the IWW, they walked out. Even, to the astonishment of drinkers and diners, if a tip was about to be placed on the table. "One hundred waiters noiselessly departed into the streets," reported the *Evening World*. "Guests waited in vain while sautés cooled and salads withered and wine grew warm. A strike was on. If the guests were surprised the managers were more so."

The strikers at the Belmont—as much of an ethnic and linguistic potpourri as the rest of the city's working class—had a particular dislike for the hotel's maître d'. He had fired one employee for attending a socialist parade on May Day and was quick to rage at any waiter who placed a plate in front of a diner with the large letter *B* on the hotel's china sideways or upside down. These were only the start of a long list of grievances that led at least 5,000 workers —including busboys, dishwashers, chefs in tall white toques, and aproned chambermaids—to heed whistles in some 50 other New York hotels and restaurants and head for the picket lines.

Rose jumped into the fray, serving on the strike committee, running some of its meetings, setting up a food kitchen for picketing workers, speaking at a gathering of black waiters to urge them to join the union, writing leaflets, and phoning in strike news each day from union headquarters to the Socialist *New York Call* in time for the paper's deadline. In notes she scribbled to herself during these weeks, you can feel her simmering outrage at the miserable conditions the workers faced. Most hotel employees ate on the job, but the food was often "trimmings, refuse, leavings unclean and unwholesome. . . . Everywhere the ordinary bill of fare is hash and stew—so the boss may use up the scrapings and leavings from the plates of the patrons." Sometimes the menu was horsemeat. "Coffee in 'Help's Hall' is usually brewed from yesterday's grounds." The sleeping quarters for women workers were "bunks, one above the other. Ten, fifteen, crowded into one room, in a dingy out-of-the-way corner. . . . No ventilation; rarely a ray of sunlight." In one hotel, the women had to wash themselves and their clothing in the same tub where meat and poultry were cleaned. A waiter could be fined for forgetting a napkin, dropping a spoon, or smiling in the dining room. Hours were long—sometimes up to 14 a day—and some chambermaids and bellhops earned as little as $12 a month plus tips. Cooks labored in basement kitchens where the temperature might reach 125° Fahrenheit.

Reflecting the militant spirit of the IWW, Rose suggested to the waiters a few tactics they might use in the future. If dairy companies "put the grease from sewerage in butter and sell it, that's called good business," she said. "But if you put kerosene oil in a custard pie, that's sabotage." Why not, she proposed, serve restaurant customers salt in the sugar bowls, sour milk in cream pitchers, vinegar instead of water? Worried hotel managers distributed photographs of Rose to front-desk clerks in case she tried to register at a hotel as a well-dressed guest and then begin organizing the staff.

For maximum publicity, shrewd Wobbly organizers concentrated on high-end hotels like the Belmont and the Waldorf Astoria, and well-known restaurants like Delmonico's and the Luncheon Club of the New York Stock Exchange (where the whistle was blown at half past noon, just as 150 members had been seated). In the Waldorf Astoria kitchen, bellhops were conscripted to wash pots and pans, and hotel executives to mix sauces. Hundreds of undercover private detectives donned evening dress to patrol hotel lobbies, corridors, and dining rooms for signs of further trouble. Managers scrambled to replace their waiters with doormen, manicurists, shoeshine attendants, elevator operators, and college students brought in by train from New England. (The anti-labor Charles W. Eliot, recently retired as president of Harvard, had often encouraged his students to help break strikes.)

Those who had joined the walkout kept a close watch for strikebreakers arriving at the city's railway stations. Inside Grand Central, several dozen waiters assaulted a much larger group of men, throwing in their faces supplies of red pepper purloined from restaurants. The waiters were correct in recognizing the men as being en route to break a strike—it was just not, as the waiters had thought, their own. Rather, they had been recruited to replace striking transit workers in Boston. Sneezing uncontrollably from the pepper, victims, perpetrators, police, and bystanders all fled the station, tears streaming down their faces.

Much of the time Rose was at union headquarters on 44th Street near Sixth Avenue or at the nearby hall where strikers gathered, just off Bryant Park, in easy range of the picket lines that ringed the midtown hotels. (The building had long hosted both labor meetings and rehearsals for Broadway musicals. While Rose, Elizabeth Gurley Flynn, and others addressed striking waiters, the ceiling above them sometimes resounded with dancing feet.) Rose edited the union's press releases, and it was she who, on its behalf, announced a lawsuit against the city for arresting a group of picketers. She drew great applause at a Carnegie Hall rally when she brought news that furnace tenders, mechanics, electricians, and a plumber from the Hotel Netherland had joined the strike, shutting off the electricity as they left.

Speaking to such audiences was more challenging, but perhaps more satisfying, without loudspeakers. "Styles of speech have changed," observed Flynn decades later, "with the radio and public [address] systems, which have . . . calmed down the approach. Then we gesticulated, we paced the platform, we appealed to the emotions. We provoked arguments and questions. We spoke loudly, passionately. . . . Even when newly-arrived immigrants did not understand our words they shared our spirit. At all our indoor mass meetings there were speakers in many languages—Jewish [Yiddish], Russian, Polish, Italian, German and others. Our foreign-born comrades . . . were magnificent orators. They inspired us to more beautiful and moving language in English."

The waiters' strike was the first time that Rose worked with the man who was the central figure of the IWW, William D. "Big Bill"

Haywood. It was he who had called the very first meeting of the Wobblies to order seven years earlier with the declaration, "Fellow workers. . . . This is the Continental Congress of the working class!" With one eye sightless from a childhood accident (although he didn't correct people who assumed he'd injured it fighting strikebreakers), thick black hair, and what a journalist described as a "massive, rugged face, seamed and scarred like a mountain," this broad-shouldered son of a Pony Express rider was a legendary troublemaker.

As a boy in Utah, Haywood had roamed free, exploring abandoned mines; as a man he worked as a card dealer in a saloon, a surveyor, a cowboy, and a miner, where underground his right hand was crushed by a carload of rock. Such happenings were common in the western gold and silver mines of Haywood's time—which included those owned by the Phelps Stokes family in Nevada. A miner who worked ten years had one chance in three of suffering a serious injury, and one in eight of being killed. At one point Haywood even carved his own 160-acre homestead out of the wilderness. When his wife went into labor and no one else was there to help, he delivered his own child. When he needed to defend himself while organizing miners, he became famous for using his fists—and sometimes more. Once attacked by a Colorado sheriff's deputy, he pulled out a revolver and wounded the man. (Amazingly, a court ruled that he had acted in self-defense.)

Haywood arrived in New York with the aura of someone coming from a battlefield. Though the city's labor wars were stormy, those of the Rocky Mountains rose to another dimension of violence entirely, descended from the recent gunslinger days of the frontier. Angry miners did not hesitate to use one of the tools of their trade, dynamite, against company installations. Their opponents—the county sheriffs, federal troops, and armies of private detectives deployed by the mining companies—had no scruples about legal niceties when they put down a strike. In one notorious battle, rebellious miners hijacked a train that became known as the Dynamite Express, while the corporate forces that eventually suppressed them imprisoned more than a thousand men in boxcars and a makeshift stockade.

"An uncouth, stumbling, one-eyed giant with an enormous head which he tended to hold on one side" was the way birth control activist Margaret Sanger, a fellow Wobbly, described Haywood. He "looked like a bull about to plunge into an arena. . . . His great voice boomed; his speech was crude and so were his manners; his philosophy was that of the mining camps." He had "stubby, roughened fingernails, uncreased trousers, and shoddy clothes for which he refused to pay more than the minimum." His head bore the scars of a beating by a mining company's hired gunmen, and he had a well-known appetite for drink and women. New York knew all about him: five years earlier, when he and two union comrades had been on trial in Idaho for plotting to assassinate an anti-labor former governor, 40,000 men and women with banners in English and Yiddish had marched through Manhattan in a dramatic show of solidarity.

Haywood enjoyed his role as the bad boy of the American left. In one debate with a more moderate Socialist leader, he called for "a little sabotage in the right place at the right time." The dispute caused a bitter split in Socialist ranks, but Graham and Rose had become friends of his, and they stuck by him.

At New York's Amsterdam Opera House, Haywood and Rose spoke to a rally of 3,000 striking waiters and hotel workers, while another 2,000 stood outside. "Rose Pastor Stokes was greeted with applause when she entered the hall, and another outburst came when she rose to speak," reported the *Sun*. "Half way through her talk she was interrupted to receive a big bouquet of American Beauties and a smaller bunch of white roses." When she left the opera house there were more cheers, men raising their hats high as she swept down the aisle. It is striking, the bouquet: Elizabeth Gurley Flynn, who had never left the working class, was also a powerful orator and spoke to the waiters many times, but there is no record that she ever was given a bouquet. These workers seemed to recognize that Rose, born one of them, now lived in a world where flowers were abundant, but she was still on their side.

She felt exuberant when she spoke to such audiences. "Your 'Jungle' may reach the readers," she wrote somewhat boastfully to Upton Sinclair, "but I have the joy of reaching the earnest men and women who have never so much as *heard* of your book—who may yet read much some day." Graham also gave several speeches backing the strike, but Rose was the member of the couple whom the workers wanted to hear. An admiring waiter wrote to her that he was worried she appeared in a weakened state when she gave one speech, telling the audience that she "had only had a bowl of soup and a few slices of bread during the day." He urged her to take better care of herself, because "it is you who is giving us the courage to keep up the fight." Another wrote that "your words are engraved upon my mind and they return during the day with that melodious sound of your voice."

At one rally, she urged the strikers to stick together, no matter whether "Russian, Pole, Irishman, Frenchman, or Greek." The Brooklyn Bridge, she explained, "is suspended by . . . wire as fine as a hair. But this wire is wound in with countless other wires until it makes a cable strong enough to support the bridge."

She then read aloud a letter from a hotel manager, which, she said, a friend had sent her on condition that she keep the names of the sender and recipient secret. "I see that Mrs. Stokes intends to befriend the International Hotel Workers," he wrote, calling them "the most contemptible, low-lived people in the world. They thieve alone, and when they organize they thieve together." Then she paused, looked at her audience, and asked them, "Wouldn't you think he was talking of Wall Street?" The crowd "broke into cheers, which lasted for a long time," according to the *Times*.

The unnamed "hotel manager" was in fact a hotel owner—Graham's Uncle Will, and he was enraged to have his letter quoted. "The thing for Rose to do," he wrote to Graham's brother Anson, ". . . is to collect all the Russian, Polish, Turkish, Greek, Armenian, Bulgarian, Servian and Italian waiters, put them back on ships and take them back to their native lands."

In addition to his Kentucky stud farm, construction companies, a small railroad, and more, W.E.D. Stokes owned one of New York's more luxurious hotels. It stretched—and, reborn as an apartment building, still stretches—for an entire block on Broadway, between 73rd and 74th Streets. With Persian carpets, mahogany paneling, abundant marble, chandeliers, and a Turkish bath, it was called, echoing a Stokes family name, the Ansonia. This immense, turreted, white-brick-and-limestone edifice, frosted with Beaux Arts balconies, cornices, scrollwork, and satyrs, was, Stokes claimed, the largest hotel in the world, and possibly its 2,500 rooms made this true. There was a swimming pool in the basement, an English grill on the roof, a telegraph office, and in the lobby a fountain with live seals. The Ansonia was popular with opera singers, boxers, dancers, gamblers, and gangsters—one of whom, a co-investor with Stokes in another business, moved directly into the hotel after a stint up the river at Sing Sing prison. Stokes kept a menagerie of chickens, pigs, geese, goats, and a pet bear on the hotel's roof, which led to a row with the city health authorities.

Stokes had been much in the news some months earlier, when he had taken three bullets in the legs during an argument with two women the press euphemistically referred to as chorus girls. When the two were put on trial, it was a spectacular case that kept New Yorkers riveted for months: a stash of his love letters to one of the women with whom, as a newspaper delicately put it, Stokes admitted to a "highly advanced friendship"; three mysterious Japanese servants who he claimed held him down while he was shot; tears in the courtroom from the two defendants; and a sympathetic jury that finally acquitted them. After the trial came a lucrative engagement for the two women on the vaudeville stage, in an act called "The Shooting Girls." Whatever worries Graham's parents had about Rose's increasing militancy staining the family name had once again been outweighed by their dismay at the headlines about Uncle Will.

When W.E.D. Stokes found his hotel a target of the waiters' strike, he was not about to let any union organizing slow down business. After 40 of the Ansonia's waiters walked out, he had 40 waitresses from a hotel in New Jersey standing by to replace them. When he heard a rumor that Rose had persuaded Graham to give $6 million to the union's strike fund, he fired off a choleric letter to her: "You have upset the minds of thousands of waiters, buses [busboys] and cooks who came here from distant lands, some, perhaps with the honest intention of becoming good American citizens. You have made them dissatisfied, unhappy and caused them to lose their positions. . . . The sooner this country gets rid of this rotten trash the better for it."

After the $6 million rumor reached the press, one newspaper declared that such a contribution to the waiters' strike would be "the biggest tip on record." There was, of course, no such contribution. But Uncle Will continued to boil with anger at the way Rose had backed the strikers. His next attack on her would be far worse.

Like many labor struggles of these years, the strike was less than a resounding success. Some waiters did win better wages and conditions, but the citywide triumph they had hoped for was not to be. They lacked a big strike fund, and without such a war chest their efforts were hamstrung. A spirited effort by Rose to organize thousands of hotel chambermaids into a branch of the IWW also fizzled out. In less than two months, the waiters voted to go back to work, while union activists among them found their names on an employers' blacklist.

Despite these disappointments, for Americans outraged by the vast inequalities of the day, it had been exhilarating to see 800 striking waiters at one point blocking Fifth Avenue, the artery that was the epitome of Gilded Age wealth; the police had to fire revolvers in the air to disperse them. And to know that throughout the city thousands of diners in tuxedos and evening gowns had been taken by surprise and left staring at empty place settings instead of the lobster or filet mignon they had ordered. For Rose, the memory lingered. Many months later, she and Graham had lunch in a restaurant where she noted proudly that "the headwaiter is a little fearful of me."

The year 1912 also saw another major strike led by the IWW, this one more successful. Some 25,000 workers in Lawrence, Massachusetts, most of them immigrants and women, walked out of the city's textile mills to protest an abrupt cut in wages. Both the 240-pound Haywood in his trademark Stetson cowboy hat, with his sightless right eye always turned away from press photographers' cameras, and the petite, blue-eyed, 21-year-old Flynn again played leading roles. Local police and thousands of state militia battled the rebellious workers, beating and arresting them and in midwinter spraying them with freezing water from fire hoses. The city was put under martial law. Several strikers were killed. Haywood came to New York to raise money for the strikers, and Rose and Graham spoke at one such rally, so the city's radical community found themselves following the events in Lawrence closely.

One unusual feature of the strike connected it to New York. To speed them away from violence and from households running out of food, many Lawrence workers put their children on trains out of town. They were housed by allies elsewhere, which meant that even people hundreds of miles away could feel that they were part of the textile workers' fight. "Take the Children" was the headline on a plea in the *New York Call.* "Workers and strike sympathizers who can take a striker's child until the struggle ends are urged to send their name and address to the *Call.* Do it at once." For *Il Proletario,* an IWW Italian-language paper in Brooklyn, the appeal was "*Sian Figli Nostri*" — Make Them Our Children. When the first trainload left Lawrence for New York, it was shepherded by Flynn and Margaret Sanger, who was as ardent about workers' rights as she was about birth control. There were 119 children on board, some of the smaller ones with name tags pinned to their ragged coats.

A crowd of 5,000 waving red banners and singing the "Internationale," the world socialist anthem, greeted them when they arrived under the great glass-and-iron roof at Grand Central. Some had fallen asleep on the train and had to be carried. The older ones were hoisted jubilantly onto their welcomers' shoulders, given a hot meal, warm clothes, and medical exams at a nearby union hall, and then turned over to the volunteers who had offered to care for them. Some children spoke little English and had to be sorted out among host families accordingly. Another trainload came the next week, and more strikers' children were sent to other cities.

The distance the children traveled was not just geographical, for some who took them in were well off. Boys and girls often found themselves awed and delighted to be in more spacious homes than the cramped tenements with shared beds they were used to. The country remained more divided than ever between rich and poor, but at moments like this it seemed possible to bridge that gap.

Just as the hopes of the nation's workers were raised in this period of dramatic strikes, American artists and intellectuals felt themselves at the dawn of a new age of creativity, of which the battle for workers' rights seemed a part. For both labor and intellectual ferment, New York was the epicenter. To Graham and Rose, Caritas Island became more of a summer and weekend retreat. Besides the draw of New York, Rose never got over her profound discomfort at employing servants on the island— "I hated the relationship with all my being"— but Graham did no housework, and she found caring for 14 rooms far more than she could manage herself. In New York, the couple stayed in his parents' mansion at 230 Madison Avenue, where Rose felt similarly uncomfortable. Finally Graham's mother—her hand still controlling the family's purse strings—bought them a smaller city home of their own, an ivy-covered redbrick townhouse with a mansard roof at 88 Grove Street in Greenwich Village.

With its twisting streets and alleys, so different from the checkerboard grid that covered most of Manhattan, the bohemian Village was full of low, old, brick row houses, sometimes with passageways leading to tiny courtyards or stables converted to studios. These might be shabby, but were enticingly so, like similar neighborhoods on the Left Bank in Paris. The low rents of the Village attracted writers and artists. One evening a few years after Graham and Rose moved there, six people climbed to the top of the great marble arch in Washington Square, hung lanterns and balloons, lit a bonfire, and proclaimed Greenwich Village an independent republic.

"Everywhere," wrote the critic Malcolm Cowley, looking back on the era, "new institutions were being founded—magazines, clubs, little theaters, art or free-love or single-tax colonies, experimental schools, picture galleries. Everywhere was a sense of comradeship and immense potentialities for change." Like the adjoining Lower East Side, the Village had a vibrant bar and café life, where intellectuals, workers, and activists debated the latest book or strike or play in the Yiddish theater. Women could join these discussions unchaperoned, argue with men, and boldly defy custom by adding their own cigarette smoke to that floating above the tables. One major topic for talk was the revolutionary 1913 "Armory Show," which introduced many Americans to the bold revisioning of the cubists, the brilliant colors of fauvism, and other modern art by the likes of Henri Matisse, Georges Braque, and Pablo Picasso. The exhibit gained added luster in the eyes of the Greenwich Village avant-garde when it outraged conventional critics: the *Times* declared its artists "cousins to the anarchists," and the *Tribune* insisted the paintings were the work of "foolish terrorists" who wanted "to turn the world upside down." When the show traveled to Illinois, the lieutenant governor ordered an investigation of it as an affront to decency.

On his frequent visits to New York, Big Bill Haywood suggested that when the revolution came, workers would have time to produce and enjoy art and literature. As if in proof, he combined his wild-man-of-the-frontier persona with a penchant for reciting long passages from Shakespeare, a love born in his boyhood when he had worked as a theater usher in Salt Lake City. He further indulged it during the year he spent in prison in Idaho on a murder charge of which he was in the end acquitted, a period he referred to as "my vacation," when "I didn't have anything else to do but read." In his spare time in New York he visited artists' studios — he himself had designed many of the IWW's best posters — and sat in Washington Square writing poems. When Haywood's Wobbly comrade Flynn gave her lover, the Italian anarchist Carlo Tresca, a book inscribed, "I love you, Carlo. Thine, Elizabeth," it was not Karl Marx but poetry by Elizabeth Barrett Browning.

The Greenwich Village circles in which Rose and Graham now moved included such figures as the muckraker Lincoln Steffens, the future Catholic radical activist Dorothy Day, and the heiress Mabel Dodge, of whom Steffens wrote, "She read everything, she believed — for a while — everything, she backed everything." Dressed in flowing white satin robes, with an emerald-green shawl around her shoulders, Dodge was, writes one historian, "a lady who somehow contrived to look aristocratic and earthy at the same time." An avant-garde bloodhound on the trail of the latest trends, she organized her friends to try everything from hallucinogenic mushrooms to a new form of music called jazz. She became renowned for hosting elegant Evenings, as she called them, with a capital *E,* in her high-ceilinged apartment near Washington Square, filled with silks, brocade, and Italian antiques. Much of it was decorated in white: white linen drapes, a white marble fireplace, and a white porcelain chandelier.

The Anarchist Evening, the Suffrage Evening, or the Expressionist Evening might be so crowded that her pastel chaises longues overflowed and some people sat on the white polar bear rug. Young women in evening dress and editors in three-piece suits mingled with workmen in denim, radicals in Russian peasant blouses, and hobo poets from the streets who might be asked to recite their work. There would be an invited speaker or two and a moderator who led an intense debate. Were the two sexes irreconcilable antagonists? Was industrial sabotage justified or could socialism be achieved by strikes and voting alone? Was psychoanalysis a revolutionary advance or a plaything of bourgeois dilettantes? And then, near midnight, came a buffet of Virginia ham, turkey, cheeses, and liqueurs. Among the rotating array of guests were Graham and Rose, who lived a few blocks away. Dodge, always seated regally in a large armchair, occasionally asked Graham to moderate one of the discussions.

Her salons "burst upon New York like a rocket," wrote Margaret Sanger. The participants might include "Wobblies with uncut hair, unshaven faces, leaning against valuable draperies. . . . Everybody was looking for an opportunity to talk. Each believed he had a key to the gates of heaven; each was trying to convert the others. . . . Just before the argument reached the stage of fist fights, the big doors were thrown open and the butler announced, 'Madam, supper is served.' Many of the boys had never heard those words, but one and all jumped up with alacrity from the floor."

Also within a few blocks of Rose and Graham was the red-brick building that housed *The Masses,* an irreverent monthly edited by their friend Max Eastman. It was financed in part by English Walling's fortune, but named, of course, after the working class that everyone was certain would be at the forefront of the great transformation to come. The handsome Eastman, with his wavy blond hair and deep-set eyes, was, in the words of one contemporary, "the fair-haired apostle of the new poetry, the knight errant of a new and rebellious generation . . . a yes-sayer of the joy and adventure of living." Although the magazine's editorial meetings were renowned for their combative debates, Eastman himself, a skillful recruiter of writers, artists, and donors, ultimately made most decisions about what finally appeared in print.

Radical but never doctrinaire, including among its writers both visionaries and pragmatists, *The Masses* published pioneering feminists, biting drawings, some of the era's best fiction, and on-the-scene reportage from the great labor battles. Eastman eagerly embraced every progressive cause, organizing, for instance, the Men's League for Woman Suffrage. The magazine's cartoons helped pioneer the style of having a one-line quotation as a caption, which would later be adopted by *The New Yorker*. One showed anti-vice crusader Anthony Comstock dragging a woman behind him to a judge's bench, raising a disapproving finger, and saying, "Your Honor, this woman gave birth to a naked child!"

The Masses, unsurprisingly, never reached the masses; circulation averaged around 12,000. Still, it was one of the liveliest journals this country ever produced, although its lifetime was fated, as we shall see, to be brutally cut short. The black-and-white drawings of its star artist and cartoonist, Maurice Becker, featured well-fed, tail-coated robber barons, a preacher with his hand on a stock ticker, street urchins, and the homeless sleeping on park benches or tenement fire escapes. Both Anna and English Walling wrote for *The Masses*, as did Leroy Scott; for a time Scott was an editor there as well. Rose published several poems in the magazine, and when Max Eastman appeared at a legislative hearing to protest that a newsstand company was refusing to sell the journal, she and Graham went with him to show their support.

A "slapdash gathering of energy, youth, hope," the critic Irving Howe later wrote, *The Masses* was "the rallying center . . . for almost everything that was then alive and irreverent in American culture." In its orbit and at Mabel Dodge's salon, people as varied, as she put it, as "Socialists, Trade-Unionists, Anarchists, Suffragists, Poets . . . Psychoanalysts, I. W. W.'s, Single Taxers . . . Modern-Artists, Clubwomen, Women's-Place-is-in-the-Home-Women" all talked, argued, and fell in and out of love. This extraordinary enclave in history was without the bitter sectarian divisions that would before long fracture the American left.

The more fiery and revolutionary her star guests, Dodge felt, the better. Progressive intellectuals often liked to imagine themselves as mixing with the proletariat. And so they idealized figures like the saintly ex-railwayman Eugene Debs and Haywood, with his burly miner's build and the aura of dynamite in his past (Max Eastman even wrote him into a novel), prison veterans both. Haywood could frequently be found at Mabel Dodge's salons, as could Emma Goldman. In her militant defense of labor, her time behind bars, and her sexual politics, Goldman, with her pince-nez and defiantly outthrust chin, offered genteel New Yorkers something thrillingly transgressive. Despite her more demure manner, Rose, too, having come from the world of immigrant poverty, held the same allure for well-off guests at these salons, an appeal only enhanced when she was in the news for leading strikes.

This was an era when, Dodge recalled, "barriers went down and people reached each other who had never been in touch before." Nor were Graham Stokes and English Walling the only "millionaire socialists" who seemed to be crossing class barriers. William F. Cochran, heir to a prosperous carpet manufacturing business, was fox hunting in Maryland one day when, as he recalled, he reined in his horse and asked himself, "What am I doing this for?" He, too, joined the socialist movement, as did Rufus Weeks, a vice president of the New York Life Insurance Company and a generous donor to *The Masses* and similar causes. If such people could break free of their class, was not a new world possible?

When Debs, as the Socialist Party candidate, received over 900,000 votes for president in 1912, more than double what he had won four years earlier, it looked as if that new world was fast approaching. It was approaching elsewhere as well, for socialism was an international movement. Its leaders from different countries knew each other, for they met periodically at conferences and felt themselves part of a growing crusade that transcended national boundaries. In a way that would be unthinkable today, Keir Hardie, the former Scottish miner who was the leading socialist voice in the British Parliament, campaigned with Debs in 1912 for two months, speaking at 44 rallies, including one at a mining camp in Colorado. (The two men had been friends ever since Hardie had once visited the American in prison years before. "Walk right in," Debs greeted him, "and make yourself at home.")

Debs didn't win the election, of course, running in the popular vote a distant fourth to the victor, Woodrow Wilson. But his supporters could take heart that ex-president Theodore Roosevelt, who came in second as an independent Bull Moose candidate, had been pushed far enough left to adopt many socialist ideas: a living wage, a ban on child labor, an inheritance tax, better workers' compensation, and unemployment, medical, and old-age insurance. Socialists and other visionaries felt they had the wind at their backs.

"Whether in literature, plastic art, the labor movement," declared the journalist Hutchins Hapgood, part of the Greenwich Village crowd, ". . . we find an instinct to loosen up the old forms and traditions, to dynamite the baked and hardened earth so that fresh flowers can grow." Disease, exploitation, and injustice would vanish; women would be the equals of men; workers would own their factories; music, literature, and dazzling new modern art would be enjoyed by all. "Our ears catching the first murmur of a new experience," wrote Max Eastman in 1913, "we ran after the world in our eagerness." No one foresaw any storm clouds.

When she wasn't on a speaker's platform, Rose was writing—or translating. Working with a friend, she rendered into English a collection of poetry by Morris Rosenfeld, the best-known Yiddish poet of the day, who had been born near Augustów and now lived in New York. Rose's mother had read his poems aloud to her when she was a child. The intense, depressive Rosenfeld had worked in clothing sweatshops, endured the worst of Lower East Side poverty, and wrote about events like the Triangle Shirtwaist fire. "No Yiddish writer before Rosenfeld," writes Irving Howe, "had touched so closely the intimate experience of his audience, all the buried anger of the immigrant's days." Rose was among the few people at this time doing anything to bring the literary voices of working-class Eastern European Jews to an English-language audience. And few women were active in the world of print in any manner: in the 1900 census, male journalists outnumbered female ones by more than 12 to 1.

In addition to poetry, she wrote about labor issues and other political events of the day. Although almost all of this work now reposes, to borrow the words of the writer Francis Steegmuller, "in that particularly deathly death reserved for political newspaper pieces," these articles still offer us a map of her mind. She took many ideas from her speeches: the inadequacy of traditional charity (an effort to "extinguish the fires of hell with thimbles full of water"), the class struggle as central, and the need for an alliance between the working class and enlightened professionals. But everything was subordinate to the dream of socialism. She favored suffrage for women, for instance, because it would hasten "the day of industrial liberation — the basis for every other conceivable kind of true freedom."

It was in her speeches, not her writing, that she shone. "Her clouds of red-brown curly hair shook loose as she spoke," remembered Elizabeth Gurley Flynn, "forming a lovely frame for her large expressive brown eyes and her clear-cut cameo-like features. She had a tiny scar on the tip of her nose from a cut when she fell as a child, sliding down the banister of her tenement house. It gave her a piquant, retroussé effect." In 1913, a veteran socialist wrote her, "None of the men who spoke — with all due respect to Mr. Stokes — got the grip on that crowd that you did. . . . For days after you left they talked about your address." However, people did begin to notice one change: more and more, Rose did her speaking tours alone.

11

Not the Rose I Thought She Was

I N JUNE 1913, GRAHAM'S FATHER died of a stroke. As the ever-dutiful steward of the family enterprises, Graham now was the one in charge at the office on William Street in downtown Manhattan, from which the Phelps Stokes real estate business built, bought, sold, and managed New York apartment buildings, particularly on Manhattan's fashionable Upper East Side. He continued to make periodic business trips to supervise the family's silver mines in Nevada and the Nevada Central Railroad. Sometimes his work involved lobbying. At one point, for example, Congress was considering a bill to change rates and regulations for railroads that carried the US mail, which would have been costly to the Nevada Central. Graham wrote a long letter to President Wilson arguing against the bill. He then enlisted his brother Anson to send a copy, with a cover note from his office at Yale, where he was the university's second-highest official, to a Nevada senator who was a Yale man.

Now in his forties, Graham seldom appeared on the platform with Rose. Even in the excitement of their first years of touring together, he enjoyed speaking far less than she did. "At the ends of meetings," she would later write, there were always "workers pressing forward for a handclasp and a word. . . . To me the experience was like healing." She loved the faces "of toilworn men, of careworn women—of pale children who would live to see the Dawn of a

New Day. I could not get close enough to them when the speeches were done. . . . But Graham always wearied. I could not understand how it was with him. 'Come on, Girlie, I am tired to death!' he would moan. 'Let's get out of this, come!'"

It was not the office on William Street that Graham yearned to get back to; some days he did not go there at all. More to his liking was spending time at the New York Public Library, researching a book about the economic motives of the Founding Fathers. His work went slowly, though, and then the historian Charles Beard published a much-discussed book on the same subject. Graham's was never finished. He lacked the writerly discipline of his friend English Walling, who wrote or edited a long string of works about socialism. He did better, however, with a project that put some of his medical knowledge to work. Long a hay fever sufferer, he devised eye drops made from rose petals that gave him relief, and sold the rights to a pharmaceutical company.

In 1913, in a small leather book with a flimsy, largely symbolic lock, Rose began keeping a diary. She wrote in it only sparingly, and abandoned it after two years, but for that time it gives us a new and intimate window onto her feelings. To the diary she confided that she felt "terribly, unbearably restless" when "all is in turmoil in society" and she found herself on Caritas Island "quietly reading, writing, housekeeping." She vowed "to spend at least half my year in the work of the people *direct*. My writing bears upon the same theme, arises from the same motive, but it is not *enough*."

That year she again plunged into a labor battle, supporting New York garment workers when 110,000 of them walked off the job. Enthusiastically accepting an invitation to serve on the strike committee, she found herself "hearing in silence poor Graham's laments at my leaving him alone on the Island for an indefinite time. He is very dependent on my presence and dreads the thought of my going into the strike without him. . . . As I left the house for the station, he called after me, 'Deary, be careful! Don't get into trouble with the police!'"

Almost as if seeking a kind of martyrdom—a theme that would become steadily more pronounced in her life in the coming years—

Rose worked herself into exhaustion midway through the six-week strike, after packing in up to half a dozen speeches or interviews a day, talking to shirt makers, vest makers, and buttonhole makers. She also opened three lunchrooms to feed men and women on the picket line, and regularly called on the public for contributions of money and clothing. The alarmed lawyer for the Manufacturers and Merchants' Association warned his clients that "Haywood, and Rose Pastor Stokes may come in at any time and raise trouble."

Graham's only involvement was to chair a large support meeting at Carnegie Hall, a gathering that turned tense as New York's sheriff and two dozen deputies appeared. Rose read some Wobbly poetry aloud and Upton Sinclair spoke. An IWW agitator who had previously called for union cooks to poison the soup they made for capitalists was scheduled to speak, and the sheriff had declared that he would not tolerate such things being said. In the end, despite being taunted by various speakers, the sheriff did not take the bait and no one was arrested. Undoubtedly, Graham was relieved and Rose disappointed.

She knew that her oratory had a powerful effect. "Men wept," she wrote in her diary after one talk before male garment workers. "And when I finished speaking they applauded wildly." At a rally at Union Square, reported the *Tribune,* "her fiery words [were] greeted with cheers from socialists, anarchists and plain workers alike." After another meeting, the headline in the *New York American* read, "Girl Workers Stirred to Tears by Mrs. Stokes." Yet, like any good performer, she had a self-critical eye. Of a talk given when she was cold and tired, she wrote, "This meeting was widely reported, but I have rarely made so poor a speech."

Addressing a rally of strikers at the Brooklyn Labor Lyceum, Rose was jarred when a 14-year-old girl, Christina Volpe, mounted the platform and read a list of hostile questions: "Why do you preach picketing and violence and have my people clubbed by the police?" "Who wants this strike—the working men and women or the labor leaders?" Rose reached for the piece of paper, found handwriting that looked like an adult man's, and accused the girl of being "a spy of the bosses." It turned out that the questions had been given to

Volpe by a reporter from the Republican *Brooklyn Times,* who had promised that if she asked them, she would get a set of furs and her picture on the newspaper's front page.

The attack jarred Rose, for she clearly felt some guilt that she did not have to make the kinds of sacrifices any striking worker must endure. In response she spoke openly about the class leap she had made. "I wear good clothes and I belong to the idle class," she said. ". . . But there was a time when I did have to work just as you do now. There was a time when I froze in the cold, just as you do now; when I starved for want of food because of the lack of decent wages." She described her tenement home, her going to work at age 11, her six younger brothers and sisters, her 16-hour days of rolling cigars. "But the time will come when I will have to go back to work again among you. It will come when all the wealth belongs to the men and women who create it."

A decade later, she would indeed have to return to work, although not for the reason she hoped.

Each labor battle of this era only seemed to trigger more. In 1913, some 25,000 silk workers went on strike in Paterson, New Jersey, across the Hudson River from New York. They had endured ten-hour days amid acid fumes from dyes, in mills often unheated in winter. Tuberculosis and other respiratory diseases took a painful toll. They demanded better safety conditions, an end to child labor, increased wages, and an eight-hour day. Three hundred silk mills were shut down, and 1,300 strikers went to jail. Many of these silk workers had volunteered to take in children of the Lawrence strikers the year before, and people sometimes spoke of Paterson as "Red City."

As in factories, mills, and mines throughout the country, Paterson employers deliberately hired immigrants from many different ethnic backgrounds—they regularly sent recruiters to nearby Ellis Island—hoping that would make it harder for their workers to organize. But the IWW, involved with this strike from the beginning, was determined to transcend such divisions. Elizabeth Gurley Flynn warned the strikers not to be "tricked by racial prejudice, for they'll try to tell you that the Jews are going to work and then they'll tell you that the Italians have gone back." At strike meetings, Big Bill Haywood encouraged members of each group to come forward and address the crowd. These Paterson rallies sometimes featured speeches in nine languages. In the working class, Haywood thundered, no one is a foreigner.

Rose traveled to Paterson to address a meeting of more than 2,000 strikers and their supporters, urging them to stick together and slamming the press for its hostile coverage. Both Flynn and Haywood were soon jailed. "What are you two doing with all these foreigners?" the Paterson police chief asked them. The chief searched Haywood to see if he was carrying a weapon. He wasn't. When Haywood later told this story to an audience of strikers, he milked it for every possible drop of suspense. "But I had a gun," he said. "I always carry one and I carry it here. I am prepared to show you the weapon, which can always be found in the upper pocket of my vest." He then thrust his hand into his pocket and pulled out his bright red IWW membership card. "This is the highest caliber gun in the United States."

The upheaval in Paterson caught the attention of the Greenwich Village intelligentsia, many of whom crossed the river to New Jersey to march in picket lines. Emma Goldman noted the adoration that "well-educated literary writers" had for the rough-hewn Wobbly leader. "They follow Haywood much as a bunch of giggling girls go wild over the physical prowess of a quarterback." As the strike dragged on month after month, mill owners resisted the demands of the silk workers—whose finances grew ever more precarious. Rose chaired a meeting at Cooper Union where one of the strike leaders, out on bail, spoke and passed the hat for funds. She proposed a picket line in front of Fifth Avenue's luxury department stores, where workers could brandish their signs "in the faces of the indifferent ladies who *wear* the silks" they produced.

She also had a hand in arranging an event that is far better remembered than the strike itself. According to Mabel Dodge, the idea originated one evening at the Greenwich Village home of a public high school teacher who was Big Bill Haywood's lover whenever he visited New York. Haywood complained that the strike was getting no publicity in the city, even after a bystander, Valentino Modestino, had been killed on his own porch by a stray bullet while holding his baby daughter in his arms. "God!" Haywood said, "I wish I could show them a picture of the funeral of Modestino, who was shot by a cop. Every one of the silk mill hands followed his coffin to the grave and dropped a red flower on it. . . . If our people over here could have seen it, we could have raised a trunkful of money to help us go on. Our food is getting mighty scarce."

"Why don't you bring the strike to New York and *show* it to the workers?" Dodge claimed she then asked him. "Why don't you hire a great hall and re-enact the strike over here?"

"Well, by God! There's an idea!" Haywood answered. "But how?"

"I'll *do* it!" called out a broad-shouldered young man with tousled brown hair whom Dodge did not then know. His enthusiasm was unbounded: "We'll make a Pageant of the strike! The first in the world. . . . Why hasn't anyone ever thought of it before!"

The impetuous young man was John Reed, who soon would become the star reporter for *The Masses* and, for style, dash, and passion, the best American journalist of his generation. His ambition, he told Lincoln Steffens, was "to write my name in letters of fire against the sky." Tall, brawny, disheveled, and exuberant, with a famously unruly mop of hair, Reed had grown up in great comfort in what he called the "unfertilized soil" of provincial Portland, Oregon. As a Harvard student, he had joined innumerable clubs, swum and played water polo for the college, and led the cheering section at football games. After a walking tour of Europe and a taste of the Left Bank, he moved to New York, which he found even more exciting: the docks, Chinatown, streetwalkers, gamblers, and immigrants from every nation on earth. Although his background, like Graham's, was privileged, he had something Graham lacked, a zest for connecting with all kinds of people.

The world was at his feet, waiting to be described and evoked. In the next few years he would fill the pages of *The Masses* and other magazines with his vivid eyewitness accounts of strikes across the country, of the down-and-out in New York City, of a massacre of miners in Colorado, and more. Lusting for immersion in every experience, he would give his fellow radicals the chance to identify with revolutionary upheaval in Mexico, where he dodged bullets and trekked through the desert with rebel leader Pancho Villa. Reed's colorful writing portrayed Villa as a kind of exotic Robin Hood, confiscating landowners' corn, cattle, and gold and giving it to the poor. ("It's so much Reed," commented a fellow writer, "that I suspect it is very little Mexico.") A long article about the strike in Paterson had been Reed's first major piece for *The Masses*. In the course of reporting it, to his delight, he had been jailed for four days. He simultaneously enjoyed being a prison celebrity and mixing with the working class.

Reed embodied the bohemian spirit of Greenwich Village more than anyone, writing:

> . . . *we are free who live in Washington Square,*
> *We dare to think as Uptown wouldn't dare,*
> *Blazing our nights with arguments uproarious;*
> *What care we for a dull old world censorious*
> *When each is sure he'll fashion something glorious?*

The glorious thing he wanted to fashion now was a pageant. Pageants were something of a fad at the time, although generally staged for tamer purposes, such as celebrating a town's centennial. For this one, Dodge rented Madison Square Garden and Reed wrote the script, directing a huge cast of striking workers in rehearsals. Using his cheerleading skills, he conducted them in labor songs, appropriating a Harvard tune for one of them. Ebulliently, he conscripted New York's radical intelligentsia into helping him, recruiting Rose, along with Upton Sinclair and Lincoln Steffens, for the pageant's "press committee." The pageant, everyone expected, was certain to raise the big money so urgently needed for the workers' strike fund.

In Paterson writing for the *New York Call*, Rose asked one cast member, a young woman, if she was worried about stage fright. Not at all, she replied. "We know we can make a strike pageant because we're strikers. We're rehearsin' every day, in the real strike. That's easy. The only strikers that ain't going t' find it s' easy is the ones that must take the parts o' the policemen. My! Jes' think of a striker tryin' t' play he's a real policeman!"

When the day of the performance arrived, Paterson silk workers marched the last part of the way to Madison Square Garden through cheering crowds. Many had been reduced to one meal a day for weeks, and before a final rehearsal, they fell ravenously on food their supporters had prepared for them. Rose was at the Garden that night, as letters ten feet high in red lights spelled out *IWW* atop the building. (These were turned on only at the last minute, since the organizers guessed, correctly, that police would immediately search for the switch to turn them off.)

John Reed had recruited a painter and theater designer to make a 200-foot-wide backdrop showing the silk mills of Paterson. The Garden's massive interior was bright with red banners on the walls and red sashes, ribbons, and flowers worn by the highly sympathetic crowd. Acting out what Reed called "the wretchedness of their lives and the glory of their revolt," most of the 1,147 participating strikers played themselves on a stage almost as long as a city block, dragging themselves off to work to the sound of factory whistles and whirring looms, then joyfully pouring out of the mills shouting "Strike, strike!" Some took other roles: hired detectives clubbing workers, strikebreakers, women sending their children out of town for safety, and mourners dropping red ribbons and carnations on the coffin of the martyred Modestino. His family reenacted their own grief, and the diminutive Flynn and the giant Haywood delivered the same speeches they had given at the graveside. There were songs in Italian, German, and English.

The final scene reenacted a strike meeting, the workers onstage with their backs to the audience, while Flynn, Haywood, and several others addressed the Garden crowd as if all its members, too, were on strike—the ultimate dream of New York's bohemia. A capacity audience of 15,000 stood for the whole performance, booed the police, wildly cheered the strikers, and, at the end, joined in singing the "Internationale."

The pageant was not, unfortunately, enough to stave off a punishing defeat in the five-month-long battle. For while the strikers and their sympathizers were singing "Arise, ye prisoners of starvation!" Paterson workers were coming ever closer to starving. In addition to the usual odds any strikers face, they were also up against increasing mechanization of the silk industry brought about by new high-speed looms. In return for the $5 million in unpaid wages they had lost by going on strike, the silk workers in the end gained almost nothing except places on an industry blacklist. However glorious the pageant, after the cost of renting the Garden, preparing the huge stage, transporting workers and their families by train from New Jersey, and other expenses, the event lost money.

The two main organizers, John Reed and Mabel Dodge, didn't help matters by immediately afterward embarking on a vacation in Paris and at her grand hilltop villa in Tuscany—a restored fifteenth-century Medici palace—their budding love affair taking precedence over the struggle for revolution. Still, the unprecedented spectacle in Madison Square Garden was a high point, perhaps *the* high point, of solidarity between America's labor movement and its artists and intellectuals. For a magical moment the pageant dramatically put the silk workers in the public eye and seemed to hold out a vision of a better future that would unfold not just onstage, but across the land.

Rose kept up a busy schedule of speaking, at one point visiting eight different college campuses in a single week. She also addressed a convention of hoboes in Manhattan, a conference on workplace safety, the Harlem Neighborhood Association, various church congregations, and a synagogue where many of the members were clothing manufacturers. Alexander Berkman, colleague and former lover of Emma Goldman, asked Rose to "say a few words" at a benefit for *Mother Earth,* Goldman's anarchist monthly, "for you are our comrade in spirit."

The press remained entranced with Rose, and she was as shrewd as ever at using that attention to promote the issues she cared about. When an admiring reporter for the *St. Louis Post-Dispatch* met her in a hotel dining room to gather material for a profile, Rose, knowing how journalists can make use of overheard dialogue, asked the waiter who brought them their breakfast about his hours, pay, and working conditions, and if he was a union member. (He was.) She then filled him in on the New York waiters' strike.

In one 1913 speaking tour of the Northeast, officials from Wellesley College would not allow her on campus. They were, she wrote Graham, "afraid of contaminating their gentle students with the virus of that *terrible* R. P. S." In Ohio, $90 was stolen from her hotel room. When a bellhop appeared to be the culprit, Rose turned the discovery into a political statement: she refused to prosecute, telling a newspaper, "I would rather lose the $90 than see the boy's life ruined." Talking at Carnegie Hall, she shared the platform with visiting Belgian socialist leader Émile Vandervelde and may have told him about the time she was fired from a cigar factory because a manager spotted a copy of his book under her work table. No longer was she the Rose who, to please her in-laws, had worn a small crucifix at her wedding. Socialism was now her faith. "How can you love God, whom you have not seen," she asked one audience, "if you do not love your fellow man, whom you have seen?"

Her increasing self-assurance was obvious to those who knew her. Previously, Rose "appeared to me so self-conscious and without sufficient breadth in life," Anna Walling's sister, a writer and translator, said in a letter. "Now I find her an experienced, understanding, subtle woman, quick to absorb and quick to give . . . quite a different person [from] the Rose I thought she was three years ago."

Rose was successfully managing a number of remarkably disparate roles: hostess to house parties of the country's leading radicals on Caritas Island, daughter-in-law who had learned to fit gracefully into the gatherings and overseas travels of Graham's family, speaker who could make middle-class audiences care about the survival struggles of a garment maker or restaurant busboy—and someone who could fire up a crowd of striking workers in either English or Yiddish. An Ohio newspaper compared her to three-time presidential candidate William Jennings Bryan, the most famous orator of the day.

Her increasing prominence was clearly not easy for Graham. After spending the first part of his life in the shadow of his parents and the ancestors who mattered so much to them, he now lived in the shadow of his wife. When he married Rose, he surely thought of himself as someone who would help her come to know the far wider world in which he lived: the books she had not yet read, the countries she had not yet seen, the influential people she did not yet know. And she, at the beginning, felt the same way, awed by the well-known writers and intellectuals in Graham's circle and grateful to learn from them. Now it was the other way around: he was the one in need of help, but neither of them could acknowledge it.

It is hard to look at Graham in this period without seeing him as adrift in the world. His projected book had come to naught, he had failed in several attempts to win elective office, and he was only a peripheral figure in the socialist movement. He may well have envied his brothers, who had found themselves in their work: Anson was becoming highly influential in the administration at Yale; Harold was making a successful career in journalism that would culminate in many years at the *New York Times;* and the prominent architect, Newton, was also the editor of an encyclopedic, multivolume, illustrated history of Manhattan and its buildings which is still admired today. Graham's time spent managing the clan's holdings stemmed from a sense of family obligation rather than any inherent interest of his. The many dusty boxes of his business correspondence reveal neither lust for wealth, nor excitement about new ways of acquiring it, nor even any satisfaction in successfully concluding a deal. It was as if being a Phelps Stokes was for his brothers a source of self-confidence but for him mainly a burden.

In contrast, Rose's world was expanding. In 1914, she was elected a member of Heterodoxy, an unusual group that had begun meeting two years earlier. Mabel Dodge, another member, called it a club "for unorthodox women, that is to say, women who did things and did them openly." Members included Flynn, feminist Charlotte Perkins Gilman, novelist Fannie Hurst, and many other accomplished women, although Rose was a rare Jewish immigrant among them. Frustratingly for us, the group's lunch meetings, at a Greenwich Village restaurant every other Saturday, were off the record. We know little more than the cost of the meal, 85 cents. Flynn described Heterodoxy as "an experience of unbroken delight to me! It has been a glimpse of the women of the future, big spirited, intellectually alert, devoid of the old 'femininity' which has been replaced by a wonderful freemasonry of women."

Among Heterodoxy's writers, artists, activists, educators, and professionals in their floor-length dresses were, unusually for the era, both straight and lesbian women and at least one black member. A startlingly high proportion of them—one third, more than triple the rate for American women at the time—had been divorced. "No one was there," wrote Flynn, "because her husband or father was famous." It must have been exhilarating for Rose to be in such company. One of the few accounts of a Heterodoxy meeting describes how, as the writer Amy Lowell was reciting some of her poetry, "it was all so sad that Rose Pastor Stokes turned around and laid her head on her neighbor's shoulder and cried . . . sobbing an obbligato to Miss Lowell's sonorous voice."

Although the intellectuals of Greenwich Village paid tribute to the idea of egalitarian relationships and at least a few couples tried to practice what they preached, Graham, socialist or not, had more traditional ideas. "Graham has been disagreeable most of the day," Rose wrote in her diary in 1914. They were then staying at a hotel in Florida, and she had "ventured to interject a suggestion" when he was talking with the hotel manager. "It is not customary to interrupt," he told her.

"Now and often before," Rose wrote, "my interest in the subject doesn't count. Neither does he seem to realize that an interruption kindly caused and in good faith cannot be half so much a breach of good manners as an annoyed reproof in public." Graham was no less irritable when Rose suggested "taking advantage of an opportunity" to give talks on socialism as they passed through Jacksonville on their way home. "We certainly have different notions of opportunity," he grumbled.

Their quarrel seems to have passed, for a few months later she referred in a letter to how much they had enjoyed eating peanuts together on a bench in Central Park after seeing lion cubs in the zoo.

In another she called him her "Glorious Inspiration" and assured him that even being able to write to him was a "deep, deep blessing." Some of her friends, though, were increasingly puzzled by the marriage. "I often wondered," Emma Goldman later wrote, "how Rose could live side by side with Stokes who was such a lifeless and bloodless creature."

For anyone restless in marriage, Greenwich Village offered alternatives. In Mabel Dodge's salon, in the speeches and writings of Goldman, among the staff of *The Masses,* monogamy was regarded as already on the junk heap of history. Marriage was to love, declared Goldman, as capitalism was to labor. And, of course, it was far easier than capitalism to overthrow. Dodge, for instance, had a succession of lovers in addition to John Reed, including Big Bill Haywood. Reed, in turn, moved on to the journalist Louise Bryant, who during the time they were together became involved with at least two other men, one of them a young and unknown playwright, Eugene O'Neill. When Reed and Bryant eventually decided to get married, their friend Boardman Robinson, a *Masses* cartoonist and illustrator, called it a scandal. Naturally, the demon of jealousy made many of these couplings and uncouplings far less smooth than theorists of free love might have planned. None of this, however, was for Graham and Rose. Whatever the temptations either of them may have felt in these surroundings—and about this they left no clues —they shared a strong belief in marital fidelity, and there is no evidence in these years that either of them ceased to practice it.

The restlessness Rose felt took a different form. She had made voyages to Europe, the Middle East, and South America with Graham; now, for the first time, she went abroad with someone else. In the spring of 1914, she headed off for a two-month trip to England with Olive Dargan, who had been encouraging her to write plays. On this trip, Rose read her way through the dramas of Chekhov and Strindberg. One day in London the pair visited the East End neighborhood where Rose had lived from age three to nine. "The women gathered about us," Rose wrote later, "and told us of a 'Little girl who lived here years ago; then went to America, grew up, and married a fine gentleman—a millionaire.'"

The two women met British socialist and labor leaders, attended lectures at the Royal Albert Hall, and joined mass marches for women's suffrage. Britain, like the United States, was being shaken by a wave of strikes, and Rose sensed—as did many worried British business leaders—a revolutionary mood in the air. The left was rising everywhere: Europe now had ten million socialist voters, and there were millions more sympathizers in countries where people as yet had no meaningful vote, like Russia. At international meetings the leaders of socialist parties gathered to pledge eternal solidarity with one another. A new day seemed at hand, on a continent so often riven by nationalism and war.

Graham became distraught that Rose was staying away so long. "Can not you leave me," she wrote him from the Hertfordshire countryside, "to sing my songs in this Nature's paradise for a few weeks longer?" He was impatient to have her back, complaining, "I have had no letter from you since your letter of the 20th which I received about five days ago. Five days seems an awfully long time to wait to hear from you, dear love of mine. . . . My position alone here has been so different from yours!" As often would be the case, his anxieties took the form of irrational worries about money. Claiming that she was writing to him without Rose's knowledge, Dargan assured Graham that they were spending only 18 shillings a week on room and board, and asked his forgiveness for her encouraging Rose to stay in England "longer than the date which you had generously fixed."

Rose called on Graham's vacationing mother and sister in London, but declined an invitation to sail home with them. Instead, she took a second-class berth on a ship to Montreal, where the press would not be looking for her, arriving back in New York in mid-June 1914.

At the end of that month, Archduke Franz Ferdinand, heir to the throne of the Austro-Hungarian Empire, wearing a high, plumed hat and riding through the streets of Sarajevo with his wife in an open car, was assassinated by a Serbian nationalist. It was the spark that soon flamed into a great inferno. A month later, several of the empire's squat, steam-powered gunboats on the Danube River began shelling Serbia. These were the opening shots of the cataclysm that would kill more than nine million soldiers and an untold number of civilians. It would upend the lives of tens of millions more, including Rose and Graham Stokes.

12

I Didn't Raise My Boy to Be a Soldier

FROM WHAT SEEMED A SAFE distance, Americans intently followed the war's opening moves. New York crowds flocked to Times Square and Herald Square, named after the newspapers whose offices were there, to read in their windows the latest telegraphed bulletins, posted in huge red type on newsprint. Police estimated that more than 300,000 people filled the streets leading to Times Square. "A great cheer went up," the *Times* reported, as the window bulletins announced that Britain had declared war on Germany. But "the spirit of the crowd was always good humored," almost as if it were rooting for a sports team.

Socialists, however, were appalled by the way their European comrades seemed to have forgotten their internationalist solidarity and been swept up in the contagion of clashing patriotisms. "When the war broke out I was struck dumb," wrote Big Bill Haywood, who had been to Europe in earlier years and counted some of its labor leaders as friends. "For weeks I could scarcely talk."

Radicals blamed the war on bankers and munitions makers; a *Masses* cartoon by Maurice Becker showed top-hatted plutocrats aiming giant cannons at each other, using the helpless bodies of workers as ammunition. Things were not so simple, though, for Europe's working classes went to war quite willingly. Socialists for years had vowed that workers might fight the capitalists but never each other. Across the continent, that dream now lay shattered. The parliamentary deputies of Germany's Social Democrats, Europe's strongest socialist party, heeded Kaiser Wilhelm II's plea and voted for a package of measures to finance the fighting. (In *The Masses* the year before, English Walling had presciently warned that the German party would succumb to militaristic fervor if war came.) The French Ministry of the Interior maintained a secret roster of radicals considered likely to dodge the draft; to officials' amazement, 80 percent of them promptly showed up to do military service. In Britain, where there was as yet no draft, huge crowds of young men, many labor unionists among them, jammed army enlistment offices. When Keir Hardie, the British labor leader who had once dined at the University Settlement and later campaigned with his friend Debs, told a meeting in his Welsh coal-mining constituency that his country should not join the fighting, the crowd erupted in jeers and choruses of "Rule Britannia." A shouting, cursing mob then surrounded the house where he spent the night.

Despite quietly selling Britain and France a wide array of armaments and other supplies, the United States remained officially neutral. And despite some differing opinions about how dangerous German militarism might be, American socialists for the moment were united in wanting to keep their country out of the war. English Walling was typical, condemning German aggression but finding France and Britain driven by imperial ambition as well. Along with Anna Walling and Emma Goldman, Rose joined the Women's Peace Party, headed by social worker Jane Addams, which brought together women of varying politics united by their opposition to the fighting. The following year several of its leaders would attend a conference in neutral Holland of women from countries on both sides of the war, and other nations as well, which called — in vain — for peace talks.

The bloodiest conflict that history had yet seen, the First World War daily brought new horrors. Europe's armies were equipped with machine guns and artillery of staggering destructive power, but none were prepared to face such fire themselves. Millions of French infantrymen went into battle dressed as if for parade, in bright blue jackets, with hats and pantaloons of brilliant red. German cadets in student caps headed off to the front through cheering crowds, while most of that country's troops wore leather helmets—incapable of stopping a bullet—with decorative spikes on top. For all of them, encountering the full firepower of the machine age was like marching into a furnace.

In less than a month, as German forces swept through almost all of Belgium and plunged deep into France, more than 300,000 French soldiers, resplendent in red and blue, were killed or wounded. An astonishing 27,000 of them died on a single day, August 22, 1914. The Germans, too, found themselves mown down like so many stalks of hay if they attacked into machine-gun fire. Fields and roads were strewn with shattered wagons, trucks, ambulances, red double-decker London buses that had been rushed to France to transport troops, and the corpses of horses and men. Dead bodies—when they had not been pulverized into tiny fragments by high-explosive shells—often had to be dumped into mass graves. Nor were any of the combatants prepared even for the shattering noise of industrialized warfare. "Louder and louder grew the sound of the guns," remembered one British officer, ". . . under a sky of brass, shaking with the concussion of artillery, now a single heavy discharge, then a pulsation of the whole atmosphere, as if all the gods in heaven were beating on drums the size of lakes."

On the Eastern Front, where Germany and its ally, Austria-Hungary, battled Russia, the toll was also staggering. Russia, too, had gone to war with great enthusiasm, even changing the German-sounding name of its capital, St. Petersburg, to Petrograd. But the tsarist military, as corrupt and top-heavy with incompetent court favorites as the rest of the empire's bureaucracy, was no match for the Germans. In their first major battle, more than 30,000 Russians were killed or wounded and 92,000 captured. From one entire army corps of more than 25,000 soldiers, only a single man escaped. Its commander committed suicide. In the midst of all the slaughter, special trains still carried fresh flowers each week from Crimea, in the south, to decorate the tsar's palace in Petrograd. In a wave of pogroms, looting, and deportations, the retreating Russian military vented its frustrations on Jews. When a new German offensive swept deep into Russia, the territory it overran included Augustów.

Many Americans sympathized with the Allies, for Germany had, after all, brazenly invaded France and Belgium, imposing a ruthless occupation. But leftists were dismayed that Britain and France were allied with their longtime villain, imperial Russia, a regime far more autocratic than Germany's. Few of them were cheering for either side. John Reed railed in *The Masses* against "the editorial chorus in America which pretends to believe . . . that the White and Spotless Knight of Modern Democracy is marching against the Unspeakably Vile Monster of Medieval Militarism. What has democracy to do in alliance with Nicholas, the Tsar? . . . This is not Our War."

Though he abhorred it, Reed was eager to report on the fighting firsthand, and rushed off to Europe to cover the conflict from both sides. He saw mass graves swarming with grey maggots in the Balkans, visited a hospital full of shell-shocked soldiers in Berlin, and spent time with British noncommissioned officers who were veterans of colonial wars, "debauched, diseased little men, with a moral sense fertilized by years of slaughtering yellow, brown and black men." In Russia he was followed by police spies. In vain he looked for soldiers who felt, as he did, that businessmen and jingoist politicians had started the war and now expected the working class to fight it. He was disappointed to find most British socialists eager to do battle and to meet a former Serbian socialist leader who was now a captain, claiming he was happy to be in the trenches with his men. For the frustrated Reed, the war was a story—unlike the Paterson silk strike and the other struggles he had covered—with no heroes.

Although working-class internationalism in Europe had vanished in the smoke of artillery fire, Rose and other American radicals felt there were still battles to be fought close to home. Despite the war, the wave of strikes that had begun five years earlier continued at full pitch. A bloody battle by Colorado coal miners against a Rockefeller-owned company ignited a conflict that saw more than 70 people killed before it ended in December 1914. More were killed or wounded when Polish American workers struck a Standard Oil refinery in New Jersey in 1915, one of 1,405 strikes or lockouts that year. In 1916, New York City was paralyzed by a walkout of trolley, subway, and elevated railway workers, who threw rocks and bricks at trains driven by policemen or strikebreakers. The war at home showed no signs of truce.

Ever since her years breathing tobacco dust, Rose's lungs had been sensitive to the coal smoke that was such a constant part of urban life and train travel. But she kept up her lecture schedule, denouncing the slaughter in Europe as a product of capitalist rivalry. She also spoke at mass meetings on behalf of Elizabeth Gurley Flynn and other IWW organizers being prosecuted for their role in the Paterson strike. Flynn was acquitted of all charges by a jury — Rose, at her side in the courtroom, gave her a kiss when the verdict was announced. Another comrade was less lucky. The Irish-born Patrick Quinlan would spend two years in prison for inciting violence, though the Paterson police had arrested him before he could even make a speech. He had passed more than a week on Caritas Island the year before the strike and returned for another stay while out on bail. In the guestbook, he wrote, "a slave's dream."

Once he went to prison, Rose lobbied New Jersey officials, wrote articles on his case, raised funds, and sent him a string of letters to try to keep his spirits up. The experience of gathering signatures on a petition for his freedom provoked her to write a short story with this wry ending:

> "Excuse me, sir, but won't you sign this petition to get Pat Quinlan out of prison?"
>
> He was a big, good-natured Irish cop. Out of prison! His business was to help people into it. His arm was half-raised for an eloquent flourish of refusal, as he took a step past her. Then he turned suddenly.
>
> "What did you say his name was?"
>
> "Quinlan," said the young woman, "Pat Quinlan."
>
> "Here, give me that," said the cop, "where's your pencil? No man with a name like that should be in prison."

At one point Rose found herself barred from the campus of the University of Cincinnati, speaking instead to the local Woman Suffrage Association, where a crowd of more than 500 overflowed the hall because so many students wanted to see the woman judged too dangerous for them. Graham, as usual these days, remained at home.

Although he wrote her, "Dear Girlie, I shall count the days and even the hours till you are back again!" there were signs of strain. "Today marked a deep change in me—mentally—spiritually—in my attitude toward G.," Rose wrote in her diary in 1915. "He *accused me of loafing.* Blurted it out quite innocently—because I stayed in bed late in the morning. I returned on the 22nd after a week's speaking tour in Penn. and Ohio, with a bad bronchitis and a stay-in-bed temperature. I didn't give up the rest of the tour (tho I had to speak one night with a temperature of 102°) until I completely lost my voice. . . . I have merely been trying to get stronger and reduce my temperature to normal. 'Loafing!' I didn't reply. What's the good? But it put the iron into my soul, and this time I feel it's there to stay. The terrible loneliness of one's soul in such moments!"

Others, too, began noticing Graham's irritability. Joanna Cooke, a socialist writer, spent a night with the couple during the 1916 New York transit strike, which they talked about over dinner. Much to her surprise, Cooke found Graham hostile to the strikers. Were his politics changing? "Graham was furious against the men," she would write to Rose a dozen years later, recalling the evening. "I saw it was no use to speak—& you said very little. He was peremptory and dogmatic. I was at his table and I could not begin a quarrel. . . . I felt a dreadful fear that unhappiness was on the way."

Another friend, labor organizer Matilda Rabinowitz, visited Caritas Island around the same time. Rose, with "the light of an afternoon sun falling on her hair, bronze and copper waves held in a loose knot," sang verses from Goethe that were set to music by Schubert, as one of her younger sisters accompanied her on the piano:

> *Knowest thou the land? So far and fair!*
> *Thou, whom I love, and I will wander there.*

Knowest thou the house with all its rooms aglow,
And shining hall and columned portico?

The sunlight now fading swam over the beamed ceiling and
the warm wood grain of the walls, playing on a portrait in
a gilt frame, on a piece of venetian glass, a bowl of flowers.
A low, lovely room, looking out through wide and open
French door[s] on the Long Island Sound.

. . . The singing moved me deeply. From where I sat I
could not see Rose's face. But I noticed how tense were her
clenched hands behind her back and though her head was
tilted backward, her shoulders drooped wearily. As she finished the song and turned to me her smile was one of great
sadness. She sat down beside me and took my hand. Her
brown eyes, the shade of her hair almost, glistened with
tears.

At the dinner table, "G was a dour host. . . . There was a repressed
atmosphere and little conversation. [Rose] was animated enough,
but as she looked across the table at her husband her smile would be
distorted, as if she wanted to cry. He would scarcely look up when
spoken to, and he winced at the gay laugh of [Rose's] sister. . . . He
was tall and lean with a kind of caved-in look, as if he were holding
his breath. He rose from the table . . . mumbled an apology about
some pressing work and left." As Graham "went by his wife's chair
she half turned to touch him and smiled. But he brushed by without the slightest pause."

Adding to her frustration, Rose could still not escape being seen
as Cinderella. When a newspaper advertisement for a talk in New
Jersey promoted her as the "Former Factory Girl . . . Who Won,
Married and Converted one of America's Millionaires," she scribbled on it, "One of the disgusting ways in which comrades sometimes advertise my meetings — even now — ten years after my marriage!" For different reasons, the "converted" must have left Graham
also upset at the advertisement.

In part to avoid such labeling, she grew determined to establish herself more firmly as a writer. John Reed's Paterson pageant had shown how drama could be a tool in the battle for social justice, and for several years now Rose had been writing plays. She and Graham had watched from box seats as the first of them was performed, *The Saving of Martin Greer,* in which an elderly man is driven to attempt suicide by his failure to find a job. "If the audience was looking for something very grim and earnest," commented the *New York Times* reviewer, "it was not disappointed."

Significantly, several of her plays focus on women who in some fashion renounce something or become martyrs. Her 1916 drama, *The Woman Who Wouldn't,* featured a working-class heroine, Mary Lacey, whose determined independence reminds one of the wife now getting under Graham's skin. Mary helps support her family while her millworker father is out on strike. Discovering that she is pregnant, she also learns that her fiancé is involved with another woman, although he claims he still wants to marry Mary. To her family's horror, she rejects the idea of wedding a man who is untrue—even though this will leave her the mother of an illegitimate child. She leaves home in disgrace, supporting herself as a cleaning woman, waitress, and, after the baby is born, wet nurse. Years later, along with her young daughter, she returns for a visit, now a famous labor leader who has endured prison for her activism. Her former fiancé begs her to marry him, but, telling him her life is dedicated to the labor movement, she again spurns a marriage to someone she cannot love.

Rose had more success with *In April,* which drew some favorable reviews in its New York debut and, alone among her plays, was performed elsewhere in the United States and Britain. Once again a martyr was featured, a young woman of the tenements living with her mother, who is beaten and mistreated by her drunken stepfather. The young heroine remains loyal to her mother, but in doing so she sacrifices the chance to marry.

In 1916 Rose was approached by Alice Guy Blaché, a French film director living in the United States and one of the rare women directors anywhere. Guy Blaché wanted to work with Rose on a film on something they both cared about: birth control. They drafted a script together and, along with Graham's radical sister Helen, gave it a trial reading. Again striking the note of martyrdom, the plot centers on a young working-class woman crusading for birth control who is put on trial for her beliefs. The film made the conservative, rather than free-love, argument for contraception: it would reduce adultery and prostitution because wives would be willing to let men satisfy their sexual urge at home. Even so, the project foundered when Rose and Guy Blaché were unable to get studio backing.

Under the Comstock Act of 1873, a sweeping crackdown on all manner of "obscenity," distributing contraceptives or information about them was a federal crime. Similar legislation was on the books in many states, including New York. Behind these laws lay a lingering Victorian prudery about sex and men's fear that giving women more control over their reproductive lives would inherently threaten male power.

This historical moment also saw many people riled up against contraception for an additional reason. The first years of the twentieth century were a high point of imperialism. The European powers had just finished dividing almost all of Africa among themselves. In an elaborate 1911 ceremony the British king and queen were crowned emperor and empress of India. The United States had seized colonies from Spain and ruthlessly defeated a lengthy rebellion in one of them, the Philippines. Yet such triumphs felt fragile to any enthusiastic imperialist who was aware that there were a lot more yellow, black, and brown people in the world than white ones. *They* were certainly not doing anything to limit their birth rates.

There was consequently much talk among America's Protestant elite about the importance of large families and the danger of "race suicide." A widely popular book, by Edmond Demolins, was titled *Anglo-Saxon Superiority*. A woman should be "a good wife, a good mother," one speaker who admired this book told the National Congress of Mothers (a predecessor of the PTA) in 1905, "able and willing to perform the first and greatest duty of womanhood, able and willing to bear, and to bring up as they should be brought up, healthy children . . . numerous enough so that the race shall increase and not decrease.

". . . The man or woman who deliberately foregoes these blessings," he went on, "whether from viciousness, coldness, shallowheartedness, self-indulgence, or mere failure to appreciate aright the difference between the all-important and the unimportant,—why, such a creature merits contempt as hearty as any visited upon the soldier who runs away in battle."

The speaker was President Theodore Roosevelt. All patriotic American couples, he believed, should bear at least three, and ideally four, children, and families of "better stock" (Anglo-Saxons, of course; it didn't need to be said) should wage "the warfare of the cradle" by having at least six children. To refuse to have children was "the cardinal sin, against the race and against civilization."

By 1916, he was president no longer, but he and others continued to fulminate on the subject, and the Comstock Act was still enforced. Emma Goldman had been promoting birth control for years, imagining it as part of the liberation of both women and men in the anarchist future she dreamed of. As a young woman, she had been a nurse and midwife on the Lower East Side and had seen for herself "the fierce, blind struggle of the women of the poor against frequent pregnancies. Most of them lived in continual dread of conception; the great mass of the married women submitted helplessly, and when they found themselves pregnant, their alarm and worry would result in the determination to get rid of their expected offspring. It was incredible what fantastic methods despair could invent: jumping off tables, rolling on the floor, massaging the stomach, drinking nauseating concoctions, and using blunt instruments. These and similar methods were being tried, generally with great injury."

As early as 1909, Rose had written an article saying that the real cause of "race suicide" was not "those parents who deliberately restrict the birth-rate," but the overwork and extreme poverty that drove so many people to early deaths. Now, in addition to her work with the Women's Peace Party, she joined the National Birth Control League. At one event for the cause in early 1916, Rose displayed her political savvy. She was master of ceremonies of a dinner of several hundred people—the first time that Margaret Sanger would be speaking to such a large and wealthy audience. But as Sanger entered the banquet room, Rose pulled her aside and said that she'd just been talking to one of the other speakers on the program, a physician. "He has a speech ready in which he intends to blast you to the skies for interfering in what should be a strictly medical matter," Rose quickly explained to Sanger. ". . . We meant to have you come at the end of the program but now we're going to put you first so that you can spike his guns." The maneuver worked: after hearing Sanger eloquently make her case for access to birth control, and seeing a dozen people in the audience rise and offer to support her, the doctor knew he would have no chance. He abandoned his prepared talk, and spoke on another angle of the subject entirely.

Having grown up with six siblings who sometimes did not have enough to eat, Rose found the criminalization of birth control an outrage—especially when any woman wealthy enough to see a sympathetic private doctor could find out whatever she wanted. "What is good for the up-town gander is certainly good for the down-town goose," she told one audience. "It makes no difference whether birth control is practiced in Fifth avenue or in Hester street."

In April 1916, Emma Goldman was sentenced to 15 days in the Queens County Jail for promoting birth control. Rose was in the courtroom to show support, as she would be when Sanger was put on trial for the same offense. From jail, Goldman wrote her a warm letter of thanks, telling Rose she was "glad that my arrest has brought us closer together," and promising to call as soon as she was released.

It was to honor Goldman that 3,000 people assembled in Carnegie Hall on May 5, 1916, under the watchful eye of police in the aisles, and Rose set off a near riot by condemning the Comstock Act and announcing that she would break the law by distributing birth control leaflets on the spot. Her speech, and the resulting pandemonium, were what seized the next day's headlines and eclipsed anything said by the other speakers, or by the chair, Max Eastman, who struggled in vain to keep the chaotic rush for leaflets under control.

The event "was a demonstration to welcome Emma Goldman on her release from prison," reported the *Times,* ". . . but Mrs. Stokes ran away with the meeting." Goldman did not seem to mind. She reprinted excerpts of Rose's speech in her magazine, *Mother Earth,* noting that Rose had also passed out the forbidden leaflets on another occasion several weeks earlier, and welcomed her to the company of "true revolutionaries."

Today the birth control technique recommended in these leaflets — douching — would not pass muster medically.* Using a syringe, Rose wrote, a woman should inject glycerin into the vagina "just before you take the risk," as she delicately put it. "IMMEDIATELY AFTER the risk has been taken," the woman should douche extremely thoroughly with a solution of warm water and peroxide. Was this the kind of birth control she and Graham used? It would certainly not have made for a very relaxed or spontaneous sex life.

Rose's Carnegie Hall speech was reported across the country. Although she failed to get arrested, she succeeded in deeply upsetting Graham's family. When she offered to tell the press that she spoke for herself alone, his mother wrote her, "*Don't* write to the papers. It will make me all the more conspicuous." Mrs. Stokes declared herself "heartsick" about "your deliberate publicity on a subject which should have been left to other people." She apologized for being "not cordial" in talking to Rose, "but the tears were so near the surface, I feared I could not keep them back."

It was not just the family's matriarch who was upset. "The notoriety and newspaper discussion brought about by the Carnegie Hall episode has been hard for all of us," Graham's brother Anson wrote to Rose. The cause of birth control "is *not* advanced by defiance of law and its sworn upholders." Instead, he suggested, one could "get

---

* Although in 1916 Sanger was fitting women with diaphragms at her Brooklyn clinic before the police shut it down and sent her to jail, douching was still the most widely used contraceptive method in the United States. After condoms, it was also the technique most recommended by doctors. Only in the 1920s would research reveal its high failure rate and physicians begin to realize that some of the chemicals involved could be harmful. Douching kits would still be advertised in the 1930s, and sold door-to-door by saleswomen dressed as nurses.

changes in laws brought about by legal means." Other stored-up resentments were aired in his letter as well: "You have appeared, I think, more than once in defense of strikers . . . but in such cases in the future your word will lose influence, unless you express public regret for defying the police." On the subject of birth control, he added, "My own opinion is that sexual restraint is the wisest thing to advocate."

"My deliberate running counter to the vicious law that keeps mothers and wives ignorant of methods of contraception was prompted by . . . sympathy so deep, that it would be foolish in me to try to express it to you," Rose replied. "I believe the crying needs of the people to be a higher law than any on our statute books." As to sexual restraint, she added, "I wish you could read the seven or eight hundred letters I have piled up before me now. They would convince you that it is not enough." She also asked that her comments be forwarded as "a Round Robin to the family." As the duel of letters continued, she pointed out that sometimes legal means were not enough to bring about change. What about the Boston Tea Party? Skillfully adjusting her rhetoric to her audience as always, Rose also cited to the clergyman Anson the example of Jesus chasing the money changers from the Temple.

In addition to the great value the family placed on propriety, Anson had a specific reason for not wanting the Stokes name associated with anything controversial or illegal. He had gained great influence in his long tenure as secretary of Yale University and was widely considered a leading candidate to be the school's next president.

There were other signs of tension in the air. One evening at the Madison Avenue mansion Rose noticed the absence of Helen, the family member she felt closest to, and asked where she was. "With some feeling," according to Rose's diary, Graham's mother said, "Out on the street distributing trade union papers!" She then added, "If anyone had told me a few years ago that one of my daughters was out on the street . . ." To preserve decorum, she stopped short. Rose tried to smooth things over by saying, "One's attitude does change." But her mother-in-law replied, "No, I haven't changed my attitude a bit!"

There was, however, one Stokes who felt positive about birth control: Uncle Will. His interest came not from enthusiasm for women's rights, but from wanting to prevent the births of people he considered undesirable. He hoped, he wrote Rose, "to eliminate the failings in human beings, as we have eliminated them in the thoroughbred running horse and the trotting horse." Obviously contraception would be of help in eradicating "the great degeneracy in the human race in America." A friend of his, he added, had developed a drug to induce abortion in mares, and, he had no doubt, it would work on humans too. He asked for any birth control literature Rose could send him.

For years to come, women from Maine to Alaska would write Rose hundreds of desperate letters pleading for birth control information. She answered them all, sent women her leaflets, and urged them to join the National Birth Control League. Without using their names, she sometimes incorporated their stories into her speeches. One woman had had five children in five years and left her husband rather than risk having more. Sometimes men wrote as well. An elevator operator at New York's Savoy Hotel, earning $25 a month plus tips, told her that he and his wife had two children, were barely getting by on his income, and feared they could not manage with a third. A socialist in Virginia wrote that "in the sixteen years I have been married my wife has borne six children, four of whom are now living, the other two died in infancy. Both my wife and I love our children dearly, but if we had only known how to keep from having so many we would have been much better off." Now, he added, his wife's health was shaky, and "we both feel that it would be a calamity to have any addition to our family. Therefore, not knowing any contraceptive methods we are forced to forego the pleasures of matrimony. . . . Our family physician refuses to give us any information whatever." He had asked a friend to try to get help from another doctor, "but he would not furnish any information. He said he did not know but what my friend and I were agents of the Federal Government and were trying to get him in trouble."

Meanwhile, over everything else loomed the shadow of the First World War. It continued to spawn new terrors: poison gas, flamethrowers, and German dirigibles dropping bombs from the skies above London. July 1, 1916, the start of the Battle of the Somme, was the day of greatest bloodshed in British military history; more than 21,000 British soldiers were killed or fatally wounded. The French and German armies suffered similar carnage in a months-long struggle over the French fortress at Verdun; by the year's end, that battle alone claimed 300,000 lives. Under the unrelenting bombardment, officers and men began losing their minds, filling hospital after hospital with cases of shell shock.

On the Eastern Front, the Germans and their Austro-Hungarian allies moved deep into Russia, forcing the inept army of the tsar into chaotic retreat. Although news sent by war correspondents was heavily censored, there were rumors that, in the face of catastrophic casualties, thousands of Russian soldiers had deserted. Millions of Russian war refugees were living in tents or makeshift shelters. A tight Allied naval blockade had cut off food imports by Germany and Austria-Hungary, leaving tens of millions of adults and children severely malnourished. Far from the battle lines, their death rates rose. Desperate for workers for war industries, Germany began conscripting hundreds of thousands of Russian, Eastern European, French, and Belgian civilians as forced laborers. The Germans built an electrified border fence to prevent people from fleeing occupied Belgium for neutral Holland. Hundreds died trying to cross it.

It seemed obvious to many Americans, not just those attending the Socialist and Women's Peace Party rallies that Rose spoke to, that the United States should not join this slaughter. You didn't have to be on the left to sing a song that became enormously popular, "I Didn't Raise My Boy to Be a Soldier":

> *I didn't raise my boy to be a soldier,*
> *I brought him up to be my pride and joy.*
> *Who dares to place a musket on his shoulder*
> *To shoot some other mother's darling boy?*

Public opinion in the United States, however, had begun to shift after the passenger liner *Lusitania,* at one point the largest ship afloat, was torpedoed and sunk en route to England by a German submarine in 1915. Nearly 1,200 people perished, including 94 children and more than 120 Americans. The outrage, stirred by banner headlines, was fully understandable, but Americans paid less attention to another side to the story. Besides the doomed passengers, also on board the ship were 4.2 million rounds of ammunition, 51 tons of shrapnel shells, and other munitions that American manufacturers had sold to the British. The United States was trying to have it both ways: to profit from such sales but stay out of the war.

The sinking, however, provoked demands for America to take vengeance by joining the war on the Allied side. On this subject, no one was more vociferous than Roosevelt. Frustrated at being out of office, angry at his country for having such a small army, TR was as eager for battle as he had been nearly two decades earlier when (after making sure correspondents were on hand to record the feat) he led his Rough Riders charging up Cuba's San Juan Hill in the war against Spain. An increasing number of Americans shared his martial enthusiasm, among them Graham's Uncle Will.

The war party in the United States, strongly backed by munitions and other corporations reaping high profits from their sales to the Allies, began to call for "preparedness," a code word for a massive increase in American military spending. Nine days after Rose's tumultuous 1916 appearance at Carnegie Hall, 135,000 marchers demanding preparedness paraded through New York City, "perhaps the greatest procession of civilians that the world has ever seen," declared the *Times* effusively. The mayor's carriage, National Guard detachments, prancing horses, marching bands, Boy Scouts, fife and drum players in Revolutionary War garb, judges, bankers, haberdashers, actors, socialites, railroad presidents, and nurses, as well as thousands of men wearing red, white, and blue neckties and carrying American flags, took 11 hours to pass a reviewing stand filled with politicians and military officers. The parade route up Broadway and Fifth Avenue took the marchers not far from the Stokes townhouse at 88 Grove Street.

Despite campaigning for reelection that fall on a promise of keeping the country out of war, President Woodrow Wilson was already engineering a large naval buildup and privately talking with congressional leaders about entering the conflict. He also laid the groundwork for that move by shamelessly fanning the dark undercurrent of xenophobia that had long run through American society. "There are citizens of the United States," he warned Congress, "I blush to admit, born under other flags . . . who have poured the poison of disloyalty into the very arteries of our national life." And what should be done with the disloyal? "Such creatures of passion, disloyalty, and anarchy must be crushed out."

13

Let the Guilty Be Shot at Once

"WHY DO NOT WE BREED human beings to endure hard work?" asked a book published at the beginning of 1917. "Let us have a Registry for our laboring classes, and breed them." Workers could be bred to weigh 400 pounds, the author suggested, and to carry or lift up to a thousand pounds.

The Right to Be Well Born was the work of W.E.D. Stokes, a devotee of the new movement for eugenics. The science of breeding that he had mastered with his beloved trotting horses could, Uncle Will was confident, easily be applied to humans. "My sole object is to lead my countrymen to a vision of the need of breeding better men and better women.

"Our pure healthy New England blood" was mixing disastrously with "the rotten, foreign, diseased blood of ages, which the gates of our immigration laws now swing wide open and allow to flow in among us." Immigrants were the "scum of the earth" intimately connected with the "evils of labor unions." He wrote of seeing a mass of immigrants in New York, "blind, halt, lame and deformed; many of them with unusually large heads ... many had long beards." Among the group, furthermore, "there were men of all shades of color." Worst of all, they were lined up to be sworn in as American citizens, "their votes as good as yours and mine."

The solution: ban intermarriage between the "races," establish a

"Human Registry" of genetic information on everyone, and allow only native-born Americans to vote. (As with so much else in Uncle Will's life, the publication of his book was accompanied by a lawsuit. He refused to pay its printer, a vanity press that he contended had used the wrong size paper.)

Stokes was merely expressing the racism and nativism that had long simmered in America, but began boiling over in the first decades of the twentieth century. In addition to the waves of immigrants from Europe, starting around 1910 millions of black Americans began leaving the South for other parts of the country, including Stokes's New York. In response, he demanded "a Colored Registry, or our grandchildren will be marrying mulattoes." Black people might have superior musical talent, he felt, but he was certain they had little else, for "the mind of the negro gets its maturity at the end of the second or third or fourth grade."

Already dismayed by Rose's socialism, he would have been still more horrified had he heard her speaking about racial equality on a southern tour she finished just before *The Right to Be Well Born* appeared. Remarkably, some of her fellow socialists were equally upset. At South Carolina's all-black Benedict College, she had organized 27 students into a chapter of the Intercollegiate Socialist Society. But doing so was dangerously "impolitic," she was told by her host in the state, a professor at the very white University of South Carolina. It would be a "calamity," he declared, if anyone at white colleges found out "that Negro chapters had been organized. . . . Meeting a Negro on terms of social equality was *unthinkable*. Said he, should the I.S.S. place Benedict College in the list on its letterhead it would be the end of all effort. I was appalled at this attitude."

That was how Rose described the situation in an exasperated letter to ISS headquarters, which she started writing on the train home. She ended by saying defiantly that having spoken at Benedict, "I naturally took the opportunity to organize too. William McKinley Scott will be secretary of the 27. Won't you send him the study course, please?"

Rose's approach did not prevail, despite Graham's position as president of the ISS. For many socialists—as for many other white

Americans—the idea of human brotherhood did not extend across racial lines. The month after Rose's speaking tour another official of the group visited the South and asked about setting up chapters on black campuses. To do so, the cautious Graham declared, "would make it quite impossible for us to work in the white colleges, and set back the Socialist cause for many years."

At the time of her trip south, Rose was at the height of her rhetorical powers. In Washington, DC, her audience included someone she described as "an anti-Socialist lecturer" she had once debated. He approached her after her talk. "'I wish our side had you,' he said. 'I have heard them all on your side, and you're the most dangerous one they've got.'" She filled a hall in Richmond, Virginia, for three hours, and people wouldn't leave even when the lights were turned out. "We have had no one in Chapel Hill during . . . the last 16 years who has left so fine an impression," wrote the dean of the graduate school at the University of North Carolina. In South Carolina, "the whole city was charmed," a fellow socialist reported. "Mrs. Stokes cannot come to Columbia too often or stay too long."

Graham did not share her pleasure when Rose was received like this, and always complained when she was away. "Two whole days have passed without a letter from you!" he told her petulantly, noting that he had written her every day. To shorten their time apart, he joined her in Baltimore for the last leg of her trip home. Her letters to him are loving, but never express a craving for his presence, as he so often does for hers.

On Graham's mind now was the war. Although the United States was still officially neutral, the Germans were enraged that American business was selling Britain and France ammunition, barbed wire, iron, steel, beef, oats, and more. By the war's end, Britain would be spending fully half its military budget in the United States, with J. P. Morgan & Co. acting as London's agent and collecting a 1 percent commission on every purchase. The firm soon started performing the same service for the French. Tsarist Russia was also a customer for American manufacturers. (Theoretically, American corporations were free to sell to Germany as well, but with that country cut off by an Allied naval blockade, doing so was virtually impossible.) Creating hundreds of thousands of jobs, the war's surge of demand provided a lucrative boost for the US economy. American banks and other bondholders extended massive loans to finance such purchases, giving themselves a big vested interest in an Allied victory. By April 1917, the Allies would owe the US $2.6 billion, equal to roughly $50 billion today.

Americans who favored the Allies and were suspicious of all things German began flooding police departments and government offices with tips about sinister people who might be German spies. Paranoid though much of this was, Germany actually did have a network of undercover agents in the United States. Rose and Graham were reminded of this one summer night in 1916 when German saboteurs blew up a huge dump of ammunition destined for Allied forces on the New Jersey side of New York Harbor. The two million pounds of explosives ignited the largest blast the country had ever seen, killing seven people, including a child blown from its crib in Jersey City. The string of explosions went on for 20 minutes as bombs and shells continued to go off. Heard as far away as Philadelphia, the blasts sent a dense plume of black smoke into the air, caused $22 million worth of damage, and shattered most of the windows in lower Manhattan, where Graham's office was. Other acts of sabotage stirred yet more patriotic anger and calls for a declaration of war, as did industrial accidents, which the Germans had nothing to do with but were blamed on them. Then two things in rapid succession pushed the country further toward war.

Up to this point, German submarine captains had carefully avoided attacking American ships, but Germany was desperate to cut off the US supply line to the Allies. In early 1917 it declared unlimited submarine warfare: any ship from any country approaching Allied ports would now be a target for German torpedoes. American freighters and their sailors began falling victim, and President Wilson severed diplomatic relations with Germany. Then a shocking piece of news surfaced. Arthur Zimmermann, the German foreign minister, sent a telegram to his country's ambassador in Mexico, asking him to try to bring that nation into the war on the German side, with "an understanding on our part that Mexico is to reconquer the lost territory in Texas, New Mexico and Arizona." The delighted British intelligence agents who intercepted and decoded the message passed it on to the US embassy in London. On March 1, 1917, the story of the telegram broke, covering front pages across the United States. The clumsy Zimmermann dug himself into an even deeper hole by freely admitting that he had sent it. Newspapers, clergymen, and politicians raged against German perfidy, while submarines sank yet more American ships and public opinion swung overwhelmingly toward war with Germany.

Long before these events had occurred, however, Graham Stokes had already moved away from the antiwar stance of most American socialists. "The United States," he wrote in early 1916, "should be much better equipped than it is to face the risks of war." As the months passed, he talked more and more about preparedness. He identified much less with his fellow socialists than with the East Coast elite he had come from, which for several years now had been the part of American society most eager to come to the defense of Britain and France. Like their class counterparts in Europe, American aristocrats tended to see war as noble and their own role as leading lesser men into battle.

Even with the US still officially neutral, for example, some 100 Princeton undergraduates had left college to volunteer for the armed forces. Of the first 1,400 volunteers for the Citizens' Military Training Corps, set up in 1915, 43 were former members of Harvard's exclusive Porcellian Club, to which Theodore Roosevelt had belonged. Many Ivy Leaguers also volunteered as ambulance drivers for the Allies. At least nine Harvard graduates alone joined the glamorous Lafayette Escadrille, a squadron of American fighter pilots in the French air force, which took its name from the French nobleman who had fought beside George Washington; later joining them would be the former captain of the Princeton football team. Among those helping to finance the squadron were business titans William K. Vanderbilt and J. P. Morgan Jr. One Harvard man, a classmate of John Reed's, joined the French Foreign Legion. "I pity the poor civilians who shall never have seen or known the things that we have seen and known," he wrote home from France in 1916 before being killed, patriotically enough, on July 4. In Graham's growing enthusiasm for the war, he was very much a man of his class.

His friend English Walling became still more fervent. Seldom able to control his temper even in less contentious times, he lost it completely with his wife Anna, who was active in several pacifist organizations and published an article in the peace-minded *Masses* after her husband had broken vituperatively with the magazine over the war. In one screaming match he told her that someday she might be hanged as a traitor; in another he threw a metal cracker box at her, bruising her foot. Soon afterward he departed on a trip to Florida, as usual leaving her at home with a house full of children. From there, as the United States drew closer to war, he raged at her in a letter, calling her pacifist stance "criminal to the last degree. Neither I nor mankind, nor the genuine idealists and revolutionaries of the world will ever forget or forgive what your kind has said and done in this great hour."

For some time, Graham had been expressing his prowar feelings in a way that Rose, still earnestly lecturing about peace, was probably unaware of. A high State Department official, Frank L. Polk, had been a fellow student of his at Yale. In 1915, always writing from his downtown office, Graham started sending Polk a stream of letters about people he suspected of being German agents. There were some of these, of course, and one of the men Graham told Polk about, a German-born banker, was regarded with suspicion by many others as well. They felt vindicated when he committed suicide.

Most of Graham's warnings to Polk, however, are the stuff of fantasy. Several were about a man who had been taking aerial photographs of New York Harbor and the Connecticut shoreline (Graham himself had bought one of Caritas Island). His partner in their photography business had traveled to Austria-Hungary to take war pictures for newspapers. The pair, Graham thought, "may very likely have been in the employ of the Austrian or German government in the making of a photographic reconnaissance." On a trip abroad, a sister of Graham's, he assured Polk, had seen the same man taking pictures of the Panama Canal. He passed on to Polk rumors of German sympathizers on Wall Street holding a banquet and raising champagne glasses to celebrate the sinking of the *Lusitania,* while relaying a steady stream of hints received from unidentified "informants" of German backing for various pacifist organizations.

As time went on, Graham grasped at almost anything he could tell Polk. He forwarded, for instance, this report thirdhand: His brother Anson had met a woman at a dinner party who "remarked that she knew a German spy who had very recently come to this country from Mexico" after having been imprisoned in the Tower of London. She, in turn, claimed to have met the spy at the house of a man she refused to identify, although she let slip that he "owns a blue Pierce-Arrow car." Such wisps of gossip were likely to be of little use to real spy hunters. Polk, in his brief, polite acknowledgments of Graham's letters, never once asked for more detail.

Where did Graham's eagerness to feel part of the war effort come from? We can only guess. It was not unreasonable to see Germany as the aggressor who started the war, but clearly for Graham there was more going on. He had few conspicuous accomplishments and a busy wife who was more at ease in the world and far more famous than he—which was definitely not the life he had expected. Furthermore, he had enjoyed serving in his school and college cadet corps and had happily gone back into uniform during the Spanish-American War. And, for many people, whether at loose ends in their lives or not, the belief that you are playing a role defending your country offers a sense of belonging and the hope of heroism.

In March 1917, as American ships continued to fall victim to German submarines, Graham and English Walling helped draft a statement they called "A Socialist protest." The signers included Leroy Scott and Charlotte Perkins Gilman, but not Rose. "To refuse to resist international crime is to be unworthy of the name socialist," the statement declared. "It is our present duty to the cause of internationalism to support our government in any sacrifice it requires."

The *New York Times* ignored the manifesto, but, reflecting Rose's greater prominence, it devoted considerable space to her own change of heart about the war, under the headline "Rose Pastor Stokes Quits the Pacifists." The story quoted five paragraphs of her letter of resignation from the Women's Peace Party, a statement much more nuanced than the one Graham had signed. "I love peace, but I am not a pacifist," she wrote. "I would serve my country, but I am not a patriot." She would, she declared, "fight or serve if called upon, and I would recognize myself to be fighting or serving, not for national glory or for those petty 'spheres of influence' [but] . . . for the perfecting of human unity."

Meanwhile, the very same month, American radicals were riveted by a stunning event thousands of miles away. "Czar Overthrown in Russia," read the banner headline in New York's *Evening World*. In that war-weary country, six million refugees had fled the advancing German and Austro-Hungarian armies, well over a million families had lost husbands, sons, or fathers to the war's carnage, and the economy was in shambles. Strikes and food riots broke out in the capital, as military units joined a widespread revolt against the regime. In a matter of days, Tsar Nicholas II was forced to abdicate. A newly formed Provisional Government placed him and his wife and children under house arrest before sending them into exile in Siberia—a dramatic end to 300 years of absolute rule by the Romanov family. Jubilant crowds trampled on flags and signs featuring the dynasty's double-headed eagle. The Provisional Government ended the death penalty, freed political prisoners, and abolished the Pale of Settlement and all other anti-Semitic measures.

A new age had dawned in the very country with which American progressives had so long been obsessed. What more proof was needed that the "masses" could make a revolution and seize power? And if the Romanovs could fall, why not tyrants and moguls everywhere? John Reed was eager to see it all and tell the story, and when he left New York to do so, he found, among the socialists and anarchists returning to Russia on his ship, more than a hundred Jews going back to the country that had once so abused them. That nation would see, he wrote optimistically in *The Masses,* "the establishment of a new human society upon the earth. . . . The cumbersome medieval tyranny that ruled Russia has vanished like smoke before the wind."

Furthermore, the Provisional Government caught the attention of people around the world by promising a Russia that would be not only a democracy, but one with something that didn't yet exist in the United States—votes for women. The "receipt of the news," the *Times* reported, produced "great rejoicing among the small group of Russian women in New York whose names have become well known here," mentioning Rose, Miriam Scott, and Anna Walling. "The revolution is one of the biggest things in history," Scott told a *Times* reporter. "We who have seen it coming feel now like shouting exultantly: 'I told you so!'" Rose raised funds to purchase printing presses to send to Russia, to turn out revolutionary propaganda, for though the new government promised reforms, Russian parties on the left wanted to go further and immediately make the transition to socialism.

While Russia remained in upheaval, on the evening of April 2, 1917, President Wilson passed cheering crowds on his way to the floodlit Capitol to call for a declaration of war. The entrance to the House of Representatives was flanked by two troops of cavalry in dress uniforms with drawn sabers. The president claimed the most noble of motives, asking a wildly applauding Congress to join the battle "for the ultimate peace of the world and for the liberation of its peoples. . . . The world must be made safe for democracy."

At last, tens of millions of Americans felt, their country would proudly and decisively take part in a great struggle between good and evil. Hearing Wilson speak, Chief Justice Edward White, who as a young man had fought for the Confederates, wept with joy. Members of Congress, waving small American flags, did not debate long before agreeing to the president's request to declare war. Emotions ran high. When, during the debate, a member of a pacifist delegation insulted Massachusetts Senator Henry Cabot Lodge, who was intent on war, the senator punched the man and a fistfight ensued. Before the New York Yankees played their season opener the following week, they marched onto the diamond in formation, holding their bats as if they were rifles.

In Washington, military policemen with fixed bayonets now guarded the White House, while soldiers were stationed on bridges across the Potomac. The army spared no effort to recruit. In New York, a young woman dressed as Paul Revere galloped down Broadway on horseback, accompanied by two cars full of trumpeters. Aircraft dropped leaflets urging men to enlist. Parades were staged all over the country. For the first time since the Civil War, the United States imposed a draft. On June 5, 1917, the day that eligible young men had to present themselves to register, nearly ten million appeared. A fervor for combat swept the land. Red, white, and blue bunting was draped on everything from skyscrapers to barns to small-town storefronts. People began singing:

> *Over there, over there,*
> *Send the word, send the word, over there*
> *That the Yanks are coming, the Yanks are coming,*
> *The drums rum-tumming everywhere.*

Eager young men crowded into dozens of new army training camps. While much-bloodied European armies were suppressing mutinies and chasing down deserters, American commanders would soon face the opposite problem: as the first troops started arriving in France, some soldiers, frustrated at being assigned to rear areas, began "deserting to the front."

Enthusiasm for battle, however, was by no means universal. Despite the parades, many Americans wanted no part of the war, and three million men failed to register for the draft. Even those who were not Wobblies would have agreed with a poem an IWW newspaper published after the declaration of war:

> *I love my flag, I do, I do,*
> *Which floats upon the breeze,*
> *I also love my arms and legs,*

And neck, and nose, and knees.
One little shell might spoil them all
Or give them such a twist,
They would be of no use to me;
I guess I won't enlist.

In the Socialist Party, Graham Stokes, English Walling, and a few other prominent figures remained stirred by Wilson's claim that this was a crusade to make the world safe for democracy. Rose somewhat hesitantly agreed. But most other party luminaries, including John Reed and Eugene Debs, did not. A strong majority of delegates attending an emergency party convention defied the militarism sweeping the country by passing a resolution calling the declaration of war "a crime against the people of the United States."

Graham and his prowar friends were incensed by this. Newly inflamed with patriotism, the volatile Walling wrote an almost hysterical magazine article, "Socialists: The Kaiser-Party," in which he decried "German-drilled voters" in its ranks and said the party should be crushed. "We must isolate it, brand it and set the rest of the nation against it." Graham, meanwhile, wrote to President Wilson, warning him against a rumored plan to appoint two prominent socialists to a government commission. Though the two "have been my personal friends for many years," he told the president, "I cannot contemplate quietly their attitude in the present emergency." Their opposition to conscription and military spending he called "well-nigh treasonable." Thousands of people wrote to the president every day, of course, but Graham assumed that Wilson might pay more attention to anything said or done by a Phelps Stokes—and events the following year would prove him right.

In July 1917, Graham and Rose left the Socialist Party. They signed their joint letter of resignation "Fraternally," and told their comrades that "we withdraw not because we have ceased to be Socialists," but because party members should now join the effort "to overcome the Prussian war machine." Graham had far more martial enthusiasm than Rose, but, with mixed feelings, on this issue she followed his lead. Moreover, as she acknowledged in a magazine piece, "it is not easy to remain seated when everybody is asking as loudly and clearly as eyes and faces can ask why *you* refuse to honor your country."

With some effort, Rose for a time convinced herself that this really was a war for democracy and that the American troops marching off to join it had, as she wrote, "a look in their eyes no army ever had before." And yet, in his campaign for mayor of New York, she remained a supporter of the strongly antiwar Socialist Morris Hillquit—one of the two men Graham had just condemned in his letter to the president. Graham endorsed another candidate.

Graham, English Walling, and a small group of like-minded friends made several attempts to organize prowar socialists, but, as historian Robert D. Reynolds Jr. has written, despite much talk and many meetings, "all they lacked were followers." In embracing the war, as when Graham had embraced socialism a decade earlier, it was largely in the company of others of his own background. "For men like Stokes and Walling," raged Emma Goldman, "to thus become the lackeys of Wall street and Washington is really too cheap and disgusting."

As time passed, Graham only waxed more militant. "The true internationalist," he wrote in November 1917, assailing pacifists, ". . . hearing a cry for help, whether from Belgium or Mesopotamia or a threatened world, stands erect in his manhood, or in her womanhood, and says, 'Here I am, send me!'" To his frustration, however, the authorities were not eager to send an inexperienced 45-year-old off to display his manhood in Belgium or Mesopotamia or anywhere else.

He tried to use his medical training to reach Europe in the Medical Reserve Corps, but in vain. Several other attempts to be sent overseas failed as well, before he finally managed to get into uniform as first sergeant of the 9th Coast Artillery Corps of the New York National Guard. Graham "began drilling a regiment in one of the New York armories," wrote a wry Upton Sinclair years later, "preparing to kill any of his former comrades who might attempt an uprising."

Someone else eager to display his manhood at the front was the perennially bellicose Theodore Roosevelt. He called the war the "Great Adventure" and trumpeted a plan to organize a volunteer division, soon expanded to several divisions. It would be led by descendants of Civil War generals from both North and South and (a bow to the memory of Lafayette) of French noblemen. The force would include cavalry as well as black soldiers under white officers, and would be equipped with arms purchased with the generosity of TR and his friends. He barraged President Wilson and other high officials with letters citing officers he promised to recruit, a list heavy on Harvard and Yale men, prep school graduates, and lawyers.

Rose, meanwhile, began having increasing doubts about her pro-war stand, feelings only exacerbated by hearing the approval of people who had no sympathy for the causes dear to her. These included Graham's sister Sarah, who, during her marriage to a Scottish viscount, had become Baroness Halkett. Of all her husband's siblings, she was, Rose felt, "the least inclined to have any fellow feeling for labor." When Rose received a friendly letter from her, she wrote in the margin, "What is the matter with my stand that Sarah can talk approvingly of it?" Another letter came from Margaret Wilson, the president's daughter. "Will I not come and dine with her and her father—at the White House?" Rose wrote. "Just a quiet, family dinner. . . . A sudden wariness fills me. The White House after all—the seat of Capitalist power! What is wrong with me that I elicit such an invitation?"

Inflamed by war fever and alarmed by Socialist gains in municipal elections and a surge in IWW agitation in the Far West, Congress passed draconian laws to suppress dissent. Paranoia against foreigners ran so high that the country's nearly 1,500 newspapers and magazines in more than 30 foreign languages were now required to submit English translations of any articles dealing with the war, the government, or the Allies before publishing them. This represented a ruinous expense, and many such publications simply shut down.

The commander of Wilson's assault on the press was his postmaster general, Albert Sidney Burleson, a former congressman and the first Texan to serve in a cabinet. He sent sweeping orders to local postmasters to "keep a close watch on unsealed matters, newspapers, etc." for anything calculated to "cause insubordination, disloyalty, mutiny . . . or otherwise embarrass or hamper the Government in conducting the war." What did "embarrass" mean? In another edict, Burleson listed a broad range of possibilities, from saying "that the Government is controlled by Wall Street or munition manufacturers, or any other special interests" to "attacking improperly our allies." Improperly? In the manner of petty tyrants everywhere, he knew that vague threats inspire the most fear and so refused to spell out such prohibitions in more detail.

Burleson had the power to bar publications from the mail, and Rose watched it wielded against people close to her. One of the first periodicals to be axed was Emma Goldman's *Mother Earth*. The authorities also seized its 10,000-name subscription list—a useful roster of other suspects to pursue. Similarly targeted was *The Masses;* one item that upset the censors was a cartoon showing the Liberty Bell crumbling. "They give you ninety days for quoting the Declaration of Independence," said editor Max Eastman, "six months for quoting the Bible, and pretty soon somebody is going to get a life sentence for quoting Woodrow Wilson." Although Eastman had been a good friend, Graham did not protest when the government shut down the magazine, nor when it went after a wide range of Socialist publications, including the *New York Call*, the daily he and Rose had long supported and that she had often written for.

Before the war was over, some 75 newspapers and magazines either had issues banned or were forced to shut down altogether. Virtually everything connected with the IWW was barred from the mail, even fund-raising appeals for the legal defense of Wobblies in jail. Because it included the word "sabotage," authorities blocked the mailing of an IWW resolution *against* sabotage. One group of radicals tried to evade the dragnet by mailing out some literature using as a return address "The Christian Singing Society," but Justice Department operatives still managed to nab the package. Burleson further harassed publications and dissenters he didn't like by seeing to it that anyone who wrote to them had their letters returned, marked "Undeliverable."

Across the country, vigilante groups sprang up with names like the Sedition Slammers and the Knights of Liberty. The largest was the American Protective League, or APL, which had the support of the Justice Department, even enjoying the franking privilege of sending mail for free. Its ranks filled with businessmen who hated unions, nativists who hated immigrants, and men too old for the military who still wanted to do battle. APL members broke up left-wing or antiwar meetings and by the tens of thousands beat up or made citizens' arrests of suspected draft evaders.

Few of the suspects the APL bagged actually turned out to be guilty of anything, but the $50 bounty the government offered for every draft dodger caught encouraged numerous Americans to join raids hunting for "slackers." President Wilson voiced his approval, telling the secretary of the Navy that the raids would "put the fear of God" into draft dodgers. The APL rapidly mushroomed to at least 250,000 members, who gathered more than a million pages of wildly unreliable surveillance data on Americans they claimed might be aiding the Germans.

For corporations, who hated the IWW above all, the war was a convenient excuse to urge prosecutors, the press, and vigilantes to go after the organization. Government agents and private detectives alike infiltrated IWW locals. In Tulsa, Oklahoma, a mob wearing hoods seized 17 Wobblies and whipped, tarred, and feathered them. On September 5, 1917, in a coordinated sweep approved by President Wilson, federal agents raided every IWW office in the country —all four dozen of them—as well as the homes of Wobbly activists. From the group's Chicago headquarters alone, the raiders took five tons of material, including some of the ashes of the martyred Wobbly songwriter Joe Hill. None of this was ever returned. More than a hundred Wobblies were arrested and brought to Chicago's Cook County Jail, many in sealed boxcars, to await trial. Among them were people Rose had worked with in efforts like the waiters' strike and the struggle of the Paterson silk workers.

The ferocity in the air extended to the very highest reaches of society. Elihu Root, for example, now a special emissary of the president, was a corporate lawyer and former secretary of war, secretary of state, and senator from New York. He was the prototype of the so-called wise men who moved smoothly back and forth between Wall Street and Washington to form the twentieth-century American foreign policy establishment. "Pro-German traitors" were threatening the war effort, Root told an audience at New York's Union League Club in August 1917. "There are men walking about the streets of this city tonight who ought to be taken out at sunrise tomorrow and shot for treason. . . . There are some newspapers published in this city every day the editors of which deserve conviction and execution for treason."

By the war's end, nearly 6,300 radicals would be arrested with warrants and uncounted thousands more without them. "There is no use making the world safe for democracy," declared Max Eastman, "if there is no democracy left." Vandals smeared excrement on letters arriving at the office of the Women's Peace Party, and across the street from the White House, a jeering mob broke into the headquarters of the Emergency Peace Federation, a coalition opposing American participation in the war, to smash chairs and desks and spatter the office with yellow paint. On the Boston Common, soldiers and civilians violently disrupted a peace demonstration, broke down the door of a nearby Socialist Party office, and tossed files, furniture, and personal belongings out the windows and then onto a bonfire.

At the Capitol, six senators had voted against the declaration of war, among them Robert "Fighting Bob" La Follette, the great Wisconsin reformer who had long crusaded against militarism, corruption, and unchecked corporate power. (Rose knew his daughter Fola, an actress, labor activist, and fellow member of Heterodoxy.) Senator La Follette, who had listened to Wilson's speech to Congress with folded arms, chewing gum, now began receiving nooses in the mail. In his home state, he was burned in effigy. Among those who called for action against senators like him was Graham's Uncle Will. "An immediate secret investigation" of treasonous antiwar legislators should be launched, he demanded. "If any are guilty, let the guilty be shot at once, without an hour's delay. We need a few public examples."

Some victims of the ferocity unleashed by the war were friends of Rose's, including Emma Goldman and Alexander Berkman, now both arrested for organizing against the draft. "It took a world war to put Goldman and Berkman where they should have been years ago," declared the *Wall Street Journal*. In court, addressing the "Gentlemen of the jury," Goldman asked, "May there not be different kinds of patriotism as there are different kinds of liberty?" Her own American patriotism, she explained, was like that of "the man who loves a woman with open eyes. He is enchanted by her beauty, yet he sees her faults." Her eloquence was ignored. The jury found her guilty, and she and Berkman were sentenced to two years in prison.

One grim act of repression had a connection to the Phelps Stokes fortune. Before he moved into other businesses, Graham's father had been a partner in the family mining corporation, Phelps, Dodge & Co. (It would remain one of the largest American mining companies into the twenty-first century.) Phelps, Dodge owned, among other holdings, a massive copper mine that spread beneath a ring of hills in the desert scrubland of Bisbee, Arizona. The war had sparked a huge demand for copper, a half ounce of which went into every rifle cartridge. Bisbee's mines ran around the clock. In late June 1917, workers organized by the IWW began a strike at the company's mine and several smaller ones nearby, demanding safer working conditions, especially underground, and wages that reflected wartime inflation and the soaring corporate profits of the copper boom.

The company's response was to help the local sheriff (a veteran of Roosevelt's Rough Riders) assemble a vigilante posse of more than 2,000 company officials, hired gunmen, and armed local businessmen. Paid by Phelps, Dodge and wearing white armbands to identify themselves, they first seized the local telegraph office to prevent any communication with the outside world. Then, at 5 a.m. on July 12, led by a car mounted with a machine gun, they swept through Bisbee, broke down doors, forced nearly 1,200 strikers and their supporters from their beds, and marched them out of town.

The Wobblies seized were held for several hours under the hot sun of a baseball field, before being forced at bayonet point into a train of two dozen freight cars and cattle cars with manure on their floors—the railroad was a Phelps, Dodge subsidiary. They were then hauled 180 miles through the broiling desert across the state line into New Mexico. Armed guards were stationed atop each car, and more armed men escorted the train in automobiles. After two days without food, the strikers were housed in an army stockade before eventually being released. Over the next few months, any who tried to return to Bisbee were promptly arrested. The organizers of the posse, wrote the *Los Angeles Times,* "have written a lesson that the whole of America would do well to copy."

Little wonder that Rose was disturbed at what military fervor was doing to the United States, and began reconsidering her stance in favor of the war. But it was something else that would do even more to hasten her change of heart—and which would open a breach between her and Graham.

One November day in 1917, pedestrians on Chicago's Dearborn Street could hear the sounds of cheering coming, mysteriously, through the barred windows of the fortress-like Cook County Jail. It was soon followed by laughter, excited talk, and then song after song, as prisoners banged their tin cups and wooden stools against floors and cell bars to provide the beat. The jail held many of the Wobblies who had been seized in the nationwide roundup of several months earlier, and news had just reached them, as it had other Americans, of a further upheaval in Russia.

Throughout the year, that country had seen increasing political turmoil, as hundreds of thousands of soldiers deserted the army to walk back to their villages. Then, on November 7, the Bolsheviks, the most militant faction in Russia's Social Democratic Party, staged a coup, seizing the reins of national power. Crowds under red and gold revolutionary banners flooded the streets of Petrograd. In short order, Bolshevik leaders announced that they were canceling all debts owed by the tsar's government, and, in an unprecedented breach of diplomatic protocol, they published previously secret treaties in which the Allied powers had agreed on the division of territory and spheres of influence in the postwar world to come. The Bolsheviks were committed to revolution at home and—unlike the

Provisional Government they overthrew—to pulling Russia swiftly out of the war.

For American war supporters, the loss of Russia as an ally was horrifying. However incompetent, the immense Russian army had kept millions of German and Austro-Hungarian troops tied down on the Eastern Front. Socialists, Wobblies, and others who opposed the war, however, were jubilant. At last the great proletarian revolution they had long hoped for had now begun. Rose was ecstatic; she was, after all, the woman who had said eight years earlier that the working class must take power by the ballot if possible but "with the bullet if necessary." And now in Russia, apparently, that had happened.

For some American leftists the fact that so many of the new Russian leaders, like Leon Trotsky and Vladimir Ilich Lenin, were intellectuals only added to their joy. Here, finally, was living evidence that you could be a writer or scholar and at the same time battle shoulder to shoulder with the working class. One of those taking part in that battle was John Reed, on the scene to report this second act of the Russian Revolution. He was with Bolshevik soldiers as they surged triumphantly through the tsar's palaces; he was at their side on battlefields and in street demonstrations; he gave speeches in English to uncomprehending factory workers; from a truck barreling around Petrograd he passed out Russian leaflets he could not read. He joined revolutionaries in looting the imperial Winter Palace, collecting a sword with a jeweled handle. He was thrilled when rebels called him *tovarich*, "comrade." A few of them had just returned from exile in New York, where he had known them, and their presence seemed proof that the spirit of revolution could leap national borders. One, for example, was the Russian-born Bill Shatoff, who had been a Wobbly organizer in Chicago and elsewhere and, as a printer, had secretly run off illegal birth control leaflets for Margaret Sanger. Back in his native land, he soon became police chief of Petrograd.

Such connections gave Reed an advantage over other journalists now arriving on the scene to cover what he called "the greatest story of my life." How could it not be, this apparent opening of the gateway into the future? Reed took notes during the day and transcribed them furiously in the evenings on his portable typewriter. "Radicals Rule Russia" was part of the double-decker headline that stretched across the front page of the *New York Call* above his story about the coup.

With Russia so distant, American progressives could imagine the revolution as whatever they wished it to be. In the federal penitentiary in Leavenworth, Kansas, a Wobbly inmate declared that "Bolshevism was but the Russian name for I. W. W." The revolution was putting an end to "the dark forces of Dollar Diplomacy," Rose told one audience. "Every lover of humanity and every fighter for liberty thrills to the name of Russia today." The photographs and newsreels of armed soldiers who had sided with the Bolsheviks marching in triumph through the snowy streets of the capital was electrifying proof that the old order was finally overturned.

The new government promptly began peace talks with Germany and Austria-Hungary in the great red-brick fortress of Brest-Litovsk, once a stronghold of the tsar's empire. The Bolshevik triumph and the new regime's move to negotiate an end to the war only increased fury against leftists and pacifists in the United States. On the streets of New York, off-duty sailors and soldiers attacked people they suspected of being Germans or socialists. In one of the city's restaurants, someone who failed to stand for "The Star-Spangled Banner" was beaten up. In Washington, for the same offense, a man was killed. Columbia University's president, Nicholas Murray Butler, harshly condemned any of his professors who did not back the war, saying that "what had been folly was now treason." As Max Eastman was giving a speech in Fargo, North Dakota, men in uniform suddenly swarmed the stage, forcing him to flee. Local friends warned him not to return to the hotel where he was staying; it, too, was surrounded by soldiers.

In the name of patriotism and protecting key arms industries, the battle against labor intensified. Black Americans had suffered thousands of lynchings over the years, and in the country's new climate of patriotic righteousness white people were lynched, too. One was Frank Little, an IWW organizer in Butte, Montana. Six masked men entered the boardinghouse where he was staying and seized the crutches he needed since breaking a leg in a car accident. They tied him, still in his underwear, to a car's rear bumper and dragged him to a railroad bridge at the edge of town, where they hanged him. A note pinned to his body read, "Others Take Notice. First and Last Warning." His crime was to have helped organize a strike two months earlier, after a fire in a Butte copper mine killed 164 miners.

In the midst of the biggest crackdown on left-wing politics that the United States had ever seen, government agents raided the Socialist Party's national headquarters in Chicago. Shortly afterward, Rose announced that she was applying to be readmitted to the party.

Graham was appalled. Gone was the Rose who had once had so much awe of her husband's superior erudition. "Stokes Will Not Follow Wife to Socialist Party" read a front-page headline in the *New York Tribune*. "Mrs. Stokes and I still have the same ideals and the same aims," he declared, "but we differ on the means of attaining them." When a reporter from the newspaper called on them at 88 Grove Street, they greeted him together in front of their living room fireplace, but she went upstairs while Graham described his political position, and he did the same while she laid out hers. Despite the blazing fire, it sounded like a chilly occasion.

For the first time in her life, Rose embarked on a campaign totally opposed to what her husband stood for. She was soon on the road, speaking out against the draft and the myth, as she told one audience, "that this war is being fought to make the world safe for democracy. It is being fought to make the world safe for capital." Some crowds hissed and booed, sometimes people walked out—unusual experiences for her—but she continued undaunted. Meanwhile, unceasing parades and rallies urged Americans to buy war bonds, and a torrent of propaganda, orchestrated by a well-funded new government body, the Committee on Public Information, filled the country's newspapers, bookstores, lecture halls, and movie screens. Theaters showed films with titles like *The Claws of the Hun* or *The Kaiser, the Beast of Berlin*. A popular poster showing a gorilla in a German helmet, carrying off a helpless woman, was emblazoned, DESTROY THIS MAD BRUTE — ENLIST.

Across America, friendships ruptured over the Russian Revolution and the war. At Heterodoxy, recalled Elizabeth Gurley Flynn, "a few super-patriots were shocked at the antiwar sentiments freely expressed at our meetings. They demanded the expulsion of Rose Pastor Stokes and myself. . . . When the club refused, they resigned." The luncheon group soon changed its gathering place with every meeting to avoid being snooped on by the Justice Department's Bureau of Investigation, the predecessor to the FBI.

Paranoia about spies and saboteurs knew no bounds. Tipsters flooded the bureau with reports about suspicious activities. Uncle Will, for instance, told a bureau agent about an opera singer who lived at his hotel, the Ansonia, flaunting jewelry said to be gifts from the kaiser and the Austro-Hungarian emperor. She had a son with a "German accent" who was "extremely secretive and mysterious in his manners." Another woman was "said to be a German Jewess," and a suspiciously pro-German man had supposedly "paid a clever New York Jew Attorney" $100,000 to get him out of an indictment.

W.E.D. Stokes seemed ready to believe any rumor that came his way and passed along one that a German had invented a substitute for gasoline. He wrote to officials throughout the government. To naval intelligence he reported that the German navy was preparing "nitrogen bombs," and so shouldn't American sailors be equipped with nitrogen masks? Above all, he warned his correspondents about the worst danger, "these socialistic Jews, who have no nationality, are only a race. . . . The most important thing you have to do for this country, is to get rid of these people." The solution was "to send them all back to the land they came from."

Finally he wrote a letter to Assistant Attorney General Charles

Warren, an influential Boston Brahmin who shared Uncle Will's hostility to immigrants and enthusiasm for eugenics, about one "socialistic Jew" in particular. "My nephew, J. Graham Stokes, the ex-Socialist leader, married Rose Pastor. He is as fine a young man as ever lived, but he is married to a woman who was born under a cloud with a grievance, and she is dangerous."

14

All My Life I Have Been
Preparing to Meet This

GRAHAM'S UNCLE WAS ONE OF thousands of Americans who flooded the Justice Department with warnings about people they considered subversive. And the Bureau of Investigation had its own large force of agents in the field, gathering information to use in prosecuting dissenters.

Anyone who questioned the war was suspect, but outspoken women were particularly despised. After all, wasn't going to war a measure of national virility? When the antiwar socialist Kate Richards O'Hare was sent to prison, for example, the indictment charged her with saying "that the women of the United States were nothing more than brood sows to raise children to get into the Army." Similarly, when in Oregon Dr. Marie Equi was put on trial for speaking out against conscription, the prosecutor declared her an "unnatural woman." Rose, too, was in the bureau's sights. In the words of one agent monitoring her, she felt "that President Wilson was a tool in the hands of capital [and] that the United States did not have the right to draft men into service and send them overseas to fight against their wishes."

Meanwhile, in Europe the rival armies along the front in France and Belgium remained locked in the brutal stalemate of trench warfare, with tens of thousands of men killed, wounded, or gassed each month. On the Eastern Front, by contrast, the new regime in Russia had stopped fighting. By failing to support the Bolshevik revolution, Rose and many others felt, the Allies were ignoring the only sign of hope in years of horrendous bloodshed.

As radical publications like *The Masses* were forced to close, there were ever-fewer places where she could publish, but she could still speak. Now, however, such talk was within the purview of the harsh new Espionage Act, passed in mid-1917, the legal centerpiece of the government's crackdown on dissent. This sweeping bill defined as a felony anything that would "cause insubordination, disloyalty, mutiny or refusal of duty in the military or naval forces of the United States." The act had little to do with espionage and was aimed at intimidating war protesters. Of the 1,500 Americans arrested under it, only 10 were charged with being German agents.

Press coverage of dissent grew sparse. So when Rose appeared before 350 members of the Women's Dining Club of Kansas City, Missouri, on the evening of March 17, 1918, following a quartet of singers, most of the club's members apparently did not realize that she had now rejoined the Socialist Party, backed the Bolsheviks, and opposed the draft. "Some of you may be disappointed in what you hear from me tonight," she began. "I doubt whether you will hear what you want to hear." She then proceeded to mock the official justification given for the war. "If America had entered the war for the ideal of democracy," she declared, "our armies would have gone to Europe [in 1914] when Belgium was ravished." The crowd soon started hissing, and a Navy lieutenant in uniform, in charge of the local recruiting office, strode out of the room with notes he had taken. Many others followed.

Rose spoke in a "lying and infamous manner against our President and our Government," H. W. Jones, a former military chaplain and member of the American Protective League, telegraphed Joseph Tumulty, Woodrow Wilson's chief of staff. "Such Kaiser agents should be stopped and interned and should not be loose." The telegram provoked an order from Washington to the Bureau of Investigation office in Kansas City: "Please cover her activities." Members of the Women's Dining Club, whose president was promptly visited by a bureau agent, began to fear that they, too, might find themselves in trouble under the Espionage Act simply for inviting her. The club issued a statement that its members "are each and all patriotic citizens and do not approve the disloyal remarks made by Mrs. Stokes."

What finally provided the government grounds to prosecute Rose was not the speech she had actually given that evening, but her habit of meticulously correcting any errors in press coverage of her. The *Kansas City Star* had garbled its description of her talk. She immediately wrote the newspaper, "I am quoted as having said: 'I believe the government of the United States should have the unqualified support of every citizen in its war aims.' I made *no* such statement and I believe *no* such thing. No government which is *for* the profiteers can be also *for* the people, and I am for the people, while the government is for the profiteers."

She continued to draw crowds on her Missouri speaking tour; despite the government's propaganda barrage, millions of Americans still doubted whether their country should join this war on the far side of the Atlantic. In Sedalia, she was barred from the county courthouse, which had been reserved for her talk, and had to address several hundred people on its steps "while federal agents mingled with the crowd," a newspaper reported. In Springfield, she was locked out of the theater where she was to speak—along with 200 people who had come to hear her. When she began talking to them on the street, the local police chief told her she could not speak about the war, because "in war times we want unity."

"As a concession to you," Rose said, ". . . I will discuss economic questions—our bread and butter problems."

"No, you have no permit. I would like to be chivalrous to a lady," said the chief.

"You can just give me my rights and never mind your courtesy," Rose replied.

After being arrested and taken away in a police car, she reported, "I had a long talk with the chief, practically made my speech to him. I gave him my views . . . he listened. He admitted that . . . strike violence is often instigated by the owners of the industry and not by the strikers." She was released on a $100 bond, which she forfeited when she left town the next day.

Bureau of Investigation agents followed her through Missouri and questioned people who had talked to her. Government stenographers transcribed her speeches. A stream of letters and telegrams reporting them flowed back to the Justice Department in Washington. After a speech at the Opera House in Willow Springs, her letter to the *Kansas City Star,* about the government being for the profiteers, caught up with her. In the lobby of her hotel, she was arrested by federal agents on suspicion of violating the Espionage Act. The penalty for those convicted could be a fine of up to $10,000 or a maximum of 20 years behind bars.

Two days before Rose's arrest in Willow Springs, the war in Europe had taken a turn that caused great fear among the Allies. On the Western Front, the Germans launched a huge and successful offensive. On its first day, a million artillery shells were fired into British and French trenches in just five hours. Small squads of newly trained "storm troopers" then darted forward and infiltrated Allied positions, taking large numbers of prisoners and pushing the jarred French and British forces into a long retreat. At last the deadlock of trench warfare was broken. Kaiser Wilhelm II's armies rolled on relentlessly. "With our backs to the wall," the British commander in chief, Field Marshal Sir Douglas Haig, told his soldiers, "and believing in the justice of our cause each one of us must fight on to the end." The American troops in their broad-brimmed hats beginning to arrive in France, it was clear, would be trying to stop a juggernaut that was overwhelming their far more experienced allies.

A continent away, Rose welcomed her arrest. She was held in the matron's quarters of the Kansas City Police Department, the *New York Times* reported, "a pleasant sitting room in the City Hall, with barred doors and windows," but "she told [the US Marshal] she wanted to be put in the worst part of the jail."

Graham had not yet heard that she had been charged under the Espionage Act, only that she had been prevented from talking in

Springfield. He telegraphed her: "Dreadfully troubled. Don't arouse masses of people against cause Social Democracy. Awful reports in papers here."

"Your message misdirected dear," Rose replied acidly. "Send it to Jingo Capitalist Press. Am under arrest."

Immediately he took the train to Kansas City, and hired a lawyer who won Rose's release from jail on $10,000 bail. "It was a bitter thing for me," she wrote a socialist comrade, that she had to depend on his money. He made his own political position clear, however, by announcing that he was spending another $10,000 to buy war bonds.

As she awaited trial, the national wave of paranoia only increased, spurred by the grim war news from Europe. Army intelligence deployed its own mushrooming network of agents against leftists and pacifists at home, using, as did the Bureau of Investigation, the new art of telephone tapping. Antiwar activists began hearing suspicious clicks and static on their phone lines. Soldiers, sailors, and vigilantes attacked and vandalized the office of the already beleaguered Socialist *New York Call*.

Two weeks after Rose's arrest, a mob in Collinsville, Illinois, seized a German-born coal miner on the baseless rumor that he was a spy—in fact, he had tried to enlist in the US Navy but been turned down because he had a glass eye. They stripped off his clothes, wrapped him in an American flag, forced him to sing "The Star-Spangled Banner," marched him to a tree outside of town, and hanged him. When 11 members of the mob went on trial, a jury deliberated for 45 minutes and voted to acquit them of all charges, while a military band played in the courthouse rotunda.

Delighted by Rose's arrest, Uncle Will continued his fusillade of letters to government officials. He assured Assistant Attorney General Warren that Rose had "in her apartment important information in connection with Bolsheviki, I. W. W. Socialistic and Anarchistic subjects." When Graham rushed off to join her in Kansas City—leaving neither of them home at 88 Grove Street—his uncle telephoned the Bureau of Investigation's New York office, which logged his call: "Agent received word from W.E.D. Stokes that . . . if a search was made of the premises some valuable information could be secured." The next day two agents reported that "we proceeded to the house was [*sic*] admitted by a colored maid [and] searched the house."

Ten days later, when the couple returned to New York, Uncle Will fired off another letter to the Justice Department saying that he had talked to both of them. Graham, he reported, "thinks she has gotten a good scare. . . . She, on the other hand seems to covet jail or anything else for the good of her cause." What the government needed to do, he insisted, was deport her: "Do you suppose . . . that she could be given a passport to go to Russia, the country from which she came, and let the matter end there?" He apparently made the same suggestion to Rose, for she later told an audience that a "certain gentleman in New York" had told her twice that if she wanted to go to Russia, a passport and safe-conduct pass could easily be arranged.

Rose and Graham went back to Kansas City for her trial under the Espionage Act, which began on May 20, 1918. To court she wore a long grey dress with a white collar; she went out of her way to appear at ease, laughing and chatting with supporters while the jury was selected. Spectators could see Graham's tall, gaunt figure loyally at her side at the defense table. He did his best to help her attorneys, finding, for instance, a quotation that seemed to prove that Rose was no more subversive than Woodrow Wilson had been before he became president. In his reformer days, Wilson had once written that "the masters of the government of the United States are the combined capitalists and manufacturers." One of Rose's lawyers introduced the words into the court record. The prosecution, however, referred to Rose as a "frenzied fanatic." What seemed to fire up both judge and prosecutors was the thrill of having a figure of national notoriety unexpectedly on trial in their city. "In my opinion," one prosecutor declared to the court, Rose was "the most vicious German propagandist in the United States of America now at large."

A group of women paraded through Kansas City singing "The Star-Spangled Banner" and demanding her conviction. A prosecutor told the jury—all male, of course—that in questioning the war, Rose was spurning her place among the legion of "strong, loyal women, like those we saw marching in the streets here the other day. Women who are loyal unto death for their country." He added, "There are women who work in factories in this city who are happy and contented; who have raised families; who are taking their part in the great economic machinery of this country without complaint. . . . But are these women attempting to foment and disturb this country at a time like this?" They were not. As further evidence of Rose's disrespect for traditional American womanhood, he cited her distribution of birth control leaflets.

Channeling the xenophobic spirit of the day, one prosecutor did not hesitate to remind the jury that Rose was an immigrant, speaking of "the venom that is in the heart of this foreign-born woman." Rose was asked, "Do you believe in patriotism as defined in Webster's Dictionary as the love and adoration for one's country?"

"I love all countries," she replied.

The outcome of the three-day trial was never in doubt. In a lengthy summary from the bench, Judge Arba S. Van Valkenburgh virtually outdid the prosecution in painting Rose as a criminal and the war as noble, warning the jury that "anything which in any sense and from any source weakens the manpower and fighting power of [an] Ally, is a blow at ourselves; and to the success of our common venture." After three hours of deliberation, she was duly convicted of attempting to cause insubordination and mutiny, obstructing enlistment and recruiting, and voicing falsehoods that would interfere with American military operations and help those of its enemies.

"Mrs. Stokes received the jury's verdict without the slightest trace of emotion," reported the *New York Times*. Indeed, she embraced her new status as a martyr. "I expect to continue my work," she declared, "and if I should be locked up it would make my efforts tremendously more effective." To a friend from Cleveland days, she wrote, "The thought of a long prison term that in my case may be a life term, does not appal me. It seems to me that all my life I have been preparing to meet this." Where did Rose's attraction to martyrdom come from? Surely one source is that she had long felt uncomfortable that friends whose politics she shared—birth con-

trol activists like Margaret Sanger, labor militants like Patrick Quinlan and Elizabeth Gurley Flynn, full-spectrum troublemakers like
Emma Goldman—had spent time behind bars, sometimes repeatedly, while she had been magically protected by her marriage to a
Phelps Stokes. Now at last it seemed she would share their fate.

An editorial in the *Times* celebrated the verdict against Rose for
showing how tough the country could be on "anti-American utterances." Other newspapers both large ("a salutary lesson"—the *Los
Angeles Times*) and small ("There can be no leniency for the seditious"—the *Norwich Bulletin* in Connecticut) agreed. From here
on, it was clear that there would be no more sympathetic press coverage of the charming onetime cigar worker who had married a millionaire.

As Rose left the courtroom, she patted Graham's shoulder. "Cheer
up," she said. Although horrified by the verdict, his response to it
was not without grace. "There is compensation in everything," he
told a Kansas City reporter. "Mine is that I think more of her than
I ever did in my life."

While Graham headed back to New York to march in a parade with
his National Guard regiment and Rose waited to hear her sentence,
the public's attention remained riveted on the war. In France, the
German offensive continued, advancing steadily closer to Paris. Yet
another terrifying new weapon made its appearance: a gigantic German artillery piece, its barrel more than a hundred feet long, which
bombarded the French capital from 70 miles away. Russia's with-
drawal from the war also meant that Germany could move more
than half a million troops across Europe to join the onslaught.
In late May, a German attack northeast of Paris pushed panicked
French forces back some 20 miles. By the hundreds of thousands,
Parisians fled the capital, baggage piled high on railway station plat-
forms. The threat that Paris itself might be captured while American
boys died in its defense made it harder than ever for peace-minded
Americans to speak out. Even the great dissenter, Eugene Debs, fell
uncharacteristically silent.

On June 1, 1918, as the German advance continued, tens of thousands of US troops were rushed to the front lines, and martial fervor in America grew still stronger. Rose Pastor Stokes was summoned back to the federal courtroom in Kansas City, where Judge Van Valkenburgh sentenced her to a prison term of ten years.

15

Waves Against a Cliff

IN THE WEEKS AFTER ROSE was sentenced, front-page headlines told of American troops in furious, bloody battles at Belleau Wood, Château-Thierry, and elsewhere in France as casualty lists spread across newspapers' inside pages. The Committee on Public Information, the US government's propaganda agency, fed the war hysteria with thousands of dire warnings about spies and saboteurs. It sent no less than 75,000 speakers to movie houses and lecture halls, produced 77 million pamphlets, mounted a traveling exhibit of captured German weaponry, and staged reenactments of trench warfare. A patriotic frenzy filled the air—and provided the excuse to continue the war at home against organized labor and dissent.

Nearly 6,000 wildcat strikes broke out in 1918. The Bureau of Investigation and armies of private detectives combined forces to infiltrate unions, deploying *agents provocateurs* who set up dummy IWW locals to produce incendiary leaflets that would offer the pretext for more arrests. Wobblies especially hated the detectives. "When a detective dies," said Big Bill Haywood, "he goes so low that he has to climb a ladder to get into Hell," after which even Satan would say, "We don't want him in here."

Haywood was one of some one hundred leading Wobblies whose trial in Chicago ran through the spring and summer. They were charged with violating the Espionage Act and an astonishingly wide potpourri of other federal laws. The government wanted to crush the organization. John Reed was there to record the ordeal of these "out-door men, hard-rock blasters, tree-fellers, wheat-binders, long-shoremen, the boys who do the strong work of the world." Fresh from covering the Russian Revolution and brimming with enthusiasm about it, he imagined the roles in the courtroom reversed: the Wobblies were a revolutionary tribunal, putting on trial the representative of "the old régime," the judge.

In jail, Haywood helped edit a newspaper for his fellow prisoners to keep their spirits up—handwritten, it was passed from one cell to the next. He arrived in court each day in his black Stetson hat. On the witness stand, he was the most eloquent of the defendants. He spoke of his dream of a day when there would be "no rich and no poor; no millionaires, and no paupers no palaces and no hovels . . . and where no man will have to work 13 hours in a smelter." Of this vision, he declared, "If that is a conspiracy, then we are conspiring."

Although the trial lasted four months, the jury took a mere 55 minutes, less than 30 seconds per defendant, to render its verdict. All the defendants were found guilty on all counts. The judge—"a wasted man with untidy white hair," Reed called him, "an emaciated face in which two burning eyes are set like jewels, parchment skin split by a crack for a mouth; the face of Andrew Jackson three years dead"—passed out sentences totaling 807 years of prison time and fines of more than $2.4 million, which of course no Wobbly had the money to pay. Haywood and the others were packed off in a special train to the federal prison at Leavenworth, Kansas. "The big game is over and we never won a hand," this onetime saloon card dealer wrote to Reed. "The other fellow had the cut, shuffle and deal all the time."

Labor militants like the Wobblies were one target of the government's crackdown, antiwar activists the other. The two categories often overlapped. Before the fighting in Europe ended, the United States would jail some 1,200 opponents of the war. Among them were hundreds of conscientious objectors to the draft who were sent to military prisons, where they were sometimes forced to stand on tiptoe for nine hours a day, wrists chained to cell bars. A dark, haunting drawing of this ordeal survives, by *Masses* cartoonist Maurice Becker, who underwent it himself.

Rose felt certain that, like Becker, Haywood, Goldman, and other friends, she would go to prison as well. Judge Van Valkenburgh for the moment allowed her to remain free on the $10,000 bond while her case was appealed. President Wilson felt her conviction was "very just" and even asked his attorney general why the editor of the *Kansas City Star* could not be prosecuted as well, for publishing Rose's letter.

Graham, meanwhile, continued struggling to balance his enthusiasm for the war with his marriage to someone facing a decade in jail for opposing it. "If the judge had known her as I do," he insisted to a reporter who appeared at 88 Grove Street and found him in his khaki National Guard uniform, ". . . he would not have felt that justice required such a sentence as he imposed. I am sure that 90 per cent of the trouble resulted from misunderstanding." Trying to protect Rose, he added something that surely must have enraged her when she read it in the newspaper the next day: "10 per cent of it was due to a hasty impulse, which Mrs. Stokes immediately regretted."

Meanwhile, from a Europe bled dry by four years of brutal fighting came reports that trade unionists and left-wing legislators in the Allied countries were pushing for a peace conference—anathema to their governments, which wanted only a German surrender. Graham and his small band of prowar socialists managed to persuade the State Department to let four members of their group travel to Britain, France, and Italy to lobby their European colleagues to abandon such peacemaking impulses.

Graham's National Guard service kept him in New York, but the delegates set off across the Atlantic, and soon he was receiving upbeat telegrams about successful meetings in London, Paris, and Bologna. "Dangerous tide pacifism turned back," said one. However, the real tide that was turned back was the all-or-nothing attack into which the German army had poured its last remaining manpower, aiming to capture Paris. The surge in martial enthusiasm that the envoys found in the Allied countries had nothing to do with their visit and everything to do with the collapse of the German offensive and the likelihood of an imminent Allied victory. Nevertheless, Graham proudly believed that his small group had played a key role in boosting Allied morale. When the delegation returned, he wrote, "President Wilson personally invited me and half a dozen of my most intimate associates . . . to meet him at the White House where he extended to us a most cordial expression of his gratitude."

The couple continued to live together at 88 Grove Street, but their political paths diverged ever more widely. In September 1918, the same month that Graham had his 40-minute audience at the White House, Rose addressed a crowd of a thousand in Detroit. The police broke up the gathering, forcing all the men to show their draft cards. She also spoke on the Boston Common and back home in New York. "When Mrs. Stokes, late, appeared on the platform," reported the *Tribune* of a rally for August Claessens, a Socialist politician in Harlem, "men and women jumped up to their feet, cheering, waving their hands and applauding. It was some minutes before Claessens could continue with his speech."

The Socialists nominated her as a candidate for the New York State Assembly, and when campaigning, she in no way restrained what she said. "Mrs. Stokes Repeats Kansas City Words," read a *Times* headline. The Bureau of Investigation man who followed her to the Lower East Side that evening reported, among other things, that most of the audience was Jewish. On another occasion, according to Agent O-99 of military intelligence, which was also on her trail, she told a Brooklyn crowd that "the time has come . . . we have to do away with Rockefeller, Morgan and all the Capitalist Forces."

With so many dissenters behind bars, Rose was one of the most outspoken still at liberty. Someone inspired by her example was Eugene Debs. Deeply depressed at seeing the dream of international working-class solidarity go up in flames, Debs continued to defend the free-speech rights of his comrades being jailed or prosecuted, but had largely fallen silent about the war itself. Rose's example spurred him into action. "During the war Mr. Debs said very little on the subject," his friend the lawyer Clarence Darrow recalled years later. "I have always felt that he would have gone through the period without accident except that Rose Pastor Stokes was indicted for opposing the war."

Two weeks after Rose's sentencing, Debs spoke in Canton, Ohio, having just visited three socialists serving time in jail for opposing the draft. Two of them had been hung by their wrists from a rafter. When Debs left the jail, he crossed the street to a park and mounted its bandstand. As one of the socialist prisoners strained to hear him through the bars of a cell window, the two government stenographers assigned to take down his words were perhaps surprised to find themselves transcribing the Declaration of Independence. A local activist read it aloud while Bureau of Investigation agents and American Protective League vigilantes arrested 55 young men in the audience who could not produce their draft cards.

Bending forward over the bandstand railing, extending his long arms toward the crowd, not removing his coat and vest despite the summer heat, Debs spoke for two hours, first praising "three of our most loyal comrades" he had just visited "over yonder" at the jail. "You who have never heard him talk don't know just what that means," John Reed wrote of Debs that summer. "It isn't erudition, fine choice of words, or well-modulated voice that makes his charm; but the intensity of his face, glowing, and the swift tumbling out of his sincere words." From the bandstand, Debs called Rose an "inspiring comrade," adding, "She had her millions of dollars. . . . She went out to render service to the cause and they sent her to the penitentiary for ten years. What has she said? Nothing more than I have said here this afternoon. I want to say that if Rose Pastor Stokes is guilty, so am I."

By the summer of 1918, something beyond the war itself outraged Rose, Debs, and hundreds of thousands of others on the American left: US troops were ordered to Russia to join an Allied attempt to suppress the Bolsheviks. In March, Russia had signed a peace treaty with Germany and Austria-Hungary, formally ending the war on the Eastern Front. By June, however, a full-scale civil war had broken out in Russia itself: on one side were the Bolsheviks and their allies, on the other a mixture of forces mostly led by former tsarist generals. One of the latter was a notorious anti-Semite who soon unleashed ruthless pogroms, massacring some 8,000 Jews in Ukraine.

Any hope that loyalists had of putting the tsar back on his throne vanished in July 1918, when Nicholas II and his entire family were executed by the Bolsheviks. Still, the White forces, as they were called, continued to fight in various places across the country's endless expanse. Britain, France, and Italy all urgently hoped to bring Russia back into the fight against Germany while preventing Bolshevism from infecting a Western Europe exhausted by war. The Allies sent thousands of troops, 5,700 Americans among them, to Russia's Arctic ports, to prevent stockpiled war supplies from falling into German hands and to support anti-Bolshevik Russian forces.

The European Allies pleaded with the United States to also aid the White forces nearer to Russia's Pacific coast. So President Wilson ordered 8,000 American soldiers onto ships headed for the port of Vladivostok. In the long run, Russia would prove simply too large and the White forces too fragmented and unpopular for them and the Allied troops backing them to defeat the Bolsheviks. But for Rose the fact that the Allied nations were part of this effort was dismaying, especially because one of her brothers, in the US Navy, was himself serving on a ship crossing the Pacific to carry American soldiers to Vladivostok.

To Americans on the political right, the Allied intervention conjured up rosy visions of imperial Russia restored. Uncle Will, for example, already had a candidate he wanted Washington to endorse as the country's new leader: "my friend, the Grand Duke Nicholas, the former successful Commander of the Russian Army, who is getting ready for action," he wrote to Assistant Attorney General Charles Warren. Russian soldiers would have laughed to hear Nicholas called successful. With no battlefield experience whatever, he had been appointed Russian commander in chief in 1914 because he was the tsar's cousin. After his armies suffered catastrophic losses, he was eased out of the post a year later. Regardless, W.E.D. Stokes assured Secretary of State Robert Lansing that Nicholas was the man for the job, and that Stokes was in a position to know because "I was in the same house party with him in Russia, and sat next to him at the table, and I heard him denounce Germany and the intrigues of Germany almost daily." Despite Stokes's assertion that "he impressed me more than any man I met in Russia," the grand duke never received American backing and would end his days, a decade later, in exile on the French Riviera.

Two weeks after his speech from the Canton, Ohio, bandstand, Debs was arrested and charged with ten counts of sedition. Sixty-two years old and in ill health, he was promptly put on trial. The very look of the courtroom in Cleveland's Federal Building, where his fate was to be decided, seemed to promise a grim outcome. "The judge sat high up behind a desk as long as a drygoods counter," wrote Max Eastman, who covered the trial, "and behind and above him the full width of the wall was filled with a splendorous painting. It was a painting of angels with beautiful bodies and stern faces and swords of flame, guarding the tablets of stone upon which were inscribed the Ten Commandments." The judge was a former law partner of the current secretary of war.

Rose was there to support her friend. "I can bear it for myself," she wrote to Olive Dargan, "but my heart breaks when I think of him — in prison — at his age!" Debs's attorney concluded his opening statement by saying, "We ask you to judge Eugene V. Debs by his life, his deeds and his works. If you will do that we shall abide by your verdict." When a burst of applause came from Debs's supporters, the judge exploded in fury, telling the bailiffs, "Arrest everybody you saw clapping their hands!" Rose was one of those seized, and ended up standing before the judge, according to the *New York Times,* "with bowed head and with an air which said as plainly as words: 'In trouble again.'" She and three others, considered the ringleaders of the disturbance, were fined $25 apiece.

The trial was swift, since Debs did not contest the prosecution's account of his speech. Standing as tall as ever but looking somewhat emaciated, he made a statement to the jury about his beliefs, fortified with references to the Founding Fathers and the abolitionists, which left several jury members in tears. The judge, however, denied him permission to talk about wartime "profiteering." Rose sat through the trial each day, dressed in subdued black, white, and grey, taking copious notes, and going to lunch with Debs, his legal team, and other socialist comrades.

The prosecutor pointedly recalled Debs's statement that "if Rose Pastor Stokes is guilty, so am I," and reminded the jury that she had been sentenced to ten years. They retired to deliberate for more than five hours as rain fell outside the courtroom windows. Debs's supporters remained in their seats in the courtroom until a bailiff announced that the jury would return to deliver its verdict. At that moment, Rose left the spectators' seats and went to Debs's side. "She drew her chair beside his," the *New York Tribune* reported, "and into her hands he slipped his own gaunt fingers."

Debs was found guilty of attempting to incite military insubordination, obstruct recruiting, and promote the cause of the enemy. After a day's break, the judge allowed him to make a statement before he was sentenced. It was then that he gave the speech of which journalist Heywood Broun wrote, "If anybody told me that tongues of fire danced upon his shoulders as he spoke, I would believe it." Its most famous passage goes: "Your Honor, years ago I recognized my kinship with all living beings, and I made up my mind that I was not one bit better than the meanest of the earth. I said then, I say now, that while there is a lower class, I am in it; while there is a criminal element, I am of it; while there is a soul in prison, I am not free."

Debs's words did not move the judge. Spectators gasped as he pronounced sentence on the four-time candidate for president: a fine of $10,000 and ten years in prison.

On the very day Debs was convicted, Graham told the *Times* that the Socialist Party was "not even 1 per cent loyal either to this country or to the American people's ideals of democracy." Nor, he continued, "have the working people of America ever had an abler or truer leader" than President Wilson. The rest of his family was supporting the war effort. His mother loaned part of her Madison Avenue mansion to YMCA volunteers working with the troops, his brother Anson spent several months in Europe setting up educational programs for the US Army, and his brother Harold was an artillery officer at the front.

Still, both Rose and Graham seemed to assume that their marriage would go on, even if they would no longer be entertaining labor and socialist leaders at their island home. That home, in fact, would be no more, Rose wrote a friend. "Caritas Island has been sold. . . . We have had great joy of the dear island and it is well that others enjoy it now. Graham and I are planning to build a little house in a sweet woods that we have back on the mainland a little way—just as if I were really going to live in it. Graham won[']t believe that I will ever go to prison, so I humor him—and plan everything as if I were not."

The First World War ended, with peace terms dictated by the triumphant Allies, on November 11, 1918. Although ticker-tape parades greeted the news, it remained a grim season. A worldwide influenza pandemic, its spread accelerated by the great troop movements of the war, was taking a staggering toll. Many faces on the streets of New York, as in other American cities, were covered with white gauze masks. Rose continued to live in limbo, as her case remained on appeal. "Darling—Rose—sister," Dargan wrote her, "—it has come over me like a thunderclap . . . the realization that you may be shut out from the world of sun and green things—and I cannot bear it."

The verdict against Debs was also appealed, but was upheld by the Supreme Court, and he was ordered to federal prison. Rose's similar sentence, however, was taking far longer to wind its way through the system. Was the government reluctant to turn a woman —or a Stokes—into a martyr? Possibly, for soon after her sentencing she had told one correspondent that she "had had intimations from Washington that all would be well" if she said no more about the war. But, she added, "I will not buy my freedom by paying with silence."

Women would not have the right to vote in federal elections until 1920, but New York State had recently granted them suffrage, so Rose registered to vote in the November 1918 state elections, in which she was running as a candidate for the legislature. Early one morning soon after, police raided 88 Grove Street and arrested her. She had violated the law, they claimed, because felons were not eligible to vote. Though the charge was soon dismissed, it was a pointed reminder that in the eyes of the authorities she was a convicted criminal.

When the war ended in Europe, Rose was 39. In photos she looks somber, no longer like the radiant bride of 13 years earlier. Nor could the novelty of her marriage still win her a sympathetic hearing from audiences like suburban women's clubs. In the minds of the overwhelming majority of Americans, the socialism she so passionately believed in was now associated with the revolution in Russia. That cataclysm had already seen the murder of the tsar, the tsarina, and all their photogenic children, the girls in white dresses and the boy in a sailor suit. In addition, by pulling Russia out of the war, the revolution had deprived the Allies of an army several million strong, making the job of American fighting men in France much harder. Even after the war was over, those resentments remained. When she tried to give a speech in Yonkers, New York, Rose's words were drowned out by a choir led by an Episcopal minister and singing "The Star-Spangled Banner." The mail brought her a flood of invective. "The inbreeding of centuries of hate, treachery, ingratitude, rebellion and mental and physical filth have crystallized into your distorted though clever mind," said a typical letter. ". . . We Americans will not rest until your whole nest of vipers is exterminated, by either prison terms, deportation or worse."

Yet Rose seemed almost to welcome the prospect of prison. "No great liberative movement," she told Anna Walling in a revealing letter, "can succeed without a great deal of suffering and sacrifice. . . . Ten years is a long time, at my time of life. I shall come out an old woman." She went on to describe how, in going through some old papers, she had come upon "a *dream* that I had years ago . . . and it struck me with new, strange significance. I must copy it here for you.

"I dreamed God turned me into stone and set me far out, into a wild sea. A high cliff I was, against which the waves beat with a fierce, lashing fury. . . . Then strangely through my agony there stole a sense of power and of glory: I could not fight back, true; I could not fight back. But I was a *cliff*—an immovable cliff against which the sea hurled itself in vain.—Oh God! make me to be that high cliff!"

She continued: "That dream strikes me with new force today, as almost something prophetic of these days. Much like the sensation I felt in that strange dream was present in me all through the trial, and during the morning upon which sentence was pronounced. I did not shed one tear for myself, or have an extra heart beat. . . . I felt all the immovable power of the organized proletariat of the world in me. These courts and those governments of the master-class were hurling their power against me but I was a cliff—an immovable cliff. God *had* made me to be that cliff!"

16

The Springtime of Revolution?

WAS ROSE'S HAUNTING DREAM ONE of resistance? Or of martyrdom? In public statements, too, as she continued to wait for a decision on the appeal of her case, she seemed to welcome the prospect of those ten years behind bars. "Here we are, gentlemen; you can jail us," she defiantly told a meeting in New York, as an undercover agent in the audience took down her words. "We are not afraid of jails."

For what cause would she be a martyr? Her prison sentence had been for opposing the First World War. With a century's hindsight, we can certainly admire those like her who protested it. The war remade Europe for the worse in every conceivable way, killing more than nine million soldiers, wounding another 21 million, and also leaving millions of civilians dead. It left a continent of bereaved families, maimed men, and what Winston Churchill called "a crippled, broken world."

Smoldering in its wake, in defeated Germany, was a sullen resentment and search for scapegoats that would soon lead directly to an even more destructive war and the Holocaust as well. Rose and the others who opposed America's entering the war were right to suspect that among their government's motives was fear that the country's banks might lose their loans to the Allies, and its corporations their wartime profits. Only later would it be revealed that in early

1917, Woodrow Wilson's ambassador to London had telegraphed the secretary of state, "Perhaps our going to war is the only way in which our present preeminent trade position can be maintained and a panic averted." Indeed, after the war was over, the president himself abandoned his rhetoric about making the world safe for democracy, asking, in 1919, "Is there any child who does not know that the seed of war in the modern world is industrial and commercial rivalry? . . . This war was a commercial and industrial war. It was not a political war."

After the armistice of November 11, 1918, however, there was no more war to resist. Rose's great cause now was the Russian Revolution. At this moment in history, among Americans she was not alone. "One cannot overemphasize the utopian, democratic image that surrounded bolshevism in its first months in power," writes the historian John Patrick Diggins. "The image of a 'people's democracy' . . . enraptured the entire spectrum of the American Left: anarchists, syndicalists, revolutionary socialists, democratic socialists, and even a number of pacifists, social reformers, and liberal intellectuals."

Many were people Rose knew and had worked with, like John Reed, who after returning from Russia published his epic eyewitness account of the Bolshevik seizure of power, *Ten Days That Shook the World*. It was filled with the boom of cannons, heroic street battles, all-night meetings, bold proclamations, and rough-clad workers and peasants taking over the elegant mansions of the aristocracy. Reed called the book "a slice of intensified history—history as I saw it." But it was not just history; it was a template for how to make a revolution, and proof that it could be done. Reed's prose made those Russians in their high, round fur hats seem close to America. He described how 30,000 coal miners organizing in Kharkov adopted the preamble to the IWW constitution: "The working class and the employing class have nothing in common," how an agitator addressing a vast throng had "spectacles and hair drawn flatly down," which gave her "the air of a New England school-teacher," and how everyone seemed aware of the struggle in the United States.

In a truck full of armed men heading off to do battle with counterrevolutionaries, a burly soldier shouted questions at Reed over the roar of the engine: What about internationalizing the Panama Canal? What's happening to the imprisoned California labor leader Tom Mooney? And "are the American workers ready to throw over the capitalists?" When Reed returned to Russia after his book's publication, it would not just be as a journalist but as a participant in the movement he was certain would sweep across the globe. Debs and Haywood devoured his book with admiration in their respective prison cells.

Someone else who read *Ten Days That Shook the World* in prison was Emma Goldman. "John Reed's story, engrossingly thrilling, helped me to forget my surroundings. I ceased to be a captive in the Missouri penitentiary and I felt myself transferred to Russia, caught by her fierce storm, swept along by its momentum, and identified with the forces that had brought about the miraculous change . . . a social earthquake whose tremors were shaking the entire world."

Many others felt the same way. Max Eastman, Reed's editor at the now-shuttered *Masses,* wrote a poem in praise of Lenin, the Bolshevik leader. On returning from a trip to Russia, the venerable muckraker Lincoln Steffens, another member of the Stokeses' former Greenwich Village community, famously declared, "I have been over into the future, and it works." Like so many American radicals, he was eager to see the new Soviet regime as an inspiring alternative to a world that had so recently sent millions of young men to senseless deaths.

Rose became national secretary of the Women's Division of the Friends of Soviet Russia, which agitated on behalf of the new government and raised funds for famine relief. Along with Reed, she joined a faction of left-wing Socialists, one of several American groups that, after a confusing period of doctrinal feuding and name changes, eventually merged into what would become the Communist Party. Rose served on its executive committee. According to a neighbor who informed on her to the Bureau of Investigation, she assured a group of lunch guests in 1919 "that the Bolsheviki would have complete control of the whole world, within a period of five years." In a speech that year, she declared, "It won't be long. I repeat —it won't be long."

Graham, on the other hand, wrote an angry diatribe for the *Times* against the "propaganda" of John Reed and others. He urged the United States to support White Russian leader Alexander Kolchak, who was still holding out in Siberia against the Reds. A lifelong military man, Kolchak promoted himself to admiral, crushed trade unions, and ordered thousands of executions. Graham felt, however, that the admiral was the best prospect "to establish Democracy on an enduring basis in that unhappy land."

Despite retaining his youthful love of all things military, Graham was surely frustrated that he would never receive the delirious hero's welcome that greeted shiploads of victorious American soldiers returning from Europe. He compensated for this by doing all he could to build up his credentials in the National Guard, where he had now been promoted to captain. Like Rose, he had not lost a desire to feel he was making history. He asserted, for example, that the messages about suspected German espionage he had sent his State Department friend Frank Polk during the war had been of crucial importance. "I was actively engaged in confidential work for the Government of the United States, and incidentally for the State of New York," he wrote, applying for membership in a veterans' group, "that work being of a character that in the opinion of the Secret Service agents of this country immediately familiar with it involved much risk of life." The reference to New York had to do with his National Guard unit patrolling an aqueduct, on watch for possible German sabotage, but "much risk of life" must have raised the eyebrow of any reader.

In the same letter he claimed that he had identified to Polk "the probable head of the German Secret Service in this country." He wrote a similarly self-promoting seven-page, single-spaced memo to National Guard authorities, titled "Unofficial War Activities of Captain J. G. Phelps Stokes, CA-ORC." There, he listed all the information he had passed on about supposed German spies and German backing for pacifist groups, as well as every acknowledgment

Polk had sent him, and added a lengthy description of dispatching the small group of prowar socialists to Europe in the summer of 1918. His lobbying finally won him a medal, the Military Cross of the State of New York.

Looking back at the radicals of the early twentieth century, it can feel easy, too easy perhaps, to dismiss them as naïve in thinking that the capitalist order in America could be overthrown. If there ever was a time when that seemed possible, it was 1919, a year the novelist John Dos Passos called "the springtime of revolution." There was plenty of evidence to confirm Rose's belief that the world was in upheaval. After all, Communist governments briefly held power in Hungary and parts of Germany. Ireland and Egypt were in revolt against the British. Colonial rule was shaken by new protests in India. "We are running a race with Bolshevism and the world is on fire," a worried Woodrow Wilson told his physician, as general strikes began shaking cities in Europe and both North and South America. "Margaret, all my dreams are coming true," Big Bill Haywood wrote from his prison cell at Leavenworth to Margaret Sanger. "My work is being fulfilled, millions of workers are seeing the light."

In the United States, jobless war veterans staged protests, and millions of men and women — from garbagemen, streetcar conductors, and airmail pilots to telephone operators, blacksmiths, printers, and longshoremen — joined the largest strike wave in American history. By the end of 1919, four million people, one in five American workers, had gone on strike — 3,600 walkouts that even included stage actors. Army tanks were on the streets in Cleveland, and Gary, Indiana, was placed under martial law. Around the country, troops were called out to restore order.

In Boston the police — a traditional enemy of labor — walked out, too. They were overwhelmingly Irish Catholic, although that did not stop the *New York Tribune* from condemning this "outbreak of Bolshevism." Industry redoubled its use of private detectives; the three biggest firms now employed 135,000 agents. ("Heavy, brutish-faced men," as John Reed described them, "built like minotaurs, whose hips bulged and whose little eyes . . . mingled ferocity and servility, like a bulldog's.") A mail bomb plot was discovered—36 packages addressed to prominent politicians, judges, and businessmen, all set to explode on May Day, 1919. Although all but one were safely defused, a dozen or so additional bombs went off in the following weeks, one killing a night watchman at a judge's house and another severely damaging the home of Attorney General A. Mitchell Palmer. The bombings were almost certainly all the work of a small band of Italian American anarchists (one of whom accidentally blew himself up at Palmer's house), but the government was determined to blame them on Bolsheviks. Palmer, his eye on the Democratic nomination for president, warned that May Day of 1920 would be the occasion for a full-scale attempt at revolution.

One major tool for suppressing labor unrest was the National Guard, units of which had been mobilized for just that purpose more than a hundred times in the preceding 40 years. From Washington, the War Department ordered Guard commanders to redouble their efforts to bring their units up to full strength, urging "all employers" and "prominent men" to aid this effort. But enlisting the right recruits was a tricky business, according to several internal memos by a captain who directed such efforts for one New York National Guard unit. With so many Bolsheviks and other radicals about, he wrote, the unit "must exercise unusual care lest ill-disposed persons enlist in the Regiment for the purpose of wrecking its armory."

Just who such "ill-disposed persons" might be, the writer didn't need to spell out. It was obvious to any military man what categories of recruits were potentially treacherous: Jewish (socialists or Communists), Italian (anarchists), Irish (anti-British rebels), or black (unthinkable). For convenience in such matters as recruiting and keeping order, the army's Military Intelligence Division created an "Ethnic Map of New York," with various areas of the city shaded different colors according to the dangerous categories of people living in them: red for Russian Jews, brown for Italians, green for Irish, black for "Negro."

How, then, could a National Guard unit fill its ranks while avoiding such risks? The same captain proudly described a successful method. A large truck would head out in the evening, carrying an officer, a sergeant, two drummers, two buglers, and "about fifteen enlisted men who have shown their ability as 'good mixers' in a crowd." The truck would park, the drums and bugles would attract an audience, and the officer and sergeant would give speeches. While one spoke, "the other is studying the faces of men in the crowd, looking for likely candidates." When one was spotted, an enlisted man would buttonhole him, give him a leaflet, and talk up the regiment (whose attractions included a gym, basketball court, and two tennis courts). "About two hundred and fifty recruits of fair grade have been secured by this method within the past two months."

The author of these memos, of course, was Graham, whose National Guard unit was charged with protecting lower Manhattan. Not surprisingly, many of his fellow officers, ready to defend Wall Street against all enemies, were, as Graham put it, "men of responsibility in the business world." Known as the Blue-Blood Regiment, the unit was filled with the sons of old, wealthy New York families, with names like Rhinelander, Tillinghast, and Delafield. Graham was comfortable among them, and the military increasingly became for him a kind of focus that in recent years his life had lacked.

In 1920, with the country still in ferment and President Wilson crippled by a stroke, the Socialist Party nominated as its candidate for president Convict #9653 in Atlanta's federal penitentiary. Although Eugene Debs could campaign only from his cell, he received some 915,000 votes. Throughout his imprisonment, Rose tried to keep his spirits up with letters. "I'm with you all the time," he wrote her back.

Debs so trusted Rose that he told her the great secret he had shared only with his brother and a few close friends: the woman he really loved was not his prim, reserved wife, Kate, who sometimes showed more interest in jewelry than socialism, but Mabel Curry, a warm and spirited suffragist who lived near him in Terre Haute, Indiana. Unlike Kate, Curry laughed easily and not only shared his passion for social justice but lectured on such themes herself. Before he went to prison, every time he embarked on a trip and his train passed a street near her house, they had waved a furtive farewell. Both were agonized, however, at the thought of leaving their respective mates, in an age when divorce was rare and considered shameful.

Debs introduced her by mail to Rose, and Curry was grateful for Rose's letters, and "to hear your words of understanding of my great and beautiful lover." Debs feared that his years behind bars would be a severe hardship for Mabel, and they were. She opened her heart to Rose, explaining the code words she and Debs used in their letters (which they knew would be read by wardens), and her fears about his health and loss of weight in prison. She told Rose of the gap between her conventional marriage of 26 years to "a fine kind man" and her great love for Debs "that gave all and took all," and she confessed what a strain it was to keep that secret. "I am trying hard to be of good cheer for his sake but I am really shot to pieces." Of their shared ideals, she added, "I thank God that for some reason known to him, I have been permitted to play a part in the life of this man." For Rose, seeing the depth of their feelings must have summoned up the days when she and Graham once felt so closely bound by their shared dream of reshaping the world.

Although the war was long over, repression went on. The US Post Office still barred various radical newspapers and magazines from the mails. Federal agents, local police, and American Protective League vigilantes continued to attend Rose's speeches. Thirty-two states outlawed red flags, and jailed more than 1,300 people for displaying them. Foreign-born leftists were deported. Big Bill Haywood, after nearly two years behind bars, was temporarily freed on bond, but was ill with diabetes and facing 20 years in prison if he lost his case on appeal. Then he was slapped with additional charges by the government. In disguise and with a false passport, he fled to an unhappy exile in Russia, where his death at the age of 59 would be hastened by alcohol. As his ship left New York Harbor, he claimed, he told the Statue of Liberty, "Good-bye, you've had your back turned on me too long."

Local police and federal agents deployed by Attorney General Palmer carried out what became known as the Palmer Raids. Over a two-month period they seized thousands of men and women, often without arrest warrants, in more than 30 cities, sometimes administering gratuitous beatings or throwing their victims down staircases. By the end of the largest raid, in more than 30 towns and cities on January 2, 1920, an estimated 10,000 people had been arrested. Several hundred men in chains were marched through the streets of Boston on their way to a temporary prison on an island in the city's harbor. Another 800 were held for six days in the windowless corridor of a federal building in Detroit, with no bedding and the use of just one toilet and sink. After one raid on a Russian community center near New York's Union Square, the office looked "as if a bomb had exploded in each room," the *World* reported. "Desks were broken open, doors smashed, furniture overturned and broken, books and literature scattered, the glass doors of a cabinet broken, typewriters had apparently been thrown on the floor and stamped on." And there were "bloodstains over floor papers, literature &c." The mayhem came closer to Rose when one raid's target was the office of her group of left-wing Socialists.

In March 1920, more than a year after the war ended, the US Court of Appeals in St. Louis finally ruled on her conviction. A panel of judges declared that the evidence against her was convincing, but found fault with Judge Van Valkenburgh's instructions to the jury and remanded the case back to the lower court. For the government, this meant that convicting Rose would require a new trial. The attorney general asked President Wilson whether to proceed. "I believe that Mrs. Stokes is one of the dangerous influences of the country," the president answered, but said he did not want to prosecute. "I think the country feels that the time for that is past." Late the next year, the case was at last officially dismissed and Rose's bail money returned.

So, unlike Debs, she would not be imprisoned for her wartime dissent. She was indicted again in 1920, this time for sedition, as part of a Communist conspiracy in Illinois. The state extradited her from New York, taking her by train to Chicago under guard by a female detective. But again she was not convicted. Nor would she suffer martyrdom the following year when American Legion members surrounded a Connecticut hall, preventing her from going inside to speak. The police took her into custody. When she demanded to be charged with something, however, they merely let her go. To Rose's frustration, no one seemed willing to send a Stokes to jail.

The Russian civil war continued for several years as the new regime asserted its control over the tsar's former empire. Disrupting food supplies, the bitter combat led to famine and an ultimate military and civilian death toll estimated at eight million or more. The Union of Soviet Socialist Republics, as it would be known from 1922 onward, had truly been born in blood.

But what, exactly, had been born? Soon after the Bolsheviks had seized power, Russia held the nearest thing to a democratic election the country had ever seen—but the Bolsheviks won a mere quarter of the vote. They allowed the new national legislature to convene for only a single day before soldiers with fixed bayonets occupied the meeting hall and ordered everyone out. In the minds of many foreign supporters, such suppression of dissenting views seemed necessary, given the life-and-death struggle under way to preserve the revolution.

The crushing of all opposition, however, continued after the civil war was won. All non-Bolshevik political parties were banned and newspapers and magazines supporting them shut down. A secret police force arrested or executed anyone accused of being a counter-revolutionary. During just these first few years, the death toll from such killings mounted into the tens, possibly hundreds, of thousands. In the decades to come, it would soar into the millions.

Still, some Western leftists remained enthusiasts, among them John Reed, whose young life was cut short by typhus in Russia in 1920. He was buried in a place of honor beside the Kremlin wall. Any doubts that some claim he was developing about Russia's direction died with him. Others, though, saw the shape of what was to come with striking clarity.

After her release from prison, Emma Goldman had been deported to Russia on a decrepit former troopship along with 248 other foreign-born leftists and their guards. (Looking down from the deck, she reportedly thumbed her nose at a young Justice Department official named J. Edgar Hoover, watching to make sure the ship left New York Harbor.) She arrived in Russia in early 1920 with great optimism about the revolutionary mecca: "My heart trembled with anticipation and fervent hope." But the nearly two years she spent traveling widely there left her bitterly disillusioned. Censorship was pervasive, and independent labor unions were being crushed. Her fellow anarchists, she found, had to meet in secret and were being arrested or executed without trial. As determined and forthright as ever, she protested vigorously, in person, to Lenin himself. But he told her that "free speech is a *bourgeois* prejudice, a soothing plaster for social ills." Russia "was igniting world revolution, and here I was lamenting over a little blood-letting." As gunshots that might be executions sounded through the night, she began to feel, she wrote, a "stranger in a strange land."

For Goldman, as for many others, a revolt in early 1921 by sailors at the Kronstadt naval base, on an island off Petrograd, would prove a decisive turning point. The rebel sailors demanded the release of political prisoners, freedom of speech, an end to the budding dictatorship, and a freely elected legislature. To suppress the uprising, at the cost of thousands of lives, Bolshevik troops stormed across the sea ice at night, camouflaged against the snow in white sheets. From her hotel room window in Petrograd, Goldman heard ten days and nights of artillery fire putting down the revolt, and saw groups of rebel sympathizers being led into custody. Deeply disheartened, she left Russia for good later that year.

An increasing number of other American radicals began having similar second thoughts. Rose, however, was not among them. She remained an unquestioning believer. Soviet Russia, she felt, was a true workers' state, and all other countries were fated to soon have their own revolutions. A similar rigidity was apparent in how she now saw America. In a letter to Upton Sinclair, for example, she complained of how, in one of his books, he appealed to "the public." There is no public, she said, only workers and capitalists.

Rose's dogmatism was a marked departure from the democratic spirit of the Socialist Party and its commitment to open debate and electoral politics. Something in her was clearly drawn to the idea that a revolutionary elite knew just how history was going to unfold, and that others must simply follow that lead. Years before the Bolsheviks took power, a passage in her diary seems revealing. While rallying striking garment workers in 1913, she had written, "The people are ready to rise in one great body against oppression. *But* they are still blind, blind! Only one in a 100 has some inkling of whither we are heading, and but one in many thousands has any notion of . . . *the* way. The hour has not yet come. The people have much, an infinite amount, to learn, before any permanent change can come."

Her faith in a select group of people who know "*the* way" brings to mind someone else who believed in an elite: Graham. After all, it was he who had once been convinced that the socialist movement had "appealed altogether too much to relatively inefficient and unpractical people," and that it needed "men and women of initiative, efficiency and power." Now, years later, during the very week of the Kronstadt revolt, Rose wrote this to a friend on the subject of the Soviets imprisoning dissidents: "If it is necessary to save the revolution, it must be done. I myself would want to be put in jail under such circumstances." If, she said, she ever became "a meddlesome person in a time of revolution . . . then I trust I shall get safely tucked away in some nice double-locked cell until the danger from my muddled, obstinate self is over."

For his part, Eugene Debs was dismayed by such repression. Although he still had hopes that the infant Soviet Union might change, he was an instinctive democrat and bristled at the authoritarian ways of what he called the "Vatican in Moscow." He was finally released from prison in 1921 when President Warren Harding commuted his sentence. An impatient Rose paid him a visit at his home in Indiana the next year to argue that he should be fully supportive of the Soviets. Shortly afterward, though, Debs telegraphed Lenin asking for clemency for 22 dissidents on trial for treason. Rose now had no tolerance for such "backsliding," as she called it. "He is not a proletarian revolutionist—something he succeeded for many years in making a great many workers believe he was," she wrote a friend. "For this reason, I am sorry for Debs, just as I am sorry for other men in recent political history, who turned away from the light."

To Rose's mind, someone who had "turned away from the light" even more decisively was Emma Goldman. Exiled from the United States and now living in Europe, she laid out her grim assessment of the Soviet regime in a book whose title alone enraged true believers, *My Disillusionment in Russia*. Her old friend, Rose told a public meeting in New York, should be burned in effigy.

The increasing tension between Rose and Graham was exacerbated by something Graham revealed in a letter to a cousin of his in 1921. A senior Justice Department official, he wrote, had passed on from a "secret agent" the names of "persons present at a certain secret conference of extra-fanatical Bolshevists, in this city, in which my death was planned, and at which one of the group (whose name was given me) promised, personally, to kill me. The names of his intimate associates were also given me in order that I might be on the lookout for them all." Graham did not give the names, and there is no way to know if all of this was true, for Bureau of Investigation agents often inflated their own standing by exaggerating the malevolence of the people they were watching. But Graham clearly believed the report, and it could not have made him feel any better about Rose's politics.

The strain between the couple was now visible to everyone. Years later, the left-wing writer Samuel Ornitz told Rose his memories of visiting them during this period, to discuss a Communist statement Rose and several friends were working on. "I recall a bright wintry Sunday afternoon, dining in your Grove street house," he wrote, "my wife and little son with me." At lunchtime, "Graham came down: lean, long[,] cadaverous, spectre of Capitalism, lugubrious, laconic . . . but he came to life in defense of his property, his skeleton bones clattering, his cry like a death rattle because my little boy, Arthur, lost his balance on his spindly New England chair, and his hearty young legs (he was a little over two then), lifted the table from its foundation threatening the delicate china and silver."

Later that afternoon, Ornitz recalled, he took his son for a walk.

"We walked north and when we were near 14th Street my child was attracted by the music of a brass band, playing military music." What they found was "a parade of National Guardsmen, and they were filing out of the Armory on Fourteenth near Sixth Avenue, I think, and we watched and there I saw Graham . . . drilling the guardsmen, now that war was over, to fight the revolution of the masses: while his wife was at home refining the appeal to revolution!!!"

Rose never ceased making all the proper polite gestures toward the Stokes family. She sent Graham's mother, for instance, a basket of fruit as a going-away present before an ocean cruise. But the tension with him only increased. To Graham's frustration, Rose was frequently away—speaking, attending Communist meetings, or visiting Olive Dargan, now widowed and living in North Carolina. The visits to Dargan were sometimes for several months at a time. The letters he wrote her when she was on these trips were filled with references to expenses she had incurred or small sums he was grudgingly sending her. In 1921, he told her he wanted to sell the small lot they still owned in Connecticut, where she had dreamed of building "a little house in a sweet woods." About the sale, he wrote her, "I am going to ask you to let me do it and apply the proceeds towards liquidation of your legal expenses which have amounted to date to $5633.85."

Graham was now moving into a wholly different world from Rose, having received "a wonderful invitation," as he told her, to travel "as a guest of the Navy" on the presidential yacht, the *Mayflower,* from Washington to Jamestown, Virginia. In another letter he described exuberantly how he had "had the great privilege" of meeting General John J. Pershing, the former American commander in chief in Europe, at a banquet given by a British-American friendship society. If there were any women present, he did not mention them. Instead he spoke of how the guests included "so many splendid men—men who are men all through, in body, brains, heart and high ideals. . . . There is an idealism among many of the brilliant men of the nation that is very splendid and noble and fine." Ignoring Rose's politics, he added, "But of course you understand this too."

Graham remained upset that, when in New York, Rose continued to receive at their house people he called "ingrate enemies of America," especially a Communist labor organizer and writer, Jeanette Pearl, whom he particularly loathed. "Your disregard of my feelings in this matter is so outrageous." He even threatened to fire their maid, Anna Webb, if she again allowed Pearl into the house: "I have notified Anna that unless she can succeed in keeping that woman out she . . . will have to leave my employ. If Anna goes I shall get someone to tend the door who has more regard for my feelings than my wife has shown. It has been a great imposition, Girlie, you continuing to bring or send that woman to my home, and I will not stand it any longer."

It was "my home," and "my employ," yet it was still "my wife." A few days after this angry letter, perhaps to make up for it, he sent Rose some shoes she had asked to have repaired and a photo of a new baby nephew. She thanked him, and remarked how like a Stokes the baby looked. But she added, about the woman Graham wanted barred from their home, "One word more with regard to J. P. She is my Comrade. . . . If you cannot see that great, world-shaking events have clarified my thinking for me, as they have yours, for you, there is little use, dear, in discussing the matter."

17

No Peaceful Tent in No Man's Land

Fifty thousand troops were marching past the reviewing stand, as well as 200,000 workers, many of them armed. Military aircraft flew in V formation overhead. It was November 7, 1922, and the Soviet Union was celebrating the fifth anniversary of the Bolshevik coup with a huge parade through Moscow's Red Square. Half a million people along the route offered thunderous cheers for soldiers in long greatcoats, tractors pulling artillery pieces, squadrons of cavalry with lances, and trucks wreathed in pennants carrying yet more soldiers. In front of the Kremlin, a brass band played, and giant banners proclaiming "5 Years of Soviet Power," or just the number 5, hung from the walls of the ancient fortress. Among the crowd was Rose Pastor Stokes.

She was in the American delegation to a congress of the Communist International, or Comintern, the body through which the Soviets now coordinated the actions of Communist parties around the world. Lenin addressed the congress in the gold-and-white-marble throne room of the tsars in the Kremlin, and in Petrograd its participants were feted with a ballet performance, cannon salutes, and another parade with more airplanes and Cossacks brandishing sabers.

Her fellow delegate Max Eastman was beginning to privately develop doubts about communism, but Rose had none. She was seeing, she felt certain, the culmination of the dreams of the brave Russian revolutionaries she had admired long ago. On her return, she wrote articles extolling the Soviet Union's glories for small left-wing newspapers. Her lengthy notes on the weeks she spent in "the land of my heart's desire" are filled with awed descriptions of "rosy-faced girls," construction going on everywhere, "wholesome black bread," Petrograd women who were "the backbone of the revolution," and the "well-nourished" patients and loving nurses in a children's hospital. ("I have never seen happier, healthier-looking children.") Even some small boys she noticed on the street talked out a misunderstanding—instead of having a fistfight, as she was sure would have happened in a capitalist country.

At home, her conviction under the Espionage Act, her support of Debs at his trial, her role as a Communist leader, and various brushes she had with the police won her attention and denunciation as never before. It was between 1918 and 1921 that a survey showed her to be the woman whose name appeared most often in American newspapers. Yet a mere half decade later she would disappear from the public eye.

Communists ruled the USSR, but in the United States the movement Rose had thrown herself into so passionately turned out to be powerless. Throughout the 1920s, government harassment and factional disputes kept the number of American Communists small. Finding the party's positions determined by edicts from Moscow, some of the writers and intellectuals who had at first given the movement luster became disillusioned and began leaving. Rose, however, remained, and ran (with minuscule vote totals) as a Communist candidate for Congress and then for borough president of Manhattan. She felt, she wrote in 1922, that the Soviet Union was the "sun of the world."

What attracted people to a belief system filled with such certainties, the critic Irving Howe later wrote, "was the sense that they had gained not merely a 'purpose' in life but, far more important, a coherent perspective upon everything that was happening to us. . . . With its stress upon inevitable conflicts, apocalyptic climaxes, ultimate moments, hours of doom, and shining tomorrows [Marxism] appealed deeply to our imaginations. We felt that we were always on the rim of heroism, that the mockery we might suffer at the moment would turn to vindication in the future, that our loyalty to principle would be rewarded by the grateful masses of tomorrow."

And yet, in these years the masses seemed more interested in Yankee slugger Babe Ruth, evading Prohibition, or the hope of owning a Model T Ford than in the uphill task of trying to change the world. In the right-leaning America of the 1920s, under Presidents Warren Harding, Calvin Coolidge, and Herbert Hoover, every progressive organization was in retreat. The postwar labor turmoil was over, with few gains; no more were there urgent pleas from striking workers for the golden-tongued former cigar roller to rally them.

Even the determinedly moderate American Federation of Labor lost more than a million members between 1920 and 1923, at a time when the Ku Klux Klan was reaching its all-time peak of membership and influence. Across the country, returning veterans swelled the ranks of vigilante groups. The Socialist Party was in decline, while prosecutors made use of new criminal syndicalism laws to arrest IWW members by the hundreds and essentially destroy the organization. Its very history went up in smoke, quite literally, when, in 1923, nearly all the records and correspondence seized in the nationwide raids on Wobbly offices in 1917 were burned by the Justice Department.

Several months after Rose returned from Moscow, Graham's mother, as overbearing as ever, wrote her how "very glad and thankful" she felt "that you have come home to Graham and that you *no longer hold the extreme views that have made him* so unhappy." The underlining was Rose's, and in the margin of the letter she wrote, "*Who* said so?" The letter continued, "In all the world you could not find a husband as loving and faithful, and patient, and forgiving, and forbearing as he . . . and he has always felt that you would in time realize that you had been misled." Rose scribbled at the bottom of the page, "I don't know where Mother got her notion that my views are *modified*." We do not know if she marked up this letter just for herself or to give to Graham.

However severe the strains between them, their marriage was still intact. But other parts of their shared life were crumbling. Not only was Caritas Island gone; their friends English and Anna Walling were heading down a painfully drawn-out path toward divorce. Rose and Graham no longer saw much of the other couple they had once shared the island with, Leroy and Miriam Scott. The Scotts, too, had differed strongly over the First World War and the Russian Revolution—as in the Stokes and Walling families, it was the woman of the couple who opposed the war and backed the revolution. Despite the upheavals they had managed to stay together, perhaps because they both abandoned left-wing politics. Leroy became a detective novelist, while Miriam would have a long career as a child psychologist.

On the rare occasions when Rose now found an audience willing to hear her, it was usually made up of Communists like herself. She no longer drew on the skills that had once brought her vision of a better world to life for people who did not already agree with her— making members of a church congregation or a women's club, for instance, care about the injustices that could produce events like the Triangle fire. Her language lost its spark, and there are no more accounts of her mesmerizing effect as a speaker.

She still wrote poems, but only occasionally did a magazine print one. She began doing pencil and pastel drawings, and saw a few exhibited in a show with other politically involved artists. Of a drawing of Graham, their maid Anna Webb told her, "Why that's exactly as he looks when he finds the toast slightly burned . . . that's Mr. Stokes to the life!" Graham was doubtless pleased that she was making sketches, not bombs. When she did a drawing of Anna, Rose wrote Dargan in 1923, "Graham breaks into loud praise, then cautions me against being too proud! I assure his puritanic conscience that I am only very glad and not at all proud . . . and we both laugh almost as in the old days."

At this point not only was communism a distinctly marginal force in American life, but Rose's own position in the movement became more marginal. Like many who work in quasi-underground groups, she had become obsessively wary of infiltrators and several times accused party comrades of being government spies, including her friend Jeanette Pearl, the woman whose visits to their house had so enraged Graham. Pearl objected furiously, calling Rose, in a letter to Communist Party authorities, "a highly neuratic [*sic*] woman openly living with a notorious white guard, a member of the millionaire class, who advocates 'all reds be stood up against the wall and shot.' . . . I had urged Rose to leave him. . . . This evidently came to his attention and he forbade her to associate with me declaring that he would keep me from his home if he had to use the US soldiers to do so." Pearl added an insightful Freudian twist to her Communist fervor, continuing, "I have no doubt that her charge against me is based on a subconscious desire on her part to escape the humiliation of being compelled to accept such a tyrannical ruling as to her associates." Rose's marriage caused uneasiness among other Communists as well. After 1924 she would no longer serve on the party's executive committee.

Curiously, it was just as the public lost interest in Rose that there appeared, in 1923, a novel inspired by her life.* Filled with soaring hopes, icy winds, and throbbing hearts, *Salome of the Tenements* was written by Anzia Yezierska, a fellow immigrant whom Rose had first known before she married Graham. The heroine of *Salome,* Sonya Vrunsky, is living in a dingy room on the Lower East Side when, as a reporter for the *Ghetto News,* she is sent to interview the wealthy John Manning, who dabbles in settlement house work. As they fall in love, she tells him, "I am a Russian Jewess, a flame—a longing. A soul consumed with hunger for heights beyond reach. I am the ache of unvoiced dreams, the clamor of suppressed desires. I am the unlived lives of generations stifled in Siberian prisons." He responds, "And I, I am a puritan whose fathers were afraid to trust experience. We are bound by our possessions of property, knowledge and tradition."

Manning's life includes a mansion on Madison Avenue and an idyllic Caritas-like estate on Long Island Sound. There, however, the similarities with Rose and Graham largely end—there is no so-

---

* Another, in Yiddish, *Rose of the East Side,* would be published two decades later.

cialism, and the heroine becomes a fashion designer. The couple part ways bitterly. The novel was soon turned into a screenplay for a silent film by another Russian-born Jewish writer, Sonya Levien, who, like Yezierska, had met Rose early, attended her wedding, and remained friends with her for years. Once the story reached the screen, a plot ending in divorce would never do, so in the movie, after various tribulations, the couple lives happily ever after.

Neither Rose nor Graham left any clues as to how they felt about seeing their lives turned into fiction and film, but the angry breakup of the couple in the novel must have unnerved them, especially as things between them were growing worse. The one belief they still seemed to share was in the sanctity and permanence of marriage. For Graham, it came with the weight of centuries' worth of eminent Stokes, Phelps, and Dodge ancestors, their unions and descendants etched on family trees and described at length in his father's books on the clan's genealogy. Rose clearly valued Graham's fidelity, after seeing the misery that ensued when her stepfather abandoned his entire family.

Divorce seemed unthinkable, a feeling that, for Rose, was surely reinforced by the painful experience of Eugene Debs. He and Mabel Curry had no doubt that they were meant for each other. "I want you. My heart cries for you, aches for you, and will not be still," he had written Mabel from behind bars. In another letter he assured her, "Our day . . . will come because it *must* come." Mabel promised that once he was freed from prison, he would "find nothing but devotion here and the warmest hands and heart ready to receive you." But on his release, they could not bear to break up their respective marriages and put themselves, as well as Mabel's three children, under a cloud of disgrace. Their day did not come.

For Rose and Graham, New York law added to the fear of scandal, for the state granted divorce only on grounds of adultery. With such a well-known couple, that would mean guaranteed fodder for new headlines. Still, Rose found it increasingly difficult to remain in the same house as Graham. She was desperate, she told Dargan, to escape her husband's manner of "looking fearfully injured and bearing it with stoic New England gentlemanliness. . . . Most of the

time when looking at me, he is saying, 'Bad, bad Girlie! bad Girlie!'"
Exactly what the "stoic" Graham felt is unknown. His sister Helen,
who lived next door to the couple, told Rose that Graham never
discussed his marriage with her. As far as can be told from his thousands of carefully saved letters, he confided in no one.

Others tried to avoid getting caught in the minefield between the
two of them. "I have been intending to write to you and apologize
for not accepting your invitation to come to dinner," Upton Sinclair said in a letter to Rose. "I should have felt so unhappy about
meeting Graham under the circumstances existing. I am very fond
of Graham personally, and I should like to sit down and have a heart
to heart talk with him, but to meet him and not refer to the subject
of politics—I just wouldn't know how to do that."

Rose, however, persisted in inviting people to 88 Grove Street,
and one such dinner precipitated the ultimate explosion. She had
become friends with a Communist named Irving Grossman, who
apparently brought his mother and a woman friend of hers to dinner one Saturday evening in February 1925. The next morning, Graham asked something about the other woman—it is not clear exactly what—that Rose took as a terrible insult. She stormed out of
the house the following day and did not return.

Even the furious letters they then exchanged, however, reveal
that at some level neither of them wanted to separate. "My going
would have been much harder," she wrote him, "—perhaps I had
not gone at all, who knows? If you had not said, '*it suits me!*'" Graham raged in return that before leaving, she had subjected him to
"perfectly outrageous abuse—abuse so outrageous that I could not
stand it. . . . And when in a cyclone of abuse you said you would
leave the house 'tomorrow,' I replied that *if that was the way you
felt,* I should put no obstacles in your way." But he ended by saying,
"*Come back,* Girlie."

Their very handwriting seems at war. Her script is firm, bold, or-
derly, slanting forward decisively. His, by contrast, races across the
page in a flattened, barely legible scrawl, as if poured out in haste
and fury, with the crossbar on every *T* a long, thick, imperious arc,
sometimes extending nearly halfway across the page. The letters, an-

gry and offended, continued the relationship, as if each were trying to hold on to what was left of their life together no matter how full of wounds it was. Detailed charges of hurtful things said and done were answered point by point in outraged rebuttals. Again Graham asked her to come back, and again she refused, referring to the way he had recently trained their new dog: "When you taught Bunny to sit up and look docile and pretty for her dog-biscuit, remarking to me with not a little of significance that the gesture pleased you as a 'nice' way of asking, I determined to steal my bread if I must, but never to sit up and beg like 'Bunny' to please a self-complaisant master." In a missive written about a month after she left, she declared, "We are active soldiers in opposing armies, you and I. We cannot set up for ourselves a peaceful tent in No-Man's-Land."

Graham rejected the analogy and blamed all their difficulties on her pigheadedness. "'Political differences' have little if anything to do with our trouble, Girlie," he insisted implausibly. "There are lots of people whose political differences are even greater, who have no quarrels at all. Our troubles are due, or at least 99% of them are due, to your selfish determination to disregard my feelings in our home and to do exactly as you like at all times wholly regardless of anybody's feelings but your own." Enraging her further, he changed the locks on a garage where some of their furniture was stored, so that Rose could not take any of it for her own use.

And yet she still felt torn. "I passed Graham on the street," Rose wrote Anna Walling ten months after she walked out. "He did not see me. But I caught the look in his face, his eyes; and I have been weeping myself blind over it." This was the last time she saw him.

Rose now had to worry about supporting herself. At the age of 45, she had almost no income from writing or any other source. Her friendship with Irving Grossman finally led to a job — her first real one since being a cigar worker and *Yiddishes Tageblatt* reporter 20 years earlier. She began doing advertising and public relations for a hotel his family owned in upstate New York. (Simultaneously she organized a Communist study group for its waiters.) Soon enough, the job led to something else: a passionate romance with Grossman. One hopes it brightened this time for her, for later this year she would tell a journalist that, "though living under the same roof Mr. Stokes and I have been purely 'friends' for the larger part of our married life." This remark, never further elaborated, casts a certain somber light over their two decades together.

Rose's affair with Grossman gave Graham the legal grounds he needed for a divorce in New York. Still feeling bitter and humiliated by her departure, he angrily rejected her suggestion that they end their marriage quietly in Mexico or in Rhode Island, where he owned a house and land and where divorce was possible on grounds other than adultery. Graham, Rose wrote his sister Helen, was determined to extract "his legal pound of flesh."

And this he did: testimony in court about how Rose and Grossman had been seen entering and leaving each other's hotel rooms briefly put her back in the news. The story ran on the front page of the *New York Times* two days in a row. She was portrayed as an adulterer, of course, and Graham as the betrayed husband. Rose was at a Communist meeting when a *Times* reporter first went looking for her at her mother's Bronx apartment. The next day, when he found her there wearing a grey cloak against the chill, Rose proved as skillful as ever at dealing with the press. Refusing to answer his questions, she insisted that she would only dictate a statement, and handed him a portable typewriter to take it down. Instead of shame falling on her, she declared, "it should be placed upon the shoulders of the State of New York, where it properly belongs. There is due no small measure of disgrace to any state whose laws will not permit one to get a divorce unless one is willing to be made a subject for scandal."

Her manifesto concluded: "Love is always justified, even when short-lived, even when mistaken, because during its existence it enlarges and ennobles the natures of the men and women experiencing the love. . . . The real scandal—the wife who gives herself to the husband without love and the husband who gives himself to the wife without love—the real breach is given a veneer of sanctity by the church and covered with a cloak of decency by the law."

On the wall of the apartment where she received the reporter was one of her drawings—of Graham.

Love it might be, but there were agonizing complications in her relationship with Grossman, for he was married and his wife pregnant. Before long, things took a yet more painful turn, as Grossman abandoned both wife and Rose for a third woman. "A slender young hand has plucked the sun out of my skies," Rose confided to Dargan. ". . . I try to hold the thought that our year and a half of love-life was worth the plodding lives of countless 'comfortably married' pairs. But I bleed at every cell of brain and body."

She later elaborated her thoughts about marriage and divorce in an outspoken article for *Collier's,* suggesting that loveless marriages, kept in place by restrictive laws, were no better than prostitution. "Most of us would hesitate to say how few marriages within our knowledge are happy ones," she wrote, in a way that surely would have shocked the more conventional Rose of 20 years earlier. "We would confess, if we dared, that we can count all the happy marriages we know of on the fingers of our two hands—and have some doubts about most of these!"

The country's antiquated divorce laws had caused misery for millions, and her stand brought her many letters of support, among them a warm, handwritten one from Debs. Despite "how widely our view-points may be at variance" over the Soviet Union, he wrote, he had never forgotten that Rose had been at his side during his trial. "The days have passed since last we met but not the radiance of your fine soul, and I drop you this line of loving greeting . . . that you may know I remember gratefully your loyal devotion in the days that were dark and trying and that I hold you, as all do who have the privilege of knowing you, as a lofty, courageous, noble-hearted woman and a consecrated soul in the service of humanity. Believe me, dear, brave comrade, always."

While Rose continued to draw her identity from a faith that the revolution she had seen in Russia would soon spread across the world, Graham increasingly drew his from things military. He no longer belonged to socialist groups but served instead on such bodies as the National Defense Committee of the Military-Naval Club of New York. Among his surviving papers, 18 boxes are filled with material to do with military or patriotic organizations whose meetings and dinners he faithfully attended. He embarked on writing a history of his National Guard unit, tracing its ancestry back to New York's Dutch colonial days, and also asked the War Department if its records showed whether several ancestors of his had served in the War of 1812. He won a promotion, and in letters his secretary and some of his correspondents, even when not writing about National Guard matters, began referring to him as "Major Stokes."

If the Communist Party gave Rose a sense of belonging and comradeship, his role in uniform did so for Graham. And since the military was all male, it was one place where she could never outshine him. Until he was almost 60 he would continue to have the annual physical exam required to remain on the list of reserve officers eligible to be called to active duty. Like Rose hoping for the revolution she had predicted for so long, it was as if he, too, were waiting for his own summons to glory.

Rose's article for *Collier's* brought her a rare check for $400, which she much needed, for she was fiercely determined, despite the urgings of her lawyer and her friends, to ask for no alimony. "I desire *nothing* from you but my freedom," she wrote to Graham. One thing she did expect, though, was that he would continue the $100 a month he had paid ever since Rose had left her *Tageblatt* job, to support her mother, now ill. Instead, he had his secretary write the elderly Mrs. Pastor that he planned to reduce that sum to $35 for the next six months, after which time "he hopes that your children will have found it practicable to make adequate provision for your comfort." A furious Rose returned the $35 check.

In early 1926, only six months after his divorce became final, Graham remarried. Lettice Sands, 20 years his junior, was the daughter of a railroad executive. Her family, often on the society pages, could trace its ancestry back to colonial times. Her only known public statement on any political issue would come when she and Graham signed a letter to the *Times* about strengthening a state law against cruelty to animals.

Graham's relatives doubtless breathed a collective sigh of relief at the marriage, and perhaps they breathed another later that same year when William Earl Dodge Stokes died at 74. Multiple scandals followed him to the grave: a charge of suborning perjury; a public row with two of his children; an alleged affair between his much younger estranged second wife and his own son by his first marriage; lawsuits with her over a prenuptial agreement, defamation, and other matters. In a fit of jealous rage, she charged, he had nailed shut her bedroom door. With Rose and Uncle Will now both gone from their lives, the Stokes family would seldom again fear finding their name in headlines.

Graham lived on with his new wife at 88 Grove Street, expanding the house to incorporate the building next door. They had no children. Some of the family business holdings were sold off, and Graham spent less and less time at the downtown office, leaving for weeks at a time with Lettice on frequent ocean cruises. The lengthening list of charities whose boards or membership rolls he joined ranged from the Society for the Preservation of New England Antiquities to animal protection groups like the Defenders of Furbearers. It was all far different from the daring and unusual steps away from the life expected of him that he had taken long ago. When he abandoned all his involvement with progressive politics, he also seemed to abandon whatever empathy went with it. In the depths of the Great Depression, with a quarter of the country's labor force out of work, he remarked to one visitor that at least public health was doubtless improved, because people were no longer overeating.

Stepping back fully into the rarefied and respectable world into which he had been born, he never left it again. He resumed his youthful interest in combining the traditions of different religions. At a castle in Holland he heard the Indian mystic Jiddu Krishnamurti. "There is no doubt that the same Divine Being who spoke 2000 years ago," he wrote to his mother, "spoke again last Friday. The whole emphasis now is on uncovering the Inner Light—the

Light whose tabernacle we are—and letting that Light shine." A room on the top floor of his house was filled with Christian and Hindu objects, and he gathered friends there monthly for meditation. A pamphlet on spiritual matters by "Sri J. G. Phelps Stokes" was published in India. He remained, however, a member of the vestry at the fashionable Grace Church not far from his home. He would die in 1960 at the age of 88.

The marriage of Graham and Rose ended as anything but the Cinderella dream imagined by those who had compiled scrapbooks about their wedding, their honeymoon, and their first years together. Plenty of marriages break up, of course, but when that happens we often hope that those who parted at least gained some understanding or wisdom. In Graham, at least, it is hard to see any such sign. A few years before he died, he dictated a book-length memoir, never published, titled *My Narrative*. Nearly half of it is about the trip around the world he took after he graduated from college, as if putting on center stage a time of his life when he felt no burdens. Another 60 pages discuss his ancestors and their business enterprises. At far less length, he describes his years in the settlement house movement and, very briefly, in the Socialist Party. The text ends with long lists of his National Guard posts and awards, and of the dozens of civic and military organizations he belonged to. In 266 pages, he never mentions Rose.

Rose also began a memoir—unfinished, and only published nearly 60 years after her death—but it says a great deal about their relationship, from her first enchantment to her later disillusion. Some of her other feelings, however, are censored. Omitted entirely from the book, for instance, was the love she clearly once had for Caritas Island—not a proper emotion for a Communist militant; the island itself is mentioned, in passing, only in a single sentence. Graham, Rose remarked to an acquaintance during their last years together, had "reverted to type." Given her fervent belief in the Soviet Union, he might well have said the same thing of her.

Just as he had his ecumenical shrine in his house, Rose had her own version of faith. She defiantly called her memoir *I Belong to the*

Working Class, and on the manuscript's hand-drawn opening page this title is followed by an exclamation mark. She presented everything in class terms. Graham, she wrote, "loved the people *in theory only;* there was no personal warmth in him for them. Often I thought I detected a look of contempt for some member or members of my class. He could not have dealt me a personal blow that would have hurt more." Perhaps. But what most upset him may have been that the woman who began as someone worshiping his superior knowledge turned out, in the end, to be assertive, independent, and unwilling to bend her life's course to his. If so, that was a failing he shared with men from all classes, not just his own. In his era, a truly egalitarian relationship may have been even rarer than one across the barrier of class.

One curious feeling took Rose totally by surprise when she stalked out of the redbrick Grove Street townhouse forever. At the very moment when she freed herself at last from the man who had come to oppose everything she stood for, she paradoxically seemed to lose all interest in political work. "As I look back at the last few years," she wrote Olive Dargan, "I verily believe that, if it had not been for Graham's hard opposition I'd have given up long ago my intensive activities. . . . Now that the break with Graham is complete . . . I haven't the least desire to get into crowds, to go to meetings, public or private." It was a realization that puzzled her — "queer, isn't it?" — but she shied away from exploring it further in any of her surviving letters or other writings. We can only speculate on where this feeling came from. After her ardent communism had lost her the large following she once had, and she had then been further sidelined within the Communist movement, the primary audience she had left, albeit a highly disapproving one, was Graham. It was almost as if he had been, in a way he never intended, her muse. And now she had him no more.

Rose's 20 years of campaigning came to an end. "I am not very active now, Comrade," she wrote to the Communist Party's national secretary a few months after she and Graham separated. "I look forward to the day when I can get into the fight as usual," she added, but that day never came. Although she remained a party member and joined an occasional demonstration, after 1925, the year she was divorced, she lost interest in giving speeches. "I am no longer my old self on the platform," she wrote in that letter to Dargan, "and I *will* not be less, so this is a closed chapter in my life." She continued to pay, as she and Graham had over many years, for a clipping service to send her any articles that mentioned her. But few now did.

For a time she shared a $40-a-month flat with a roommate, and then, moving to a small, heavily mortgaged cottage in Connecticut, she took in a boarder and a child for whose care she was paid $15 a week. For the first time in nearly 30 years she sometimes went hungry; at one point, after borrowing a few dollars from a sister and a brother, she owed money to the grocer and possessed only 36 cents in cash. She finally found a secretarial job at a small, Communist Party–connected relief agency.

In 1927, 48 years old and on the rebound from the faithless Irving Grossman, she fell in love again. Victor Jerome was 17 years younger than Rose. He, too, had been born in imperial Russia, in a Jewish *shtetl* a few hundred miles from Augustów. He shared both her love of literature and her politics. On one of their first dates, they went to see Soviet director Sergei Eisenstein's silent film *Battleship Potemkin,* about the famous naval mutiny during the failed Russian Revolution of 1905.

Taking college courses, scraping by with the occasional odd job as a tutor or a salesman for a printing shop, all while caring for a young son from his previous marriage, Jerome was as penniless as she. "I'm afraid I'm getting deep in love," she told a friend. "I find him so rare and fine a spirit that it would take more than human will to resist his appeal." She did not resist, and the two married quietly. From all appearances they were happy together. Jerome would eventually have a long career as a Communist Party cultural functionary, but for now, the notes and letters he and Rose exchanged when apart were full of anxieties about money. "Maybe we shall find a footing somewhere and a vista, and a few moments of beauty," she wrote him in 1928. "Oh, my darling, my darling! We must keep heart, we must."

18

Love Is Always Justified

A QUARTER CENTURY HAD PASSED since Rose first arrived in New York. The city whose streets had once been filled with horse-drawn carts and carriages was now laced together by subway lines and clogged with automobiles, while aircraft crossed its skies. Construction was about to begin on the Chrysler Building, the Empire State Building, and other skyscrapers that would reach previously unimagined heights. The click of horseshoes and the rattle of pushcart wheels on cobblestone streets had given way to an endless chorus of car and truck horns, and the smell of coal smoke and horse manure to that of diesel fumes. The flood of hopeful but impoverished newcomers who once filled the streets of the Lower East Side had thinned to a trickle, thanks to legislation pushed through Congress by anti-immigrant crusaders. The children and grandchildren of peddlers and kosher butchers were becoming professors at City College, lawyers on Long Island, doctors in Westchester. Actors who had played their first youthful roles in New York's Yiddish theater now, in late middle age, sought work in the new talkies made in Hollywood.

In early 1930, a reporter went looking for the woman to whom the nation's newspapers had once devoted hundreds of thousands of words. He found her living with Victor Jerome and his ten-year-old son in a cramped fourth-floor walk-up flat on Second Avenue near

13th Street. Rose took care of the boy while Jerome was out working or, more often, as the country sank deeper into the Great Depression, job hunting. Several newspapers picked up the story— "Once Rich 'Ghetto Rose' Now Reported Destitute," read one headline— and also revealed that she was suffering from cancer.

As the news spread, old friends and admirers sent messages, telegrams, and, from one doctor, an offer to treat her without payment. A rumor made the rounds that Graham had tried to help. The *Brooklyn Eagle* reported that "a shining black car which neighbors say is the Stokes car, has drawn up repeatedly" to Rose's tenement "and a man has alighted and climbed the four weary flights of stairs to the top floor where Rose Pastor now lives. But there is no response to his knocks." Evidence suggests, however, that this was only a fantasy that Prince Charming would again come to the rescue. Upton Sinclair and other friends—almost certainly without Rose's knowledge —appealed to Graham to help pay for her treatment. "I am now assured by friends of hers in New York, that sufficient funds for her care for a year have been raised," Graham replied to Sinclair's plea. "If I could help her without helping her work, much of which appears to me to be so very abominable, I should gladly do so, but I don't see how I can."

Rose became convinced that her best chance to prevent the metastasis of the tumor in her breast lay with Hans Holfelder, a prominent German doctor who had developed a new form of radiation therapy. Friends chipped in funds so that she could go to his clinic in Frankfurt for treatment. The two of them hit it off. Placing great faith in the English-speaking physician, she referred other patients to him and wrote letters asking American foundations to support his research. She soon made a return visit to Germany for six months of further treatment, and was invited to sit in on a lecture where Holfelder showed slides to army surgeons.

Apparently she did not know that Holfelder was an outspoken anti-Semite. He would later become a colonel in Adolf Hitler's SS and give a notorious illustrated lecture portraying cancer cells as Jews and victorious beams of radiation as Nazi storm troopers. Holfelder must have known that Rose was Jewish, but either the prestige of having a well-known foreigner as his patient mattered more or she simply charmed him, as she had so many others. "Every anti-Semite," runs a Russian proverb, "has his favorite Jew." Perhaps she was his. From his clinic, Rose wrote that "Holfelder never charged a penny for Xray or for treatment." They exchanged letters when she was back in New York, and he sent her some medicine he hoped would be helpful. To one correspondent, she wrote, "I feel I owe him my life."

In the midst of coping with cancer, she remained in debt, and she and Jerome discussed renting out a room in their apartment. "Rose, dear, here is a pale little ten dollars for some small thing you truly want," a friend wrote. Olive Dargan sent her money several times, saying of one check, "Don't hurt me by returning it. Yours is mine, and mine is yours, so long as we shall live." When she had to be hospitalized in New York, Graham's sister Helen, who remained close to her, quietly paid the bill. Despite the ominous rise of the Nazis, Rose was still convinced that her only hope lay with Dr. Holfelder. Helen and other friends contributed money to send her back to Frankfurt once more.

From shipboard, Rose wrote to a Communist friend that she was trying to convert to her faith the ship's doctor ("fairly hopeless"), its nurse (who "has budged a bit"), and—even though he was a member of a right-wing paramilitary group—her cabin steward ("after all, he's a *worker* and can be talked to. We have great talks"). She arrived in Germany in February 1933, two weeks after thousands of torch-carrying Nazi brownshirts had marched jubilantly through the streets of Berlin to celebrate Hitler becoming chancellor.

"Hitler speaks around the corner tonight," Rose wrote to Jerome. "The hall is in a rich respectable neighborhood. If I were not so ill they'd probably throw me out of the country." As her stay dragged on, she sent off a stream of desperate letters pleading with friends to send her American newspapers, and with her husband to write her "with every mail ship." A nurse's aide pocketed money Rose gave her for a telegram, and soon she was two weeks behind in paying a hospital bill. A Rose Pastor Stokes Testimonial Committee, whose members included authors Sherwood Anderson, John Dos Passos, and Langston Hughes, as well as old friends like Lincoln Steffens and Elizabeth Gurley Flynn, organized a mass meeting in New York to raise funds. From his prison cell, the famous labor martyr Tom Mooney sent a letter of support.

Rose wrote to her lawyer in New York that "the urn with my ashes will go to your office long before the summer's end." Her handwriting was shaky; as a result of the radiation treatment, she could no longer use her right hand. In her datebook, she scrawled, "Am sinking daily, cannot bear the suffering." To Dargan, she wrote, "O my darling your letters they are like your arms about me in these last hours and how I need them. Heart sinking—vision clear. Cannot write. O the years!" After asking a nurse to play some Schubert on a piano, she died in Frankfurt on June 20, 1933, a month before her 54th birthday.

In the original fairy tale, Cinderella's success requires the supernatural. The fairy godmother's magic wand transforms a pumpkin into a coach to take Cinderella to the ball, a rat into a coachman, lizards into footmen, six mice into horses, and her pauper's clothes into an evening gown of gold and silver encrusted with jewels. Later, of course, when she is back in rags but the glass slipper left behind at the ball turns out to fit her perfectly, the prince sees that she is the elegant lady who so charmed him, and he marries her.

Such stories have had particular appeal when the gap between the wealthy and the poverty-stricken is especially wide, whether between the castles and peasant huts of medieval Europe, or the grand estates and immigrant tenements of Gilded Age America. Small wonder that the drama of Rose and Graham so captured the public's attention. If love could bridge such a gulf of wealth and class, was there not hope for everyone? "The Cinderella story," wrote Tennessee Williams, "is our favorite national myth." Just as it was one answer to the dream of bridging that great gap, the hope of revolution was another. In the course of her life, Rose Pastor Stokes managed to embody the first and preach the second.

In the real world, neither a magic wand nor a political apocalypse has proven able to close that divide, which is once again widening today. The chasm between rich and poor in our second Gilded Age makes it painfully clear that much of what Rose fought for remains to be achieved. As this book goes to press, the number of billionaires in the United States has increased more than tenfold since the year 2000. And no nation on earth has such a staggering gulf between the salary levels of its CEOs and those of their workers. The chief executive of Walmart earns more than a thousand times the pay of his average employee—and that is by no means the highest such multiple. The net worth of the average American family, by contrast, is less than what it was 20 years earlier. You do not have to believe in either magic or communism to hope for an alternative.

Millions of Americans of the generation of Rose, Eugene Debs, Emma Goldman, Big Bill Haywood, and countless others nourished such hope—and not without results. Today, despite the rising inequality, we enjoy much that was inspired by those of her time who dared to dream. Would we have the eight-hour day, Social Security, Medicare, child labor laws, and so much else if American socialists and their allies had not first put such ideas on the table more than a century ago? History unfolds less in abrupt revolutions than in such increments.

The hope Rose also nourished for her marriage was a mixed story as well. However furious its ending, without it, would she have made any mark on the world? If she had not had the celebrity of her unlikely union with Graham, would Rose ever have found a vastly wider audience than she had as a writer of sentimental poetry and advice columns for the *Yiddishes Tageblatt*? Would she ever have played such a dramatic role in the battles for the rights of labor and birth control, or against the madness of the First World War? Could she, alone, have inspired so many people with the vision of a more just and equitable future? Nor could either member of the couple, singly, have attracted the extraordinary array of writers, artists, activists, and dreamers, from Maxim Gorky to Clarence Darrow to W.E.B. Du Bois, whose names fill the Caritas Island guestbook and whose weekends of conversation it would be so interesting to overhear.

Although she meant it for a different purpose entirely, part of

Rose's defiant statement on reforming divorce laws still hauntingly applies to the two of them: "Love is always justified, even when short-lived, even when mistaken, because during its existence it enlarges and ennobles the natures of the men and women experiencing the love." The love between Rose and Graham may have been short-lived and ultimately mistaken, but for a luminous few years it made the couple into figures far more memorable than either would have been alone.

Acknowledgments

If it takes a village to raise a child, it takes at least a hamlet to raise a book. My greatest debt is to family and friends who read drafts of the manuscript and gave me their feedback, most of them people who've been similarly generous for earlier books of mine. So, my deepest thanks to Deirdre English, Elizabeth Farnsworth, Doug Foster, David Hochschild, Cynthia Li, Michael Meyer, Susan C. Neilson, Ruth Rosen, and Zachary Shore. My wife, Arlie Russell Hochschild, read two separate drafts and, as always, gently pushed me to go deeper. What did he feel? Or she? Why? If Rose and Graham themselves had had the benefit of Arlie's insight into human emotions, they never would have gotten divorced.

This book, like most of its predecessors, was improved by the hand of the country's premier freelance editor, Tom Engelhardt. Those who've worked with Tom know his habit of phoning you while on one of his long walks around New York City. Even when he was demanding a rewrite that would cause me more work, it was a pleasure to imagine him, in mid-demand, striding past one of the places that figures in this story. At Houghton Mifflin Harcourt, I gratefully received more help from my editor Bruce Nichols, from Ivy Givens, and from ace manuscript editor Larry Cooper. All the excess adjectives and adverbs that Larry pruned away would fill half this page.

Aid of other kinds came from Jill Lepore, Robbin Légère Henderson, Rachel Elin Nolan, Thomas Stokes, Samuel Stokes, and John Hatch. My thanks, also, to Fred Jerome for permission to quote from the collection of Rose's papers at the Tamiment Library at New York University, and to Timothy V. Johnson, that library's director while I was working on this project. Librarians and archivists at the University of California at Berkeley, Columbia University, Yale University, the Hoover Institution at Stanford University, Bates College, the Chautauqua Institution, the New-York Historical Society, and the National Archives and Records Administration smoothed my research path as well.

The notes and bibliography in these pages make clear the debts I owe to other scholarship, both published and unpublished, especially by those who became interested in Rose Pastor Stokes and her husband long before I did. Essential guideposts, above all, were the careful studies of Rose by Arthur and Pearl Zipser, and of Graham and his circle by Robert D. Reynolds Jr.

My one regret about this book is that it can't be read by the late E. L. Doctorow, a friend and mentor whose encouragement earlier in my writing life meant more than he could have imagined. In fiction, he brought turn-of-the-century New York alive better than anyone; I'm so sorry he could not meet on the page these real inhabitants of the vanished city he conjured up so well.

The world of publishing can be a forbidding place, full of mysteriously closed doors. I would have had a much harder time finding my way through those doors had not Georges and Anne Borchardt, along with their daughter Valerie, become my literary agents 35 years ago. Their knowledge of the publishing world, and guidance through it, has always been leavened with warmth and wry humor, and I'm grateful.

Notes

Prologue:
Tumult at Carnegie Hall

page

1   *Some three thousand:* "The Birth Control Review," *Conservator,* March
     1917, p. 12. The article is signed "T."—presumably Horace Traubel, the
     magazine's publisher.
     "We have met here": RPS-Yale, Box 6. This was one of the few speeches
     Rose read from a text.

3   *"everybody shouted for":* "Mob Rose Stokes for Birth Secrets," *Oakland
     Tribune,* 6 May 1916.

4   *her name was mentioned:* Georges D. Romeike, "Who Are Talked About?"
     Journal of Education, 25 May 1922, reprinted from *American Magazine,*
     February 1922. Romeike was president of a press clipping service. Al-
     though he does not specify the time period he is surveying, it appears to
     be 1918 through 1921. A search of a modern but far from comprehensive
     database of historical newspapers, those in the Library of Congress's
     "Chronicling America" collection (accessed 21 March 2019), turns up 564
     mentions of her name in 1918 alone.

5   *break all previous records:* Chuck Collins and Josh Hoxie, *Billionaire
     Bonanza: The Forbes 400 and the Rest of Us* (Washington, DC: Institute for
     Policy Studies, 2017), p. 2.

6   *"City of the world!":* "City of Ships," in *Leaves of Grass* (1867).

1. Tsar and Queen

10   *"thinly-bearded, rugged face":* Rose Pastor Stokes 1, pp. 3–5.

"Some of my earliest recollections": To Olive Dargan[?], March 1909, RPS-Tamiment, Box 1, Folder 5.

"sunlight streaming in": Rose Pastor Stokes 1, p. 7.

11   *"the kindliest prince":* Howe, p. 7.

14   *"a plain, heavy":* Rose Pastor Stokes 1, pp. 8–13, 26, 31. Rose misidentifies the parade as marking Victoria's 60th year on the throne, which would have happened after the Pastor family moved to the United States.

2. Magic Land

15   *"'America' was in everybody's mouth":* Mary Antin, *From Plotzk to Boston* (Boston: W. B. Clarke, 1899), pp. 11–12.

16   *'Oh, Israel!':* Rose Pastor Stokes 1, pp. 35–37.

17   *In 1890, the year Rose:* Cooper, p. 13.

18   *cigar workers suffered: Bulletin of the Bureau of Labor,* vol. 18 (Washington, DC: Government Printing Office, 1909), p. 564.

19   *"It was a hard winter":* Rose Pastor Stokes 1, pp. 39–41.

she seldom made: Graham to his mother, 21 April 1905, JGPS-Columbia, Box 85. This may be a more reliable figure than the slightly lower one that Rose, always eager to stress her penury, uses in her memoir.

20   *"During my first year":* Rose Pastor Stokes 1, pp. 121, 55, 45.

"the noble-minded heroine": Boston American, 6 April 1905, quoted in Tamarkin, p. 40.

21   *"He would go":* Rose Pastor Stokes 1, pp. 57–58.

"Cut, cut, cut!": 1906? JGPS-Columbia, Box 75.

"The ventilation": n.d., quoted in Doris Francis, *Will You Still Need Me, Will You Still Feed Me, When I'm 84?* (Bloomington: Indiana University Press, 1984), p. 18.

22   *"No word, no clue":* Rose Pastor Stokes 1, p. 77.

"Count, count, count!": 1906? JGPS-Columbia, Box 75.

"always I found": Rose Pastor Stokes 1, pp. 68–69.

23   *"Once your hand":* "Stokes Bride's Own Story," New York *Sun,* 7 April 1905.

25   *"in the editor's own hand":* Rose Pastor Stokes 1, pp. 63–80.

"Don't let a day pass": 9 October 1901.

"the only hours": Rose Pastor Stokes 1, p. 81.

"I never saw": "Mrs. Stokes on 'Socialism,'" *Newton Circuit* (Newton Center, MA), 27 February 1914.

"hundreds of letters": Rose Pastor Stokes 1, p. 83.

3. City of the World

27   *"sparkling brown eyes"*: Zunser, p. 290.

     "All that had happened": Goldman, p. 3.

28   *"A great hubbub"*: "'Heart of the Ghetto,'" *Evening World*, 14 April
     1905.

30   *"just to see me"*: Rose Pastor Stokes 1, p. 80.

     "In our silent evenings together": Zunser, p. 291.

     "I also became": Rose Pastor Stokes 1, p. 85.

     one survey of the district: Population statistics from Sorin, p. 71, and An-
     binder, p. 359.

31   *grim apartment life:* "The Rise of a New Type of Socialist," *Congregation-
     alist and Christian World* 4, August 1906.

32   *"had to pick and nudge"*: Abraham Cahan, *Yekl and the Imported Bride-
     groom and Other Stories of the New York Ghetto* (New York: Dover, 1970),
     p. 13, quoted in Sorin, p. 71.

     "Was this the America": Howe, p. 67. It is unclear whom he is quoting.

     "During an election": Rose Pastor Stokes 1, p. 87.

33   *"A flirt is"*: "Some of the Striking Epigrams in Miss Rose Pastor's 'Dust-
     pan Ethics,'" *Evening World*, 8 April 1905.

     "'Free love!'": "Just Between Ourselves, Girls," *Yiddishes Tageblatt*, 7 and 22
     December 1903.

     "make demands upon him": Rose Pastor Stokes 1, p. 91.

     "to the balcony": "Just Between Ourselves, Girls," *Yiddishes Tageblatt*, 24
     September 1903.

34   *"Our children MUST"*: "Editorial" signed R. H. P., *Yiddishes Tageblatt*, 26
     August 1903.

35   *"speech to his fellow senators":* 16 March 1896.

     "the Jew makes me creep": Quoted in Simon, p. 19.

     "furtive Yacoob": *The Education of Henry Adams* (New York: Oxford Uni-
     versity Press, 1999), p. 202.

     "small, strange animals": Quoted in Simon, p. 19.

36   *"You know what"*: "Riot Mars Funeral of Rabbi Joseph," *New York Times*,
     31 July 1902.

     "If this is a free": Dinnerstein, p. 40.

37   *"Throughout the [nineteenth] century"*: *A History of the American People*, vol.
     10 (New York: Harper, 1918), pp. 98–99.

     "of education and culture": Gregory Weinstein, quoted in J. G. Phelps
     Stokes, *My Narrative*, p. 111.

     The first attempt: Allen F. Davis, "Settlement Workers in Politics, 1890–
     1914," *Review of Politics* 26(4), October 1964, p. 506.

38   *a survey of more:* The survey was in 1905. Davis, p. 27.

"My God": University Settlement Society, *Legacy of Light* (New York, 2012), pp. 82–83. In this book celebrating its 125th anniversary, the University Settlement claimed Eleanor Roosevelt as one of its own volunteers, but in fact she taught at the nearby College Settlement.

39   *"vital contact"*: Chura, p. 1, cites an early use in an 1896 book by a Princeton sociology professor, Walter Wyckoff, *The Workers: An Experiment in Reality.* It came into wider currency after a 1908 article by a Harvard student socialist, Lee Simonson.

"to shut one's self": "A New Impulse to an Old Gospel," *Forum* 14, 1892, p. 350.

"Make friends with": Poole 1, p. 71, quoting an uncharacteristically humble-sounding William English Walling, and p. 73.

40   *"I had visions"*: Rose Pastor Stokes 1, pp. 92–93.

4. Missionary to the Slums

42   *new summer "cottage"*: The building was completed in 1894. It would be surpassed the next year by George Vanderbilt's Biltmore House in Asheville, North Carolina. Graham was among the guests transported there in private railway cars for the housewarming.

42   *"some '96 fellows"*: Dodge, p. 211.

43   *police ledgers list*: Mable A. Wiley, *A Study of the Problem of Girl Delinquency in New Haven* (New Haven, CT: Civic Federation of New Haven, 1915), passim.

45   *"My son"*: J. G. Phelps Stokes, *My Narrative,* pp. 65–70.

"the wealthiest corporation": "Great Faith in This Country," *Tonopah Bonanza,* 19 October 1907.

46   *"became instead a missionary"*: Davis, p. 28.

47   *"No work for"*: J. G. Phelps Stokes 1, pp. 4, 14–15, 19.

47   *"enchanted by the very tall"*: Rose Pastor Stokes 1, p. 93.

"a look in his eyes": "The Views of a Settlement Worker: A Talk with J. G. Phelps Stokes," *Yiddishes Tageblatt,* 19 July 1903.

48   *"the tall young 'Lincoln'"*: Rose Pastor Stokes 1, p. 93.

He not only lobbied: Davis, pp. 129–130.

"Upon many stifling": Poole 1, p. 84.

49   *"were always between"*: Rose Pastor Stokes 1, p. 94.

50   *"sex expression is as vital"*: Goldman, pp. 101, 151, 84.

"a stocky figure": Fenner Brockway, *Inside the Left: Thirty Years of Platform, Press, Prison, and Parliament* (London: George Allen & Unwin, 1942), p. 298.

"I began to speak": Goldman, p. 39.

51   *"the University Settlement"*: Rose Pastor Stokes 1, p. 95.

"that by the simple device": Sinclair, p. 109.

"It moved me profoundly": Rose Pastor Stokes 1, p. 96.

53   *"I had never":* Rose Pastor Stokes 1, pp. 96, 98.

5. Cinderella of the Sweatshops

54   *"I am truly":* 22 December 1904, JGPS-Yale, Box 3, Folder 80.

"was designed": Rose Pastor Stokes 1, p. 100.

55   *"If my children fail":* Anson Phelps Stokes [Sr.], vol. 1, part 1, p. 7.

56   *"What excuse":* "Talks with Girls," *Yiddishes Tageblatt,* 12 July 1903, quoted in Enstad, p. 49.

"J. G. Phelps Stokes": 6 April 1905.

"no phase of": "Study in Pen and Pencil of Rose Harriet Pastor, the Genius of the Ghetto," *Evening World,* 8 April 1905.

the first such statistics: For Russian Jews .62 percent, for all Jews 1.17 percent, in the period 1908–1912. Julius Drachsler, *Intermarriage in New York City: A Statistical Study of the Amalgamation of European Peoples* (Ph.D. dissertation, political science, Columbia University, 1921), p. 43.

"Russian Israelite": 13 April 1905.

57   *"it was obvious":* "Stokes Bride's Own Story," New York *Sun,* 7 April 1905.

"influence the young": "Attacks the Stokeses," quoted in *New York Times,* 20 July 1905.

"All honor": "A New 'Amazing Marriage,'" 7 April 1905.

"Miss Pastor and I": 9 March 1905, JGPS-Columbia, Box 85.

58   *"You cannot realize":* 16 April 1905, JGPS-Yale, Box 3, Folder 80.

"Stokes Family Approves": *Evening World,* 6 April 1905.

"Graham's engagement," "Is it not," "much simple": 8, 15, and 20 April 1905, APS-Yale, Box 135, Folder 2459.

"filled with Poles," "groups of this": 11 and 15 December 1865, quoted in Tamarkin, p. 24.

"that there is": "J. G. Phelps Stokes to Wed Young Jewess," *New York Times,* 6 April 1905.

59   *"Miss Pastor and I":* "'We Are Already One in Soul,' Says Stokes," *Evening World,* 7 April 1905.

"millions of people": Rose Pastor Stokes 1, pp. 101–102.

"series of six articles": They ran on April 10, 12, 13, 14, 15, and 18, 1905.

"You thief!": "'Heart of the Ghetto,'" *Evening World,* 14 April 1905.

60   *"A customer takes":* "'In the Gloom of the Ghetto,'" *Evening World,* 15 April 1905.

"She is rather": "Study in Pen and Pencil of Rose Harriet Pastor, the Genius of the Ghetto," *Evening World,* 8 April 1905.

61   *"Miss Pastor is a blonde":* "Stokes Bride's Own Story," New York *Sun,* 7 April 1905.

"delightfully received": 21 April 1905, JGPS-Columbia, Box 85.

62   *"I soon grew"*: "Stokes Bride's Own Story," New York *Sun,* 7 April
1905.
"dear darling Saint!": 20 April 1905, RPS-Tamiment, quoted in Zipser,
p. 41.
"I wanted to sit," "And now that I am": Rose Pastor Stokes 1, pp. 100–101.

63   *"I believe that trade"*: "Hear J. G. Phelps Stokes," *New-York Tribune,* 5 June
1905.
"The work in the interest": "Stokes Bride-to-Be Talks to Cigarmakers,"
New York Times, 5 June 1905.

64   *"'I want the word"*: Rose Pastor Stokes 1, p. 104.
"The rector": "East Side's Poetess Is Now Mrs. Stokes," *New York Times,* 19
July 1905.
"two or three": To Anson Phelps Stokes Jr., 10 February 1919, APS-Yale,
Box 62, Folder 852.
"Mrs. Stokes objected": "Miss Pastor Weds Stokes," New York *Sun,* 19 July
1905.

65   *"I literally ran"*: Rose Pastor Stokes 1, p. 104.
"One of the butlers": Zunser, p. 293.

6. Distant Thunder

66   *"He wore a tall"*: Hutchins Hapgood, quoted in Page Smith, p. 5.

68   *"not by the labor"*: "Our God Sent Coal Operators," *New-York Tribune,* 22
August 1902.
By 1915: Peter H. Lindert and Jeffrey G. Williamson, *Unequal Gains:
American Growth and Inequality Since 1700* (Princeton, NJ: Princeton
University Press, 2016), p. 173.

69   *"Take down your pants"*: Page Smith, p. 114.

70   *"the Bay of Naples"*: Rose Pastor Stokes 1, pp. 106–107.

71   *"She is a tall"*: Quoted in "Rose Pastor Stokes," *Socialist Woman* 1(5), Octo-
ber 1907, p. 2.
"Her eye was": Lillian Baynes Griffin, "Mrs. J. G. Phelps Stokes at Home,"
Harper's Bazar 40, September 1906.
"I learned": Unpublished ms., apparently an early draft of her autobiogra-
phy, RPS-Tamiment, Box 2, Folder 6.

72   *"the road to the Patent"*: From Frank Kellogg, 26 December 1906, JGPS-
Yale, Box 2, Folder 30.
"to instruct a staff": From William Doig, 18 July 1906, JGPS-Yale, Box 1,
Folder 15.

73   *"were supplying the poor"*: Rose Pastor Stokes 1, pp. 108–114.
"wealthy women": "The Condition of Working Women from the Working Woman's Viewpoint," *Annals of the American Academy of Political and
Social Science* XXVII, January–June, 1906, p. 173.

"*through which men*": "J. G. P. Stokes Explains," 5 March 1907.

74 "*If it didn't exist*": "Stokeses Stir Up Dr. Day," New York *Sun,* 19 January 1907.

"*Through the trip south*": Rose Pastor Stokes 1, p. 114.

75 "*If such a government*": *Free Russia* 1, September 1890, p. 20.

76 *Catherine Breshkovsky:* This was how she signed her name in English, anglicized from Ekaterina Breshko-Breshkovskaia.

77 "*She was going back*": Rose Pastor Stokes 1, p. 95.

78 "*Maxim Gorky was probably*": "Maxim Gorky: Brief Life of a Great Enigma: 1868–1936," *Harvard Magazine,* July–August 2008, p. 36.

one estimate puts it: Thompson and Hart, p. 28.

"*The Massacre As I Saw It*": 24 January 1906.

79 "*The news of the Russian*": Goldman, p. 248.

7. Island Paradise

81 "*of congenial people*": "Stokes Plans a Utopia," *New York Times,* 17 December 1909.

"*come out of*": To Helena Monroe Ferguson (Helena Frank), 21 December 1906, JGPS-Columbia, Box 85.

"*a young Bulgarian*": Kent, p. 194.

"*read much Socialist*": Rose Pastor Stokes 1, p. 127.

82 "*Socialism has hitherto*": To F. H. Giddings, n.d., JGPS-Columbia, quoted in Zipser, p. 114.

"*Socialism Would Cure*": *New York Call,* 1 October 1908.

"*it would hardly*": "Few Men Viciously Idle, Says Phelps Stokes," New York *Sun,* 13 August 1912.

83 "*I can't even*": Jervis Langdon, *Samuel Langhorne Clemens: Some Reminiscences and Some Excerpts from Letters and Unpublished Manuscripts* (Elmira, NY[?], 1910), p. 12.

"*far more ominous*": To Charles F. Gettemy, 1 February 1905, quoted in Ginger, p. 290.

84 "*It was a great*": "Wage Slaves Hear from Stokes," 16 September 1906.

"*he hemmed and*": Elizabeth Gurley Flynn, in *Daily Worker,* 20 June 1943, reprinted in *Words on Fire: The Life and Writing of Elizabeth Gurley Flynn,* ed. Rosalyn Fraad Baxandall (New Brunswick, NJ: Rutgers University Press, 1987), p. 180.

"*I made no notes*": Rose Pastor Stokes 1, pp. 117–118.

84 "*now calm and low*": "Mrs. Stokes on 'Socialism,'" *Newton Circuit* (Newton Center, MA), 27 February 1911.

"*leave Methodism*": 14 July 1906, JGPS-Yale, Box 4, Folder 83.

85 *two of the three men:* Lukas, p. 381 fn.

"*darling Mother*": 6 December 1906, JGPS-Columbia, Box 85.

"one can rest": To Helena Munroe Ferguson (Helena Frank), 21 December 1906, JGPS-Columbia, Box 85.

87   *"The American nation":* *Harper's Weekly* 50, 8 September 1906, p. 1284.
      "seem to kiss": Thompson and Hart, p. 128.

88   *"I am running":* Kaun, p. 572.

89   *"rose water and":* Editorial, *New York Evening Post,* 16 April 1906.
      "standing by the": 28 April 1906, quoted in Reynolds 1, p. 23.
      "We must accept": "Gorky's Private Life His Own Affair, Says Mrs. Phelps Stokes," *Evening World,* 14 April 1906.

8. A Tall, Shamblefooted Man

90   *a horrifying scene:* ASW-Yale, Box 32, Folder 387.
      "Our love which": Anna to Hyman Strunsky, 3 March 1906, quoted in Boylan, p. 95.

91   *"I cry, Long live":* To Katia Mayson, 9 February 1905, quoted in Boylan, p. 79.
      "intense seriousness": Norman Hapgood, *A Victorian in the Modern World* (New York: Harcourt, Brace, 1939), p. 425.

92   *"We are equals," "not exactly masterly":* To Rosalind Walling, April 1906, and to Willoughby Walling, spring 1906, quoted in Boylan, p. 108.
      "He arrived shortly": ASW-Yale, Box 32, Folder 387.
      "The Revolutionaries tell me": To Willoughby and Rosalind Walling, 29 January 1906, William English Walling Papers, State Historical Society of Wisconsin, Madison, quoted in Fink, p. 322 n. 25.
      "to share permanently": 19 September [1907?], RPS-Yale, Box 5.

93   *"sports, heavy drinking":* *The Larger Aspects of Socialism* (New York: Macmillan, 1913), p. 372.

94   *"a Jewish factory worker":* Morris Hillquit, *Loose Leaves from a Busy Life* (New York: Macmillan, 1934), p. 57.

95   *"take the taste":* To Carol Mitchell Stokes, n.d., APS-Yale, Box 134, quoted in Tamarkin, p. 184.
      "th' well-known Socialist": "Mr. Dooley Discusses Socialism," *Collier's,* 2 June 1906, p. 17. Reynolds 1, p. 353, points out that this frequently quoted passage was almost certainly inspired by news reports of the second gathering of "millionaire socialists" at Graham's parents' house.
      Sarah Koten: Rachel Elin Nolan is the first scholar to notice Rose's involvement with Koten. My thanks to Nolan for sharing some of her materials with me.

96   *"All right, judge":* "Sara Koten Tells Her Own Story," *New York Call,* 13 June, 1908.
      "Are you the murderer": "Nurse Kills Doctor," *New-York Tribune,* 8 June 1908.

"there is little": "Murder by Divine Request," 9 June 1908.

"a dull, plodding": "Koten Girl Escapes Chair," New York *Sun,* 15 April 1909.

"In less than five": "Sara Koten Tells Her Own Story," 13 June 1908.

97   *"I will pay all":* "Rose Pastor Will Help," *Cleveland Plain Dealer,* 13 June 1908.

"more sinned against": Koten's destination after the trial was kept secret so she would not be followed by a horde of reporters. There is no certain confirmation that Koten took up Rose's offer of refuge at Caritas Island, but consistent with her going there is the report that on leaving the court "she was led through the crowd and hurried into a waiting carriage, being taken to the Grand Central station, where a train was boarding for the North. Her destination was not revealed other than that it was a quiet country place where she can care for her baby and be cared for herself." "Sara Koten Is Set at Liberty," *New York Call,* 21 April 1909.

"something at the bottom": "Stokeses Stir Up Dr. Day," New York *Sun,* 19 January 1907.

"I felt I could remove": To "Comrade Ells," October 1916, RPS-Tamiment, quoted in Zipser, p. 116.

98   *"We call to mind":* "Mrs. J. G. Phelps Stokes — the Socialists' Attitude Toward Charity," *Chautauquan Daily,* 15 July 1913.

"was attractively presented": Brooklyn Citizen, 25 January 1907, quoted in Zipser, p. 63.

"Mrs. Phelps Stokes made quite": Ralph M. Easley, quoted in Zipser, p. 60.

"She is immensely": "Rose Stokes in the Shirtwaist Strike," *New York Times,* 2 January 1910.

"Mrs. Stokes is a wonderful": Morris Hindus, quoted in *Intercollegiate Socialist,* April–May 1914, p. 26.

"She was very emotional": Mildred Phelps Stokes Hooker to John M. Whitcomb, 20 August [1960?], quoted in Tamarkin, p. 236.

99   *"able-bodied men":* "To the Members of the Socialist Party in the Eighth Assembly District of New York," 4 September 1908, RPS-Yale, Box 11.

"She is as much": "Sunday Afternoon Campaign Meetings," *Trenton Evening Times,* 16 October 1908.

100   *"children used to flock":* Oscar Ameringer, *If You Don't Weaken* (Norman: University of Oklahoma Press, 1983), p. 226.

101   *"It was like a sacrament":* Eastman 2, p. 57.

"That old man with the burning": Quoted in Howard Zinn, *A People's History of the United States, 1492–Present* (New York: Harper, 2005), pp. 339–340.

"He was a tall shamblefooted": Dos Passos, p. 31.

102   *"on a truck":* Poole 1, p. 196.

"but I and many women": "Debs Speaks Here in a Sea of Red," *New York Times,* 5 October 1908.

103   *"Oh, what a wonderful cause":* 26 August 1908, RPS-Tamiment, Box 2, Folder 13.

9. By Ballot or Bullet

104   *"I am a working girl," "If I turn":* Buhle et al., p. 744, Levine, p. 154, and Dubofsky 1, p. 12.

105   *"She was on the platform":* Sarah Comstock, "The Uprising of the Girls," *Collier's,* 25 December 1909.

106   *"in piecework":* Enstad, p. 142.
       "supreme, despairing": "Hunter and Moose: Parable on the Strike," *New York Evening Journal,* 6 January 1910, quoted in Tamarkin, p. 226.

107   *"My people":* Anonymous "Slavic immigrant" quoted in Robert Wiebe, *The Search for Order: 1877–1920* (New York: Hill and Wang, 1967), p. 9.
       Yet half of all male: Dubofsky 1, p. 12.
       "Morning, noon": Jacob August Riis, *How the Other Half Lives: Studies Among the Tenements of New York* (New York: Scribner's, 1914), pp. 124–125.

108   *"The police became":* Vorse, p. 33.
       "Really, I'll never put": Page Smith, p. 250.
       "Altogether too much": To Elizabeth Gurley Flynn, quoted in "Rose Pastor Stokes Tells of Strike," *Spokane Press,* 2 January 1910.

109   *"What is there":* "One on Mrs. Stokes," *New-York Tribune,* 16 December 1909.
       sent her a telegram: "Ask Mrs. Stokes for Aid," *New-York Tribune,* 13 January 1910.
       "Mrs. Stokes told": "To Strike in Philadelphia: Shirtwaist Workers Act Upon Suggestion of Mrs. Stokes," *New-York Tribune,* 5 December 1909.

110   *"Rose, any time":* 12 October 1909, RPS-Yale, Box 3.
       "The baby was": Kent, pp. 187–194.

111   *Rose declared that:* "Miss Goldman's Trial Draws Sympathizers," *Bridgeport (CT) Evening Farmer,* 21 April 1916.
       "Only the prisoner": "Twilight Sleep II," *McClure's,* June 1922, p. 64.
       "Someday I shall emerge": To Jack London, 1 April 1913, quoted in Boylan, p. 198.
       "Forget your babies!": Goldman to Anna Walling, 2 November 1912, quoted in Fink, p. 163.

112   *"it was as though a spurt":* Vorse, p. 9.
       "After reading it": Flynn, pp. 123, 48.

113   *"Take care, my son":* Vorse, p. 34.

"the very citadel": Kent, p. 193.

114   *"probably not exceeding"*: "Mrs. J. G. Phelps Stokes at Home," *Harper's Bazar* 40, September 1906, p. 795.

"a gift or loan": October 1908, JGPS-Columbia, Box 85.

115   *"the moving spirit"*: "Famous Stokes Mine Is Sold," *Tonopah Daily Bonanza,* 30 August 1908.

"I have already trod": To Olive Dargan[?], March 1909, RPS-Tamiment, Box 1, Folder 5.

"Left pamphlets": Diary, RPS-Yale, Box 13, Folder 1.

"non-producers": "A Talk with the Richest Socialist in America," *New York Times,* 23 October 1910.

"more slender": "World's New Rebellion Is Spread of Socialism; Ballots or Bullets Says Rose Pastor Stokes," *New York World,* 15 November 1909, quoted in Tamarkin, pp. 231–233.

10. A Key to the Gates of Heaven

119   *tracked down the stories:* "The Factory Girl's Danger," *Outlook,* 15 April 1911.

120   *"One hundred waiters"*: "Waiters' Strike May Tie Up All Hotels in City," *Evening World,* 8 May 1912. See also "Waiters Walk Out at the Hotel Belmont," New York *Sun,* 8 May 1912, and "Strike Call Startles Hotel Belmont Guests," *New-York Tribune,* 8 May 1912.

"trimmings, refuse": "Notes from Mrs. Stokes's Memoirs Regarding the Waiters' Strike," RPS-Yale, Box 6.

121   *"put the grease"*: *Cincinnati Times Star,* n.d., RPS-Tamiment, quoted in Antler, p. 86. There are more notes to herself of similar sabotage ideas in RPS-Tamiment, Box 1, Folder 2, although it is unclear how many of them made it into her speeches.

122   *"Styles of speech"*: Flynn, p. 62.

123   *"Fellow workers"*: John Reed to Eddy Hunt, n.d., quoted in Rosenstone, p. 121.

A miner who: Carlson, p. 48.

124   *"An uncouth, stumbling"*: Sanger, pp. 70–71.

"Rose Pastor Stokes was greeted": "Over 5,000 Strikers and Friends Meet," New York *Sun,* 1 June 1912.

"Your 'Jungle' may": 23 March 1911, Upton Sinclair ms., Lilly Library, Indiana University, Bloomington, quoted in Zipser, p. 145.

125   *"had only had a bowl"*: From "Ignatius," 17 June 1912, RPS-Tamiment, Box 1, Folder 2.

"your words are": DV[?] "Italian Waiter," 10 June 1912, RPS-Tamiment, Box 1, Folder 2.

"Russian, Pole, Irishman": "Mrs. Stokes Berates Hotel Proprietors," *New York Times,* 20 May 1912.

"The thing for Rose": 25 June 1912, APS-Yale, Box 62, Folder 846.

126   *"highly advanced friendship":* "Stokes's Story of Shooting," New York *Sun,* 25 November 1911.

"You have upset": 24 June 1912, RPS-Tamiment, quoted in Zipser, pp. 90–91.

127   *"the biggest tip":* Philadelphia *Bulletin,* 8 June 1912.

"the headwaiter": Diary, RPS-Yale, Box 13, Folder 1.

129   *"I hated":* Unpublished ms., apparently an early draft of her autobiography, RPS-Tamiment, Folder 6.

"Everywhere, new institutions": Quoted in Diggins, p. 93.

130   *"cousins to the anarchists":* Quoted in Wallace, p. 882.

"my vacation": Golin, p. 119.

"She read everything": The Autobiography of Lincoln Steffens, vol. 2 (New York: Harcourt, Brace, 1931), p. 654.

"a lady who": Churchill, p. 16.

131   *"burst upon New York":* Sanger, p. 73.

132   *"the fair-haired":* Lincoln Schuster to Victor Gollancz, 1936, quoted in Diggins, p. 93.

"Your honor": September 1915.

"slapdash gathering": O'Neill, p. 5.

"barriers went down": Luhan, pp. 83, 39.

133   *"What am I doing this":* Ray Stannard Baker, "Seeing America: A Rich Young Man Who Began to Believe in Jesus Christ," *American Magazine* LXXVIII(1), July 1914, p. 16.

134   *"Walk right in":* William Stewart, *Keir Hardie* (London: National Labour Press, 1921), p. 115.

"Whether in literature": "Art and Unrest," *New York Globe and Commercial Advertiser,* 27 January 1913, quoted in Stansell, p. 2.

"Our ears catching": Enjoyment of Poetry (New York: Scribner's, 1913), pp. 10–11, quoted in Diggins, p. 94.

135   *"No Yiddish writer":* Howe, p. 421.

"in that particularly": Francis Steegmuller, *Maupassant: A Lion in the Path* (New York: Random House, 1949), p. 139.

"the day of industrial": New York Call, 17 March 1913 and 17 October 1915, quoted in Sharp, pp. 54–55.

"Her clouds of": Daily Worker, 20 June 1943, reprinted in *Words on Fire: The Life and Writing of Elizabeth Gurley Flynn,* ed. Rosalyn Fraad Baxandall (New Brunswick, NJ: Rutgers University Press, 1987), p. 180.

"None of the men": Scott Nearing to RPS, 25 July 1913, RPS-Tamiment, Box 3, Folder 15.

11. Not the Rose I Thought She Was

136   *"At the ends"*: Rose Pastor Stokes 1, p. 131.

137   *"hearing in silence"*: Diary, RPS-Yale, Box 13, Folder 1. Fewer than two dozen of the diary's pages are filled, and, although sometimes the year is noted, the entries do not correspond to the dates printed on the pages.

138   *"Haywood, and Rose"*: "A Talk with Julius H. Cohen, Minimizer of Controversy," *New York Times,* 26 January 1913.
       "Men wept": Diary, RPS-Yale, Box 13, Folder 1.
       "her fiery words": "Fight to Finish, Cry of Garment Workers," *New-York Tribune,* 14 January 1913.
       "Girl Workers Stirred": 12 January 1913.
       "This meeting was": Diary, RPS-Yale, Box 13, Folder 1.
       "Why do you preach": "Rose Pastor Stokes Goes on Warpath," *Los Angeles Times,* 12 January 1913.

139   *"I wear good"*: "Noted Social Worker Replies Feelingly to an Attack Made on Her," 13 January 1913, RPS-Tamiment, Box 5, Folder 19. Newspaper name not visible on clipping.

140   *"tricked by racial"*: Golin, p. 12.
       "What are you two": Flynn, p. 161.
       "But I had a gun": Carlson, p. 202.
       "well-educated literary": Quoted in Dray, p. 296.
       "in the faces": RPS to Upton Sinclair, 26 May 1913, quoted in Tamarkin, p. 281.

141   *"I wish I could show"*: Luhan, pp. 188–189.
       "to write my name": Bertram D. Wolfe, introduction to *Ten Days That Shook the World* (New York: Modern Library/Random House, 1960), p. xiv.

142   *"It's so much Reed"*: David Carb, quoted in Rosenstone, p. 167.
       "we are free": Anna Alice Chapin, "The Day in Bohemia, or Life Among the Artists," in *Greenwich Village* (New York: Dodd, Mead, 1920), p. 177.
       "We know we can": "Tonight's Red Pageant at Garden," *New York Call,* 7 June 1913.

143   *"the wretchedness of"*: Quoted in Gelb, p. 55.

144   *"Arise, ye prisoners"*: Golin, p. 168.
       "say a few words": 20 January 1913, RPS-Yale, Box 2.

145   *"afraid of contaminating"*: 12 November 1913, RPS-Tamiment, Box 2, Folder 13.
       "I would rather": "Rose Pastor Stokes Blames 'System' When Robbed Here," *Lima Republican Gazette,* 24 August 1913.

"How can you love": "Mrs. Stokes on 'Socialism,'" *Newton Circuit* (Newton Centre, MA), 27 February 1914.

"appeared to me": Rose Strunsky letter fragment, c. 1912 or early 1913, quoted in Reynolds 1, p. 238.

An Ohio newspaper: "Rose Pastor Stokes Blames 'System' When Robbed Here."

146 *"for unorthodox women"*: Luhan, p. 143.

147 *"an experience of"*: Quoted in Schwarz, p. 1.

"No one was there": Flynn, p. 280.

"it was all so": Sara Josephine Baker, *Fighting for Life* (New York: Macmillan, 1939), pp. 182–183, quoted in Schwarz, p. 18.

"Graham has been": Diary, RPS-Yale, Box 13, Folder 1.

"Glorious Inspiration": [1915?], RPS-Tamiment, Box 2, Folder 13.

148 *"I often wondered"*: Goldman to Sonya Levien, 6 November 1925, Emma Goldman Papers, University of California, Berkeley, Reel 15.

a strong belief: Apparent evidence to the contrary, cited by Renshaw, p. 425 n. 16, is effectively debunked in Zipser, p. 173.

"The women gathered": Rose Pastor Stokes 1, p. 142.

149 *"Can not you"*: 7 May 1914, RPS-Yale, Box 4.

"I have had no": 2 June 1914, RPS-Tamiment, Box 2, Folder 13.

"longer than the date": 23 May 1914, RPS-Tamiment, Box 3, Folder 15D.

12. I Didn't Raise My Boy to Be a Soldier

151 *"A great cheer"*: "Multitudes Cheer at Bulletin Boards," 5 August 1914.

"When the war": Haywood, p. 280.

153 *"Louder and louder"*: Lyn Macdonald, *1914* (London: Michael Joseph, 1987), p. 90.

154 *"the editorial chorus"*: "The Trader's War," *Masses,* September 1914, p. 17.

"debauched, diseased": "The Worst Thing in Europe," *Masses,* March 1915, p. 18.

155 *"Excuse me, sir"*: RPS-Tamiment, Box 5, Folder 22.

156 *"Dear Girlie, I shall"*: 15 March 1915, RPS-Yale, Box 4.

"Today marked a deep": Diary, RPS-Yale, Box 13, Folder 1.

"Graham was furious": 1 September 1928, RPS-Yale, Box 1.

"the light of an afternoon": Unpublished notes by Matilda Rabinowitz. My thanks to her granddaughter, Robbin Légère Henderson, for making them available to me.

157 *"Former Factory Girl"*: Unidentified newspaper, Dover, NJ, 20 December 1915, RPS-Yale, Box 7.

158 *"If the audience"*: "Socialists Applaud a Problem Playlet," *New York Times,* 29 March 1914.

The Woman Who Wouldn't: Nolan traces connections between the plot of this play and some of the events in the Sarah Koten murder case described in chapter 8.

159   *"a good wife, a good mother"*: Quoted in Wallace, p. 759.

160   *"the cardinal sin"*: "Race Decadence," *Outlook*, 8 April 1911, pp. 763, 767.

    "the fierce, blind struggle": Goldman, p. 125.

    "those parents who": "'Why Race-Suicide with Advancing Civilization?': A Symposium," *Arena*, February 1909, p. 192.

161   *"He has a speech"*: Sanger, p. 188.

    "What is good": "Mrs. Stokes Defies the Law with Birth Control Talk— Emma Goldman Up Today," *Day Book* (Chicago), 20 April 1916.

    "glad that my": n.d., RPS-Tamiment, Box 4, Folder 15.

162   *"was a demonstration"*: "Mrs. Rose P. Stokes Defies the Police," *New York Times*, 6 May 1916.

    "true revolutionaries": Emma Goldman to RPS, n.d., RPS-Tamiment, quoted in Sharp, p. 111.

    "just before you take": "Information I have been sending to inquirers," RPS-Yale, Box 7.

    "Don't write to": 11 May 1916, RPS-Tamiment, Box 4, Folder 15A.

    "The notoriety," "My deliberate running": 21 and 29 May 1916, RPS-Yale, Box 4.

163   *Skillfully adjusting*: 6 June 1916, APS-Yale, Box 62, Folder 842. Also in RPS-Tamiment, Box 4, Folder 15.

    "With some feeling": Diary, RPS-Yale, Box 13, Folder 1.

164   *"to eliminate the failings"*: 23 July 1916, RPS-Tamiment, Box 2, Folder 7.

    An elevator operator: John and Helen Sweeney, 14 June 1916, RPS-Tamiment, Box 2, Folder 7.

    "in the sixteen years": H. P. Hough, 3 December 1916, RPS-Tamiment, Box 2, Folder 7.

166   *"perhaps the greatest"*: "Every Calling in the Line," 14 May 1916.

167   *"There are citizens"*: 7 December 1915.

13. Let the Guilty Be Shot at Once

168   *"Why do not we"*: W.E.D. Stokes, p. 74.

169   *"that Negro chapters"*: Rose Pastor Stokes 1, p. 139. A handwritten, marked-up draft of this letter, to Harry Laidler, 12 December 1916, is in RPS-Tamiment, Box 2, Folder 6.

170   *"would make it"*: To Harry Laidler, 25 January 1917, JGPS-Columbia, quoted in Horn, p. 115.

    "'I wish our side": Rose to Harry Laidler, 23 November 1916, RPS-Tamiment, Box 1, Folder 1.

    "We have had no one": Charles L. Raper to ISS, n.d., Catalogued Corre-

spondence Box 3, JGPS-Columbia (filed under Laidler). Also in RPS-Tamiment, Box 1, Folder 1.

"the whole city": Josiah Morse in *Intercollegiate Socialist* V(3), February–March 1917, p. 26.

"Two whole days": 30 November 1916, RPS-Tamiment, Box 2, Folder 13.

172   *"The United States"*: To "Socialist Comrade," March 1916, JGPS-Columbia, quoted in Zipser, p. 166.

"I pity the poor": Alan Seeger, quoted in David M. Kennedy, p. 181.

173   *"criminal to the last"*: March 1917[?], quoted in Boylan, p. 229.

"may very likely": 18 December 1915, Catalogued Correspondence Box 4, JGPS-Columbia.

174   *"remarked that she"*: 9 July 1917, Catalogued Correspondence Box 4, JGPS-Columbia.

"To refuse to resist": "Socialists Pledge Support to Wilson," *Washington Post*, 24 March 1917.

175   *"Rose Pastor Stokes Quits"*: 18 March 1917. The full resignation letter, dated 17 March, can be found in RPS-Tamiment, Box 5, Folder 33.

"Czar Overthrown in Russia": 15 March 1917.

"the establishment of a new": "The Russian Peace," *Masses*, July 1917, p. 35.

176   *"receipt of the news"*: "Women of Russia to Vote for Assembly," 23 March 1917.

"The revolution is one": "War Made Revolt Possible," 18 March 1917.

178   *"German-drilled voters"*: *Independent* 91, 10 November 1917, quoted in Boylan, p. 237.

"have been my personal": 29 April 1917, Catalogued Correspondence Box 3, JGPS-Columbia (filed under Lansing).

"Fraternally": To Stamford Socialist Party local, 9 July 1917, JGPS-Columbia, Box 27.

179   *"it is not easy"*: "A Confession," *Century*, December 1917, pp. 457–459.

"all they lacked": Reynolds 1, p. 284.

"For men like Stokes": "The Black Scourge of War," *Mother Earth*, June 1917, p. 102.

"The true internationalist": "Nonresistance and Anarchy Closely Allied," *New York Times*, 25 November 1917.

"began drilling a regiment": Sinclair, p. 140.

180   *He barraged*: See *The Letters of Theodore Roosevelt*, vol. 8, ed. Elting E. Morison (Cambridge, MA: Harvard University Press, 1954), pp. 1182, 1189, 1192–1195, and Seward W. Livermore, *Woodrow Wilson and the War Congress, 1916–18* (Seattle: University of Washington Press, 1966), pp. 19–31.

"the least inclined": Rose Pastor Stokes 1, pp. 147–149.

181   *"They give you"*: Jeremy McCarter, *Young Radicals in the War for American Ideals* (New York: Random House, 2017), p. 181.

"The Christian Singing Society": Preston, pp. 147–148.

183   *"Pro-German traitors"*: "Shoot Our Traitors at Home, Root Warns at Welcome Here from His Mission to Russia," *New York Times*, 16 August 1917.

    "There is no use": Kazin, p. 190.

    "An immediate secret": "Take Up Appeals to Expel Senators," *New York Times*, 2 October 1917. These words have often been erroneously put in Graham Stokes's mouth after being so attributed in David A. Shannon, *The Socialist Party of America: A History* (New York: Macmillan, 1955), p. 101. Reynolds pointed out this mistake both in his unpublished Ph.D. dissertation (Reynolds 1, p. 299) and in a short published article (Reynolds 3), but historians have continued to make it.

184   *"It took a world war"*: "By the Way," 11 July 1917.

    "Gentlemen of the jury": Quoted in Stansell, pp. 323–324.

185   *"have written a lesson"*: "Traitors at Home, Enemies Abroad," 15 July 1917.

186   *"with the bullet"*: "World's New Rebellion Is Spread of Socialism; Ballots or Bullets Says Rose Pastor Stokes," *New York World*, 15 November 1909, quoted in Tamarkin, pp. 231–233.

187   *"Bolshevism was but"*: Harold Varney, quoted in Diggins, p. 108.

    "the dark forces": "Our Ninth Convention," *Intercollegiate Socialist*, February–March 1918, p. 19.

    "what had been folly": Quoted in Stansell, p. 315.

188   *"Mrs. Stokes and I still"*: 7 January 1918.

    "that this war is being": "Rose Stokes Again a Red," *Los Angeles Times*, 18 March 1918.

189   *"a few super-patriots"*: Flynn, p. 280.

    "German accent": NARA Bureau of Investigation OG 19081922.

    "nitrogen bombs": To Lieutenant Duer Irving, 25 February 1918, NARA Bureau of Investigation OG 8000-643.

190   *"socialistic Jew"*: Stokes to Warren, 4 March 1918, NARA Dept. of Justice 9-19-1755.

14. All My Life I Have Been Preparing to Meet This

191   *"that the women"*: Kathleen Kennedy, p. 18.

    "that President Wilson was": NARA Bureau of Investigation OG 160093.

192   *"Some of you may"*: "Rose Stokes Again a Red," *Los Angeles Times*, 18 March 1918.

    "If America had entered": Agent's interview with Lieutenant Ralph B. Campbell, NARA Bureau of Investigation OG 160093.

    "lying and infamous": 17 and 20 March 1918, NARA Bureau of Investigation OG 160093.

193   *"are each and all"*: NARA Bureau of Investigation OG 160093.

    "I am quoted": 19 March 1918.

193   *"I had a long talk"*: Agent's report in NARA Bureau of Investigation OG
       160093.

194   *"a pleasant sitting room"*: "Mrs. Stokes in Jail for Disloyalty," 25 March
       1918.

195   *"Dreadfully troubled"*: NARA Bureau of Investigation OG 160093.
       "It was a bitter": To "Comrade Drake," 14 October 1918, RPS-Tamiment,
       Box 4, Folder 15.
       Army intelligence: See "The Father of American Surveillance," in Adam
       Hochschild, *Lessons from a Dark Time and Other Essays* (Berkeley: Univer-
       sity of California Press, 2018).
       "in her apartment": 24 March 1918, NARA Bureau of Investigation OG
       160093.
       "Agent received word": Report by H. J. Jenzer, NARA Bureau of Investiga-
       tion OG 160093.

196   *"we proceeded"*: Report by J. S. Gillies, 3 April 1918, NARA Bureau of
       Investigation OG 160093. The search was conducted on March 25.
       "thinks she has gotten": Stokes to Charles Warner, 13 April 1918, NARA
       Dept. of Justice 9-19-1755.
       "certain gentleman": At the New Star Casino, 10 November [1918?], RPS-
       Tamiment, Box 2, Folder 6.
       "In my opinion": Kathleen Kennedy, p. 62.

197   *"strong, loyal women"*: The transcript of the trial appears in *American State
       Trials: A Collection of the Important and Interesting Criminal Trials Which
       Have Taken Place in the United States, from the Beginning of Our Govern-
       ment to the Present Day,* vol. 13, ed. John D. Lawson (St. Louis: Thomas
       Law, 1921).
       "Mrs. Stokes received": "Mrs. Rose P. Stokes Convicted of Disloyalty," *New
       York Times,* 24 May 1918.
       "The thought of a long": To Flora Rauh, 25 July 1918, RPS-Yale, Box 3.

198   *"anti-American utterances"*: "When the Pacifist Comes to Face the Test," 25
       May 1918.
       "a salutary lesson": "Pen Points," 4 June 1918.
       "There can be no": "Editorial Notes," 5 June 1918.
       "There is compensation": *Kansas City Times,* 24 May 1918, quoted in *Ameri-
       can State Trials,* p. 895.

15. Waves Against a Cliff

200   *"When a detective dies"*: Quoted in Lukas, p. 9.

201   *"no rich and no poor"*: *Evidence and Cross Examination of William D. Hay-
       wood in Case of Wm. D. Haywood, et al.* ([Chicago?]: Industrial Workers of
       the World, 1918), p. 109.
       "a wasted man": "The Social Revolution in Court," *Liberator,* September
       1918.

"The big game": Melvyn Dubofsky, *"Big Bill" Haywood* (New York: St. Martin's, 1987), p. 121.

202   *"very just"*: Wilson to Gregory, 24 June 1918, in NARA Dept. of Justice 9-19-1755.

"If the judge had": "Ten-Year Term for Mrs. Stokes," *New York Times*, 2 June 1918.

"Dangerous tide": "Unofficial War Activities of Captain J. G. Phelps Stokes, CA-ORC, 12 December 1922," memorandum, JGPS-Columbia, Box 93.

203   *"President Wilson personally invited"*: Stokes family newsletter, 15 April 1954, JGPS-Columbia, Box 38.

"When Mrs. Stokes, late": "Socialists Urged to Curb Tongue or Risk Being Jailed," 15 August 1918.

"Mrs. Stokes Repeats": 10 July 1918.

"the time has come": Biddle to Van Deman, 4 November 1918, Randolph Boehm, ed., *US Military Intelligence Reports: Surveillance of Radicals in the United States, 1917–1941* (Frederick, MD: University Publications of America, 1984), Microfilm Reel 8.

"During the war": Clarence Darrow, *The Story of My Life* (New York: Scribner's, 1934), p. 69.

204   *A local activist read*: "Allies Seek Plunder, Debs Tells Socialists," *New York Times*, 17 June 1918.

"three of our most": Loren Baritz, *The American Left: Radical Political Thought in the Twentieth Century* (New York: Basic, 1971), p. 95.

"You who have never": "With Gene Debs on the Fourth," *Liberator*, September 1918.

"inspiring comrade": David Karsner, *Debs: His Authorized Life and Letters* (New York: Boni and Liveright, 1919), p. 234.

206   *"I was in the same"*: 24 and 12 July 1918, NARA Bureau of Investigation OG 8000-643.

"The judge sat high": Eastman 2, pp. 52–53.

"I can bear it": 4 July 1918, RPS-Yale, Box 3.

"We ask you": "Arrest Applauders at Trial of Debs," *New York Times*, 10 September 1918.

207   *"She drew her chair"*: "Debs Guilty; Penalty May Be 20 Years," 13 September 1918.

gave a speech: Which repeats and expands on less noticed words he had written earlier, as an epigraph to *Labor and Freedom: The Voice and Pen of Eugene V. Debs* (St. Louis: Phil Wagner, 1916).

"If anybody told me": Quoted in Ginger, p. 396.

"not even 1 per cent": "Nearing Opposed by Some Socialists," *New York Times*, 13 September 1918.

208   *"Caritas Island has"*: To Flora Rauh, 25 July 1918, RPS-Yale, Box 3.

208   *"Darling—Rose"*: 29 June 1918, RPS-Yale, Box 1.

     "had had intimations": To Harriet Viets, 18 June 1918, RPS-Yale, Box 3.

209   *"The inbreeding"*: Everett Marshall to RPS, 17 November 1919, RPS-Yale, Box 2.

     "No great liberative": 15[?] June 1918, ASW-Yale, Reel 10, Folder 50.

16. The Springtime of Revolution?

211   *"Here we are"*: *Revolutionary Radicalism: Its History, Purpose, and Tactics; Report of the Joint Legislative Committee Investigating Seditious Activities* (Albany, NY, 1920), part 1, vol. 2, p. 1434 (commonly referred to as the Lusk Committee report).

212   *"Perhaps our going"*: *Papers Relating to the Foreign Relations of the United States, 1917*, supplement 2, *The World War*, vol. 1 (Washington, DC: Government Printing Office, 1932), p. 518.

     "Is there any child": "President Wilson's Speeches Defending the Peace Treaty," *New York Tribune*, 6 September 1919.

     "One cannot overemphasize": Diggins, p. 109.

213   *What about internationalizing*: Reed 1, pp. vii, 42, 311, 234.

     "John Reed's story": Goldman, p. 450.

     "I have been over": *The Autobiography of Lincoln Steffens*, vol. 2 (New York: Harcourt, Brace, 1931), p. 799.

     "that the Bolsheviki": Mrs. Frederick Towne to agent John T. Cooney, report dated 22 August 1919, NARA Bureau of Investigation OG 160093.

214   *"It won't be long"*: Zipser, p. 248.

     "to establish Democracy": J. G. Phelps Stokes, "We Hail and Honor the Struggle of the Russian People Against the Tyranny of Bolshevism," *Struggling Russia*, 22 November 1919, p. 524.

     "I was actively engaged": To Lieutenant Alexander R. Thompson, 8 September 1921, JGPS-Columbia, Box 37.

     "Unofficial War Activities": JGPS-Columbia, Box 93.

215   *"the springtime of revolution"*: Diggins, p. 111.

     "We are running a race": Anthony Read, *The World on Fire: 1919 and the Battle with Bolshevism* (New York: Norton, 2008), p. 160.

     "Margaret, all my dreams": Quoted in Page Smith, p. 564.

     "outbreak of Bolshevism": 21 September 1919.

     "Heavy, brutish-faced": "The Social Revolution in Court," *Liberator*, September 1918.

216   *"all employers"*: Major General J. McI. Carter, chief, Militia Bureau, quoted in 29 November 1919 memorandum below.

     "must exercise unusual": "Memorandum" by J. G. Phelps Stokes, chairman, and T. J. Oakley Rhinelander, vice chairman, Recruiting Committee, 29 November 1919, JGPS-Columbia, Box 38.

     "Ethnic Map": I was made aware of this by Mike Wallace's splendid

Greater Gotham, pp. 1031–1034. He reproduces this map in black and white; the original, in color, can be easily found online.

217 *"about fifteen enlisted":* "Recruiting Methods in This Command," 16 November 1920, JGPS-Columbia, Box 38. This memo is signed only by Stokes.

    "men of responsibility": "Memorandum" by J. G. Phelps Stokes, chairman, and T. J. Oakley Rhinelander, vice chairman, Recruiting Committee, 29 November 1919, JGPS-Columbia, Box 38.

218 *"to hear your words":* n.d., RPS-Yale, Box 1.

    "a fine kind man": 19 April 1919, RPS-Yale, Box 1.

    "that gave all": n.d., RPS-Yale, Box 1.

    "I am trying hard": 25 May 1919, RPS-Yale, Box 1.

    "I thank God": n.d., RPS-Yale, Box 1.

    "Good-bye, you've had": Haywood, p. 361.

219 *"an estimated 10,000 people":* Regin Schmidt, *Red Scare: FBI and the Origins of Anticommunism in the United States, 1919–1943* (Copenhagen, Denmark: Museum Tusculanum Press, 2000), p. 178.

    "as if a bomb": 9 November 1919, quoted in Kenneth Ackerman, p. 116.

    "I believe that": 4 October 1920, *The Papers of Woodrow Wilson,* vol. 66, ed. Arthur S. Link (Princeton, NJ: Princeton University Press, 1992), p. 184.

221 *"free speech is":* Goldman, pp. 477, 502–503.

    "stranger in a strange land": Antler, p. 90.

222 *"The people are ready":* Diary, RPS-Yale, Box 13, Folder 1.

    "appealed altogether": To F. H. Giddings, n.d., JGPS-Columbia, quoted in Zipser, p. 114.

    "If it is necessary": To Daniel Kiefer, 3 March 1921, RPS-Tamiment, quoted in Zipser, p. 227.

    "Vatican in Moscow": Debs to William Z. Foster, 23 July 1924, quoted in Salvatore, p. 336.

    "He is not a proletarian": To Daniel Kiefer, 1 February 1922, RPS-Tamiment, Box 4, Folder 15F.

223 *"burned in effigy":* Goldman to Sonya Levien, 6 November 1925, Emma Goldman Papers, University of California, Berkeley, Reel 15. See also Goldman, p. 611.

    "secret agent": To Dr. William C. Lusk, 12 January 1921, JGPS-Columbia, Box 33.

    "I recall a bright": 11 December 1932, RPS-Yale, Box 2.

224 *"I am going to ask":* 3 January 1921, RPS-Yale, Box 4.

    "a wonderful invitation," "had the great privilege": 28 September 1920 and October 1920, RPS-Tamiment, Box 2, Folder 13.

225 *"ingrate enemies," "Your disregard":* n.d. and 19 December 1921, RPS-Yale, Box 4.

    "One word more": 29 December 1921, RPS-Yale, Box 4.

17. No Peaceful Tent in No Man's Land

227   *"the land of my heart's desire":* RPS-Tamiment, Box 5, Folder 24.
       name appeared most: See note to page 4.
       "sun of the world": Worker, 11 March 1922, quoted in Sharp, p. 169.
       "was the sense": "A Memoir of the Thirties," in *Steady Work: Essays in the
       Politics of Democratic Radicalism, 1953–1966* (New York: Harcourt, Brace &
       World, 1966), pp. 358–359.

228   *"very glad and thankful":* 23 April [1923?], RPS-Tamiment, Box 4, Folder
       15.

229   *"Graham breaks":* 24 September 1923, RPS-Yale, Box 3.
       several times accused: See letters to and from Rose, Pearl, and C. E. Ru-
       thenberg about this, November 1924, RPS-Yale, Box 3.

230   *"a highly neuratic":* Pearl to CEC of WP [Central Executive Committee,
       Workers Party], 10 November 1924, RPS-Yale, Box 3.
       "I am a Russian Jewess": Yezierska, p. 37.

231   *"I want you":* n.d., 28 March, and 11 April 1921, quoted in Salvatore, p. 313.
       "looking fearfully injured": 24 September 1923 and 7 June 1924, RPS-Yale,
       Box 3.

232   *"My going would":* 11 and 12 February 1925, RPS-Yale, Box 4.

233   *"When you taught":* 18 February 1925, RPS-Yale, Box 4.
       "'Political differences'": 6 March and 2 April[?] 1925, RPS-Yale, Box 4.
       "I passed Graham": 28 October 1925, ASW-Yale, Reel 10, Folder 50.
       "though living under": "Rose Pastor Stokes Won't Fight Divorce," *New York
       Times,* 19 October 1925.

234   *"his legal pound":* 7 June 1925, RPS-Yale, Box 4, and RPS-Tamiment, Box
       2, Folder 6.
       "it should be placed": "Rose Pastor Stokes Won't Fight Divorce," *New York
       Times,* 19 October 1925.

235   *"A slender young":* 2 September 1926, RPS-Yale, Box 3.
       "Most of us would": "There Are No Bad Divorces," 13 February 1926.
       "how widely our view-points": 27 and 19 October 1925, RPS-Yale, Box 1.

236   *"I desire nothing":* 23 May 1925, RPS-Yale, Box 4.
       "he hopes that": E. P. Behringer to Anna Pastor, 31 March 1926, RPS-Yale,
       Box 4.
       she and Graham signed: "Animals for Science," 14 March 1951.

237   *he remarked that:* Rose to Olive Dargan, 27 January 1932, RPS-Yale, Box
       3. She is summarizing a comment Graham made to her brother-in-law
       William Fletcher.
       "There is no doubt": 17 July 1929, JGPS-Columbia, Box 85.

238   *"reverted to type":* Clare Sheridan, *My American Diary* (New York: Boni
       and Liveright, 1922), 8 March 1921, p. 70.

"loved the people": Rose Pastor Stokes 1, p. 132.

239   "As I look back": n.d., but clearly late 1925 or 1926, RPS-Yale, Box 3.
"I am not very active": To C. E. Ruthenberg, 18 June 1925, RPS-Yale,
Box 3.
"I am no longer": n.d., but clearly late 1925 or 1926, RPS-Yale, Box 3.

240   *"I'm afraid"*: To Jeanette Pearl, n.d., RPS-Yale, Box 3.
"Maybe we shall": 4 July 1928, RPS-Yale, Box 4.

18. Love Is Always Justified

241   *He found her living:* "Reveal Operation on Rose Stokes," *New York Evening
Post,* 20 March 1930.

242   *"Once Rich": Washington Herald,* 21 March 1930.
"a shining black car": "East Side Hears Stokes Seeks to Aid Former Wife,"
25 March 1930.
"I am now assured": 12 June 1930, JGPS-Columbia, Box 94.

243   *"Holfelder never charged"*: To Joseph Brodsky, n.d. 1933, and draft of letter
to unknown correspondent, RPS-Yale, Box 1.
"Rose, dear": Jane Burr, 20 January 1933, RPS-Yale, Box 1.
"Don't hurt me": 3 December 1930, Olive Tilford Dargan and Rose Pastor
Stokes Correspondence, Tamiment Library, New York University.
"fairly hopeless": To Max Cohen, 15 February 1933, RPS-Yale, Box 3.
"Hitler speaks": 23 February 1933, RPS-Yale, Box 4.

244   *"the urn with my ashes"*: To Joseph Brodsky, n.d. 1933, RPS-Yale, Box 1.
"Am sinking daily": RPS-Yale, Box 6.
"O my darling": Letter received 26 June 1933, quoted in Kathy Ackerman,
pp. 32–33.
"The Cinderella story": Where I Live: Selected Essays (New York: New Di-
rections, 1978), p. 15.

245   *The chief executive:* Sarah Anderson and Sam Pizzigati, *How Taxpayers
Subsidize Giant Corporate Pay Gaps* (Washington, DC: Institute for Policy
Studies, 2018), pp. 2, 4.

Bibliography

NATIONAL ARCHIVES AND RECORDS ADMINISTRATION FILES

The 1918–1921 Department of Justice case against Rose Pastor Stokes is now in NARA files as RG60 Class 9 Litigation Case Files (European War Matters) A1 COR 9. But its case number, in this voluminous file itself, and as cited by previous scholars, is 9-19-1755, and so that is how I've referenced it in the notes.

The primary Bureau of Investigation file on Rose Pastor Stokes is NARA OG 160093. Some additional material on her can be found in other OG (Old German) files. At this writing, the OG file series is available online at www.fold3.com.

OTHER ARCHIVAL MATERIAL

Anna Strunsky Walling Papers, MS 1111, Manuscripts and Archives, Yale University Library (cited as ASW-Yale).

Anson Phelps Stokes [Jr.] Family Papers, MS 299, Manuscripts and Archives, Yale University Library (cited as APS-Yale).

James Graham Phelps Stokes Papers, MS 1587, Manuscripts and Archives, Yale University Library (cited as JGPS-Yale).

James Graham Phelps Stokes Papers, Rare Book and Manuscript Library, Columbia University (cited as JGPS-Columbia).

Rose Pastor Stokes Papers, MS 573, Manuscripts and Archives, Yale University Library (cited as RPS-Yale).

Rose Pastor Stokes Papers, TAM.053, Tamiment Library, New York University (cited as RPS-Tamiment).

Stokes, J. G. Phelps. *My Narrative*. Unpublished ms., in private hands.

DISSERTATIONS

Fairman, Deborah. *"Unhampered Child of Liberty": Modernity, Representation, and American Jewish Women, 1890–1930*. Ph.D., English, University of Massachusetts, Amherst, 1998.

Reynolds, Robert Dwight, Jr. *The Millionaire Socialists: J. G. Phelps Stokes and his Circle of Friends*. Ph.D., History, University of South Carolina, 1974. (Cited as Reynolds 1.)

Scholten, Pat Lee Creech. *Militant Women for Economic Justice: The Persuasion of Mary Harris Jones, Ella Reeve Bloor, Rose Pastor Stokes, Rose Schneiderman, and Elizabeth Gurley Flynn*. Ph.D., Speech Communication, Indiana University, 1978.

Sharp, Kathleen Ann. *Rose Pastor Stokes: Radical Champion of the American Working Class, 1879–1933*. Ph.D., History, Duke University, 1979.

Sigerman, Harriet Marla. *Daughters of the Book: A Study of Gender and Ethnicity in the Lives of Three American Jewish Women*. Ph.D., History, University of Massachusetts, Amherst, 1992.

Stuart, Jack Meyer. *William English Walling: A Study in Politics and Ideas*. Ph.D., History, Columbia University, 1968.

Tamarkin, Stanley Ray. *Rose Pastor Stokes: The Portrait of a Radical Woman, 1905–1919*. Ph.D., American Studies, Yale University, 1983.

BOOKS, PAMPHLETS, AND ARTICLES

Ackerman, Kathy Cantley. *The Heart of Revolution: The Radical Life and Novels of Olive Dargan*. Knoxville: University of Tennessee Press, 2004.

Ackerman, Kenneth D. *Young J. Edgar: Hoover, the Red Scare, and the Assault on Civil Liberties*. New York: Carroll & Graf, 2007.

Anbinder, Tyler. *City of Dreams: The 400-Year Epic History of Immigrant New York*. Boston: Houghton Mifflin Harcourt, 2016.

Antler, Joyce. *The Journey Home: How Jewish Women Shaped Modern America*. New York: Schocken, 1997.

Baron, Salo W. *The Russian Jew Under Tsars and Soviets*. 2nd edition. New York: Macmillan, 1976.

Boylan, James. *Revolutionary Lives: Anna Strunsky and William English Walling*. Amherst: University of Massachusetts Press, 1998.

Bronstein, Jamie L. *Two Nations, Indivisible: A History of Inequality in America*. Santa Barbara, CA: Praeger, 2016.

Brown, Stan, and Michael J. Brown. *The Story of Austin, Nevada, and the Nevada Central Railroad*. Privately printed, 1999.

Buhle, Mari Jo, Paul Buhle, and Dan Georgakis. *Encyclopedia of the American Left*. 2nd edition. New York: Oxford University Press, 1998.

Carlson, Peter. *Roughneck: The Life and Times of Big Bill Haywood*. New York: Norton, 1983.

Chura, Patrick. *Vital Contact: Downclassing Journeys in American Literature from Herman Melville to Richard Wright*. New York: Routledge, 2005.

Churchill, Allen. *The Improper Bohemians: A Re-creation of Greenwich Village in Its Heyday*. New York: Dutton, 1959.

Cooper, Patricia A. *Once a Cigar Maker: Men, Women, and Work Culture in American Cigar Factories, 1900–1919*. Urbana: University of Illinois Press, 1987.

Davis, Allen F. *Spearheads for Reform: The Social Settlements and the Progressive Movement, 1890–1914*. New York: Oxford University Press, 1967.

Debs, Eugene V. *Letters of Eugene V. Debs* (3 vols.), ed. J. Robert Constantine. Urbana: University of Illinois Press, 1990.

Diggins, John Patrick. *The Rise and Fall of the American Left*. New York: Norton, 1992.

Dinnerstein, Leonard. *Antisemitism in America*. New York: Oxford University Press, 1994.

Dodge, Phyllis B. *Tales of the Phelps-Dodge Family: A Chronicle of Five Generations*. New York: New-York Historical Society, 1987.

Dos Passos, John. *U.S.A.: The 42nd Parallel, 1919, The Big Money*. New York: Library of America, 1996.

Dray, Philip. *There Is Power in a Union: The Epic Story of Labor in America*. New York: Doubleday, 2010.

Drinnon, Richard. *Rebel in Paradise: A Biography of Emma Goldman*. Chicago: University of Chicago Press, 1961.

Dubofsky, Melvyn.
1. *When Workers Organize: New York City in the Progressive Era*. Amherst: University of Massachusetts Press, 1968.
2. *We Shall Be All: A History of the Industrial Workers of the World*. Chicago: Quadrangle, 1969.

Eastman, Max.
1. *Love and Revolution: My Journey Through an Epoch*. New York: Random House, 1964.
2. *Heroes I Have Known: Twelve Who Lived Great Lives*. New York: Simon and Schuster, 1942.

Enstad, Nan. *Ladies of Labor, Girls of Adventure: Working Women, Popular Culture, and Labor Politics at the Turn of the Twentieth Century*. New York: Columbia University Press, 1999.

Feldman, Jay. *Manufacturing Hysteria: A History of Scapegoating, Surveillance, and Secrecy in Modern America*. New York: Pantheon, 2011.

Finan, Christopher. *From the Palmer Raids to the Patriot Act: A History of the Fight for Free Speech in America*. Boston: Beacon Press, 2007.

Fink, Leon. *Progressive Intellectuals and the Dilemmas of Democratic Commitment.* Cambridge, MA: Harvard University Press, 1997.

Fischer, Nick. *Spider Web: The Birth of American Anticommunism.* Urbana: University of Illinois Press, 2016.

Flynn, Elizabeth Gurley. *The Rebel Girl: An Autobiography, My First Life (1906–1926).* New York: Masses & Mainstream, 1955.

Fraser, Steve. "1919: The Year the World Was on Fire." *Jacobin,* January 13, 2019.

Freeberg, Ernest. *Democracy's Prisoner: Eugene V. Debs, the Great War, and the Right to Dissent.* Cambridge, MA: Harvard University Press, 2008.

Gelb, Barbara. *So Short a Time: A Biography of John Reed and Louise Bryant.* New York: Norton, 1973.

Ginger, Ray. *Eugene V. Debs: A Biography.* New York: Collier, 1962.

Ginsberg, Alan Robert. *The Salome Ensemble: Rose Pastor Stokes, Anzia Yezierska, Sonya Levien, and Jetta Goudal.* Syracuse, NY: Syracuse University Press, 2016.

Gitelman, Zvi. *A Century of Ambivalence: The Jews of Russia and the Soviet Union, 1881 to the Present.* New York: Schocken/YIVO, 1988.

Goldman, Emma. *Living My Life.* The Anarchist Library, https://theanarchistlibrary.org/library/emma-goldman-living-my-life.pdf. Originally published by Knopf, New York, 1931.

Golin, Steve. *The Fragile Bridge: Paterson Silk Strike, 1913.* Philadelphia: Temple University Press, 1988.

Haywood, William D. *Bill Haywood's Book: The Autobiography of William D. Haywood.* New York: International, 1929.

Henderson, Robbin Légère, and Matilda Rabinowitz. *Immigrant Girl, Radical Woman: A Memoir from the Early Twentieth Century.* Ithaca, NY: ILR/Cornell University Press, 2017.

Holtzman, Filia. "A Mission That Failed: Gor'kij in America." *Slavic and East European Journal* 6(3), Autumn 1962.

Horn, Max. *The Intercollegiate Socialist Society, 1905–1921: Origins of the Modern American Student Movement.* Boulder, CO: Westview Press, 1979.

Howe, Irving. *World of Our Fathers: The Journey of the East European Jews to America and the Life They Found and Made.* New York: Schocken, 1989.

Humphrey, Robert E. *Children of Fantasy: The First Rebels of Greenwich Village.* New York: Wiley, 1978.

Kaun, Alexander. *Maxim Gorky and His Russia.* New York: Jonathan Cape & Harrison Smith, 1931.

Kazin, Michael. *War Against War: The American Fight for Peace, 1914–1918.* New York: Simon and Schuster, 2017.

Kennedy, David M. *Over Here: The First World War and American Society.* New York: Oxford University Press, 1980.

Kennedy, Kathleen. *Disloyal Mothers and Scurrilous Citizens: Women and Subversion During World War I.* Bloomington: Indiana University Press, 1999.

Kent, Rockwell. *It's Me O Lord: The Autobiography of Rockwell Kent*. New York: Dodd, Mead, 1955.

Lasch, Christopher. *The New Radicalism in America, 1889–1963: The Intellectual as a Social Type*. New York: Knopf, 1965.

Lepore, Jill. "Eugene V. Debs and the Endurance of Socialism." *New Yorker*, February 18 and 25, 2019.

Levine, Louis. *The Women's Garment Workers: A History of the International Ladies' Garment Workers' Union*. New York: Huebsch, 1924.

Luhan, Mabel Dodge. *Movers and Shakers*, vol. 3 of *Intimate Memories*. New York: Harcourt, Brace, 1971.

Lukas, J. Anthony. *Big Trouble: A Murder in a Small Western Town Sets Off a Struggle for the Soul of America*. New York: Simon and Schuster, 1997.

McGinity, Keren R. *Still Jewish: A History of Women and Intermarriage in America*. New York: New York University Press, 2009.

Meyer, G. J. *The World Remade: America in World War I*. New York: Bantam, 2016.

Nochlin, Linda. "The Paterson Strike Pageant of 1913." *Art in America* 62, May–June 1974.

Nolan, Rachel Elin. "'A Cool and Deliberate Sort of Madness': Production, Reproduction, and the Provisional Recovery of Progressive-Era Women's Narratives." *Signs: Journal of Women in Culture and Society* 43(2), 2018.

O'Neill, William L., ed. *Echoes of Revolt: The Masses, 1911–1917*. Chicago: Quadrangle, 1966.

Poole, Ernest.
1. *The Bridge: My Own Story*. New York: Macmillan, 1940.
2. "Maxim Gorki in New York." *Slavonic and East European Review*, American Series 3(1), May 1944.

Preston, William, Jr. *Aliens and Dissenters: Federal Suppression of Radicals, 1903–1933*, 2nd edition. Urbana: University of Illinois Press, 1994.

Reed, John.
1. *Ten Days That Shook the World*. New York: Boni and Liveright, 1919.
2. "The I. W. W. in Court." *The Education of John Reed: Selected Writings*. New York: International, 1955. First published in *Liberator*, September 1918.

Renshaw, Patrick. "Rose of the World: The Pastor-Stokes Marriage and the American Left, 1905–1925." *New York History* 62(4), October 1981.

Reynolds, Robert D., Jr.
1. See Dissertations, above.
2. "Millionaire Socialist and Omnist Episcopalian: J. G. Phelps Stokes's Political and Spiritual Search for the 'All.'" In Jacob H. Dorn, ed., *Socialism and Christianity in Early 20th-Century America*. Westport, CT: Greenwood, 1998.
3. "Pro-War Socialists: Intolerant or Bloodthirsty?" *Labor History* 17, Summer 1976.

Rosenstone, Robert A. *Romantic Revolutionary: A Biography of John Reed*. New York: Knopf, 1982.

Salvatore, Nick. *Eugene V. Debs: Citizen and Socialist.* Urbana: University of Illinois Press, 1982.

Sanders, Ronald. *The Downtown Jews: Portraits of an Immigrant Generation.* New York: Dover, 1987.

Sanger, Margaret. *An Autobiography.* New York: Norton, 1938.

Schwantes, Carlos A. *Vision and Enterprise: Exploring the History of Phelps Dodge Corporation.* Tucson: University of Arizona Press/Phelps Dodge, 2000.

Schwarz, Judith. *Radical Feminists of Heterodoxy: Greenwich Village, 1912–1940.* Lebanon, NH: New Victoria, 1982.

Simon, Rita J. *In the Golden Land: A Century of Russian and Soviet Jewish Immigration in America.* Westport, CT: Praeger, 1997.

Sinclair, Upton. *The Autobiography of Upton Sinclair.* New York: Harcourt, Brace, 1962.

Smith, Page. *America Enters the World: A People's History of the Progressive Era and World War I.* New York: McGraw-Hill, 1985.

Smith, Shannon. "From Relief to Revolution: American Women and the Russian-American Relationship, 1890–1917." *Diplomatic History* 19(4), 1995.

Sorin, Gerald. *A Time for Building: The Third Migration, 1880–1920.* Baltimore: Johns Hopkins University Press, 1992.

Stansell, Christine. *American Moderns: Bohemian New York and the Creation of a New Century.* New York: Metropolitan, 2000.

Stokes, Anson Phelps [Sr.]. *Stokes Records: Notes Regarding the Ancestry and Lives of Anson Phelps Stokes and Helen Louisa (Phelps) Stokes.* (In several irregularly numbered volumes.) New York: privately printed, 1910–1915.

Stokes, J. G. Phelps.

    1. *Hartley House and Its Relations to the Social Reform Movement.* New York, Pusey & Troxell, 1897.

    2. "Omniism, or We & Company, Limited," *Wilshire's* V, March 1903.

Stokes, Rose Pastor.

    1. *"I Belong to the Working Class": The Unfinished Autobiography of Rose Pastor Stokes.* Athens: University of Georgia Press, 1992.

    2. *The Woman Who Wouldn't.* New York: Putnam's/Knickerbocker Press, 1916.

Stokes, W.E.D. *The Right to Be Well Born: Or, Horse Breeding in Its Relation to Eugenics.* New York: C. J. O'Brien, 1917.

Thompson, Arthur W. "The Reception of Russian Revolutionary Leaders in America, 1904–1906." *American Quarterly* 18(3), Autumn 1966.

Thompson, Arthur W., and Robert A. Hart. *The Uncertain Crusade: America and the Russian Revolution of 1905.* Amherst: University of Massachusetts Press, 1970.

Tone, Andrea. *Devices and Desires: A History of Contraceptives in America.* New York: Hill and Wang, 2001.

Tuchman, Barbara W. *The Zimmermann Telegram.* New York: Viking, 1958.

Vorse, Mary Heaton. *A Footnote to Folly: Reminiscences of Mary Heaton Vorse.* New York: Farrar and Rinehart, 1935.

Wagner, Margaret E. *America and the Great War.* New York: Bloomsbury, 2017.

Wallace, Mike. *Greater Gotham: A History of New York City from 1898 to 1919.* New York: Oxford University Press, 2017.

Walling, William English.
  1. *Russia's Message: The People Against the Czar.* New York: Knopf, 1917.
  2. "The Race War in the North." *Independent,* 3 September 1910.

Watson, Bruce. *Mills, Migrants, and the Struggle for the American Dream.* New York: Viking, 2005.

Weinstein, James. *The Decline of Socialism in America, 1912–1925.* New Brunswick, NJ: Rutgers University Press, 1984.

Werner, M. R. "L'Affaire Gorky." *New Yorker,* 30 April 1949.

Yezierska, Anzia. *Salome of the Tenements.* Urbana: University of Illinois Press, 1995.

Zimmerman, Jean. *Love, Fiercely: A Gilded Age Romance.* Boston: Houghton Mifflin Harcourt, 2012.

Zipser, Arthur, and Pearl Zipser. *Fire and Grace: The Life of Rose Pastor Stokes.* Athens: University of Georgia Press, 1989.

Zunser, Miriam Shomer. "The Jewish Literary Scene in New York at the Beginning of the Century." In *YIVO Annual of Jewish Social Science,* vol. VII. New York: Yiddish Scientific Institute, 1952.

Photo Credits

WEDDING DAY Rose Pastor Stokes Papers (MS 573), Manuscripts and Archives, Yale University Library; EMMA GOLDMAN Apic/Getty Images; ELIZABETH GURLEY FLYNN Walter P. Reuther Library, Archives of Labor and Urban Affairs, Wayne State University; MAXIM GORKY Sputnik/Alamy Stock Photo; CIGAR WORKERS Rose Pastor Stokes Papers (MS 573), Manuscripts and Archives, Yale University Library; PHELPS-STOKES FAMILY Image from Stokes Records, vol. 3, by Anson Phelps Stokes; IMMIGRANTS ABOARD SHIP Museum of the City of New York/Byron Collection via Getty Images; NURSERY Bettmann/Getty Images; ROSE AT HER DESK Rose Pastor Stokes Papers (MS 573), Manuscripts and Archives, Yale University Library; NEWSPAPER *The Evening World* (New York, NY), 8 April 1905, Library of Congress; COAL MINERS Pictoral Press Ltd./Alamy Stock Photo; GARMENT WORKERS Bettmann/Getty Images; TENEMENT Bettmann/Getty Images; PHELPS STOKES HOME Great Barrington Historical Society Collection; GARMENT WORKERS STRIKE Universal History Archive/Getty Images; WOMEN STRIKERS Apic/Getty Images; ROSE AND GRAHAM Rose Pastor Stokes Papers (MS 573), Manuscripts and Archives, Yale University Library; EUGENE V. DEBS Fotosearch/Getty Images; JOHN REED Sovfoto/Getty Images; OLIVE TILFORD DARGAN Charlotte Young Collection P80.4.1-1-2, D. H. Ramsey Library Special Collections, UNC Asheville 28804; LABOR UPRISING PhotoQuest/Getty Images; ARREST Chicago History Museum/Getty Images; TRIANGLE FIRE Keystone/Getty Images; BIG BILL HAYWOOD Everett Collection Historical/Alamy Stock Photo; STRIKERS' CHILDREN Corbis via Getty Images; SILK WORKERS' STRIKE Bet-

About the Author

Adam Hochschild's first book, *Half the Way Home: A Memoir of Father and Son,* was called by Michiko Kakutani of the *New York Times* "an extraordinarily moving portrait of the complexities and confusions of familial love . . . firmly grounded in the specifics of a particular time and place, conjuring them up with Proustian detail." His nine other books are primarily about issues of human rights and social justice. They include *The Unquiet Ghost: Russians Remember Stalin* and *Spain in Our Hearts: Americans in the Spanish Civil War, 1936–1939.* His *King Leopold's Ghost: A Story of Greed, Terror, and Heroism in Colonial Africa* was a finalist for the National Book Critics Circle Award, as was *To End All Wars: A Story of Loyalty and Rebellion, 1914–1918.* Hochschild's *Bury the Chains: Prophets and Rebels in the Fight to Free an Empire's Slaves* was a finalist for the National Book Award and won the *Los Angeles Times* Book Prize and the PEN USA Literary Award. He has also received the Theodore Roosevelt–Woodrow Wilson Award of the American Historical Association. His books have been translated into 14 languages.

Besides his books, Hochschild has written for *The New Yorker, Harper's Magazine,* the *New York Review of Books, Granta,* the *New York Times Magazine,* the *Atlantic,* and elsewhere. These articles and other pieces of reportage have been collected in two volumes, most recently *Lessons from a Dark Time and Other Essays.* He and his wife, sociologist and author Arlie Russell Hochschild, have two sons and two granddaughters.

Index

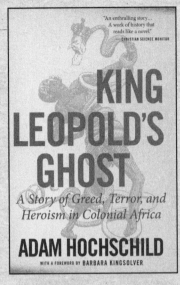

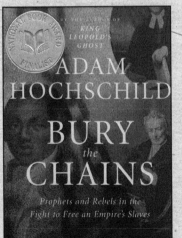